D0425933

Praise for *Unnatural Leadership*

"*Unnatural Leadership* captures the dilemmas and complexities of leading in a high-performing organization. These two executive coaches draw on their broad experience in working with some of the world's top companies to offer a compelling look at how executives think about leading in the 21st century. The book is packed with true stories from the front lines. Each page conveys what today's leader needs to do in order to achieve extraordinary results."

—Andrea Jung, chairman and CEO, Avon Products

"I've given many presentations on the connection between strong character and strong leadership. It's encouraging to read a book that recognizes this truth. It does take strength of character to break out of the comfortable, expected methods of running a company and to look a subordinate in the eye and unflinchingly say, 'I don't know.' That's what unnatural leadership is all about."

—Stephen R. Covey, author,
The Seven Habits of Highly Effective People

"This book is unnatural. It delves into the challenges, realities, and contradictions of being a leader today. Dotlich and Cairo reveal what they've learned from working with global CEOs and senior leaders, and how leaders at any level can accept their strengths and weaknesses and improve on them."

—Bill Weldon, vice chairman,
board of directors, Johnson & Johnson

"Leading today is complex. Our world is becoming more and more global, interconnected, and turbulent. In *Unnatural Leadership,* Dotlich and Cairo offer practical ideas and useful tips for dealing with the challenges of leading in a global organization."

—Joseph Berardino, CEO, Andersen

"This book strongly reinforces my own mantra, that healthy people and healthy relationships are what make healthy companies. Dotlich and Cairo have learned that the leaders who succeed in today's workplace are those who expose their vulnerabilities, admit their flaws, and embrace team members who are 'different.' As a psychologist, I applaud this trend for human reasons. As a business adviser, I acknowledge that it's a prescription for corporate success."

—Bob Rosen, CEO of Healthy Companies International
and author of *Global Literacies* and *Leading People*

"Retaining and engaging your top talent is the only way to prosper in a knowledge-based economy ˙ ˌd it's even more crucial in our volatile times. Who else will steer you through but your smart, creative, skillful people? Give them each a copy of *Unnatural Leadership,* and do it immediately. That way they'll know you're serious about winning and worth their personal commitment."

—Ed Gubman, author of *The Talent Solution*

"In this bold, thought-provoking book, Dotlich and Cairo challenge leaders, teaching them how to rethink the old sacred cows, redefine their roles, and constantly reinvent their game. A must-read!"

—Robert Kriegel, author of *If It Ain't Broke . . . BREAK IT!*
and *How to Succeed in Business Without
Working So Damn Hard*

"Don't just read this book. Devour it. Put it under your pillow so its message moves from your head to your heart. *Unnatural Leadership* is a must-read for doing business in the 21st century."

—Alan Parisse, named one of the
twenty-one top business speakers for the 21st century

Unnatural Leadership

Unnatural Leadership

Going Against
Intuition and Experience
to Develop
Ten New Leadership Instincts

David L. Dotlich

Peter C. Cairo

Foreword by Stephen H. Rhinesmith

 JOSSEY-BASS
A Wiley Company
www.josseybass.com

JOSSEY-BASS
A Wiley Company
989 Market Street
San Francisco, CA 94103-1741

www.josseybass.com

Jossey-Bass books and products are available through most bookstores. To contact Jossey-Bass directly, call (888) 378-2537, fax to (800) 605-2665, or visit our website at www.josseybass.com.

Substantial discounts on bulk quantities of Jossey-Bass books are available to corporations, professional associations, and other organizations. For details and discount information, contact the special sales department at Jossey-Bass.

We at Jossey-Bass strive to use the most environmentally sensitive paper stocks available to us. Our publications are printed on acid-free recycled stock whenever possible, and our paper always meets or exceeds minimum GPO and EPA requirements.

Library of Congress Cataloging-in-Publication Data
Dotlich, David L. (David Landreth), 1950-
Unnatural leadership : going against intuition and experience
to develop ten new leadership instincts / David L. Dotlich, Peter
C. Cairo.—1st ed.
p. cm.—(The Jossey-Bass business & management series)
Includes bibliographical references and index.
ISBN 0-7879-5618-X (alk. paper)
1. Leadership. I. Title: Going against intuition and
experience to develop ten new leadership instincts. II. Cairo,
Peter C., 1948- III. Title. IV. Series.
HD57.7 .D68 2002
658.4'092—dc21   2001005906

FIRST EDITION
HB Printing 10 9 8 7 6 5 4 3 2

Contents

Foreword

For as long as human beings have lived and worked in groups, there have been leaders. The roles and responsibilities these leaders have filled have been defined many times by the culture in which they lived. Plato argued that rulers deserve to rule only if they have undergone far-reaching education, so they have become philosophers. Confucius believed that leadership should be based entirely on merit and that ability and moral excellence, rather than birth, fitted a man for leadership.

The United States is a relatively new society, born from immigrants fleeing monarchies. It has always preferred to define leadership in an egalitarian way. The ideal American leader has been one who had proven expertise but who could also inspire confidence in followers so that they would willingly support the vision articulated for the benefit of all. For most of the twentieth century, this meant that leaders needed not only to be driven toward the attainment of organizational objectives but also to attend to the motivation and inspiration of others who would achieve these objectives.

In 1989, business management expert and author Ken Blanchard brought together two streams of leadership—task-oriented leadership and people-oriented leadership—and noted that the combination of emphasis between task and people depended on the situation. He concluded that there is no one ideal leadership style; instead, the best leadership varies from situation to situation. On the battlefield and in emergencies, he maintained, the best leadership style is directive. In day-to-day operations among professionals, the best style might be more consultative. In strategic planning requiring the buy-in of many people, participative leadership would be more appropriate. And in situations where direct reports were mature and capable of carrying out their own responsibilities, delegation would be the most appropriate leadership behavior.

Situational leadership theory still provides relevant instruction to the variety of ways leaders can be effective. But in the past decade, there has been an additional thrust in leadership thinking. There now is an emphasis not only on how leaders lead, but on what values and character they express in their leadership. Members of Generation X and their new sensitivities to the environment, human rights, and globalization demand that leaders not only get things done but increasingly to "get things done" in the "right way."

The "right way," of course, still depends on whether you are a Chinese leader in the Confucian tradition, an Argentinean leader in the Latin American tradition, or a Swedish leader in the Scandinavian tradition. But in the United States and many other cultures, leadership is increasingly associated with what Kevin Cashman has called "leading from the inside out." In other words, you cannot truly be a leader of others unless you understand yourself and have accepted your own strength and weaknesses.

This emphasis on personal characteristics and qualities, in addition to technical expertise, has added new requirements for leadership and new dimensions to training and coaching leaders. In the executive coaching and development programs that I have conducted with Peter Cairo and David Dotlich, we have helped thousands of executives learn to deal with these new leadership requirements.

For many, these new demands are "unnatural" because they suggest that leaders go against some of the conventional wisdom of the twentieth century. In this view, leaders were heroic with a get-it-done-at-all-costs philosophy and with little regard for how objectives were achieved. The increasing challenges of global leadership, combined with new demands of workers more sensitive to values, have led to what Harvard professor Joseph Badaracco calls "choosing between right and right." In such cases, leaders are required to choose between two values that are equally right. "Work-life balance" and "shareholder value," for example, may seem at odds when leaders ask employees to work for increased productivity. During such decisions, leaders need to ask themselves what they believe in and what they stand for. When this happens, they confront themselves and their own strengths and vulnerabilities. They must go inside themselves in order to lead others.

In *Unnatural Leadership,* David Dotlich and Peter Cairo explore these new leadership requirements and the challenges of helping leaders develop the necessary mind-set and skills for effective leadership in today's world. The personal challenges of moving beyond one's comfort zone (Prisoner of Experience), dealing with one's fears (Acknowledging Your Shadow Side), and revealing one's doubts about one's capacity to deal with the demands of a new world (Exposing Vulnerabilities) are explored to examine the new qualities that leaders must possess to be credible and effective. Some years ago, Will Rogers observed, "Everyone is ignorant, only on different subjects." It is important that we be clear about what we know and what we do not in a world in which we increasingly need to depend on others.

I am writing this foreword in the days after the September 11 terrorist attack on the United States. This unprecedented act of horror requires the leaders of the United States to deal not just with the complexity of determining who has committed the act and how, where and when to retaliate; it also requires the emotional leadership of the nation. It challenges leaders at all levels of the nation to ask themselves fundamental questions about life and death and to provide solace to a grieving nation.

If we are fortunate, this kind of challenge will not be frequent for leaders in the twenty-first century. Yet it goes to the heart of the need for people who have both the analytical capacity to deal with a complex world and the emotional intelligence to manage the human dilemmas sensitively that an increasingly global world presents. In Chapter Nine, "Trust Others Before They Earn It," and Chapter Ten, "Coach and Teach Rather Than Lead and Inspire," the authors discuss how today's leaders must extend themselves to others in ways that have not been natural in years past.

I am so pleased that David Dotlich and Peter Cairo have looked within themselves and their experience coaching and developing leaders in the past twenty years to examine some fundamental lessons of leadership. This is a book that could not be written by people who themselves had not confronted the vulnerabilities that they discuss for others. Having been their friend and colleague for almost a decade, I can attest to the fact that this book comes from their "inside out," as well as the inside out of leaders whom they have counseled and coached over the past twenty years.

I hope that you find their experiences helpful in your own review of what is natural and unnatural for your leadership style. In our discontinuous, contradictory world, we all need to reexamine our assumptions about our organizations, ourselves, and our life together if we are to lead everyone to a mutually beneficial life in the years ahead.

December 2001   Stephen H. Rhinesmith
West Chatham, Massachusetts

For Kathryn M. Dotlich and Athena G. Cairo
Our favorite Unnatural Leaders

Preface

In the aftermath of the tragic events of September 11, 2001, there have been many unexpected and even positive outcomes. In the midst of chaos and grief, extraordinary leaders have emerged everywhere, providing confidence, hope, and direction while acknowledging their own vulnerability and sorrow. They have offered strength and resolve without succumbing to the temptation to offer bromides or easy solutions. This tragedy and its wake will continue to redefine the course of history and will almost certainly affect and deepen our understanding of the essence of leadership for years to come. In an instant, our image of the infallible and all-knowing leader somehow seemed inappropriate for the new era that was unfolding.

We had originally intended *Unnatural Leadership* to differentiate leadership from the heroic model previously popularized in the business press. We could not know that *Unnatural Leadership* would also seem appropriate for unnatural times. But now we have all seen leaders who combine strength with vulnerability, face into paradoxes (such as combating terrorism while preserving civil liberties), and acknowledge the ever-present shadow side of their own human behavior. These individuals have emerged from crisis with stronger, clearer voices and have become examples that others want to follow. Leaders who challenge the conventional wisdom of impulsive overreaction and provide a way to create meaning out of despair and loss stand apart in their maturity and wisdom. Leaders who can combine force with compassion, can invite dissent and resolve different viewpoints, and connect with others in the world by acknowledging their own fallibility and vulnerability are best equipped to navigate global and business contexts even more complex than those we describe in this book.

As business life resumes, leadership will be permanently redefined because of where we have been and where we are going.

Leading in large organizations has always been complex and demanding. This has not changed. In writing *Unnatural Leadership,* we could anticipate and describe increasing complexity in the world, but terrorist attacks have produced one outcome no one could anticipate. Leaders must now endeavor to lead people permanently changed by events.

At this unique moment in history, we have had the privilege of observing great leadership under the most difficult conditions. We have been reminded that it is often much simpler and more human than any of us care to admit. We created the idea of unnatural leadership as a tool for describing a new type of leadership that is emerging. We believe that the barbaric acts in New York and Washington, D.C., have served to crystallize and accelerate this trend, and we hope that many of the ideas we discuss in this book will become more rather than less relevant.

December 2001   DAVID L. DOTLICH
                                                          Portland, Oregon

                                                          PETER C. CAIRO
                                                          Bearsville, New York

Acknowledgments

Americans have recently had the collective opportunity to remember how important friends, family, and colleagues are to life itself. Finishing this book has coincided with this important lesson and would not be possible without the involvement and support of the many clients and colleagues of CDR International, from whom we learn each day. During our executive leadership programs conducted around the world and in many coaching relationships, thousands of leaders have opened up their hearts and minds to provide us with their insights and experience and to help us distill what is really important about leading and working with people. Among the many leaders and clients we especially want to thank, and whose ideas run throughout this book, are these: at Johnson & Johnson, Bill Weldon, Peter Tattle, Roger Fine, Mike Carey, Russ Deyo, Sandra Tripp, and Allen Andersen; at Colgate-Palmolive, Bob Joy, Reuben Mark, Bill Shanahan, Javier Teruel, Franck Moison, Andy Hendry, and Lois Julier; at Avon Products, Andrea Jung, Debbie Himsel, Jill Kanin-Lovers, Susan Kropf, Bob Corti, and Harriet Edelman; at Intel, Craig Barrett, Pat Gelsinger, Laura Stepp, and Tony Cox; at Andersen, Joe Berardino, Norbert Becker, Philip Randall, Tom Elliott, Kay Priestly, and Xavier de Sarrau; at Novartis, Norman Walker, Antoine Tirard, Paulo Costa, and Frank Waltmann; at PG&E, Bob Glynn, Jean Brennan, Gordon Smith, and Brent Stanley; at Washington Mutual, Kerry Killinger, Linda Clark-Santos, and Brenda Bluemke; at Quantum, Jerry Maurer and Michael Brown; at Lilly, Sydney Taurel, Laura Dorsey, Lisa Cheraskin, Pedro Granadillo, and Sharon Sullivan; at Bank of America, Ken Lewis, Jim Shanley, Steele Alphin, and Kelly Kent; at Sprint, Bill Esrey, Ron LeMay, and Lynn Badaracco; at Merck, Grey Warner and Howard Levine; at BellSouth, Melanie Cadenhead and Val Markos; and at EMC, Corey Seitz.

We also have the wonderful good fortune of working with a world-class team of consultants and coaches who are unnaturally great and who teach and practice the skills we describe. Some of these are Jim Noel, Neil Johnston, Deborah Barber, Alice Portz, Mike Fruge, Mark Kiefaber, Ralph Bates, Carole France, Russ Demers, John Bradberry, Ginny Whitelaw, Rod Anderson, Neville Osrin, Saletta Boni, Peg Howell, and Ram Charan. We especially want to thank Jill Conner, who contributed to the chapter exercises in this book, taking our ideas and translating them into practical tips for leaders. Cedric Crocker and Susan Williams of Jossey-Bass can make editing seem like alchemy. At CDR International, three people deserve special thanks: Amy Renee Nielsen, who managed the project (and us) to the finish; Richard Aldersea, who as the leader of CDR International keeps everything moving forward; and most important, our colleague and friend Stephen Rhinesmith, who continually inspires us with his own unnatural leadership, as well as his intellectual honesty, creative ideas, and steadfast integrity.

Our families have supported the many nights away, telephone calls during vacations, and long hours in front of the computer necessary to complete this book: Doug, Carter, and Jeremy; and Kathy, Danielle, Justin, and Megan. Their love and support make it all possible and worthwhile.

Unnatural Leadership

Introduction

This book evolved from a series of Action Learning programs our company, CDR International, ran for Bank of America beginning in 1999. Action Learning, a process designed to facilitate leadership growth and development through work on actual business issues, was instituted after the former NationsBank merged with the Bank of America. Ken Lewis, who was then president and is now chief executive officer, brought us in to work with the company's top two thousand leaders. Besides the Action Learning program, we also provided Action Coaching (leadership coaching that fosters individual development linked to organizational goals) for Bank of America executives.

The bank's postmerger strategy was to provide full-service offerings to its customers and to that end needed its leaders to leverage various parts of the business to serve customers better. This meant understanding services outside their areas, sharing customer leads with each other, cross-selling services, and working toward the overall bank goals (rather than function unit or individual business goals).

The problem was that because attention was focused on the merger, the measurement systems lagged the new strategy. Performance was still being measured based on achieving individual and functional goals, and there were few incentives to share information and customers. Just as significant, leaders from both merged companies were a bit wary of each other, especially because the two banks' cultures were so different.

As we worked with leaders on Action Learning and Action Coaching over the next two years, we observed a phenomenon that we had not seen before. Many of the leaders who were emerging as truly effective were not displaying the traditional characteristics of leaders. The traditional leadership traits—dominant personality, highly decisive, motivational—did not seem as useful

1

as untraditional ones. The leaders who were most successful were those who could extend trust immediately and work productively with people from the other bank and other functions; these leaders were willing to give up some control in order to accomplish the bank's larger goals and were comfortable working across functions and departments. They did not need a cadre of trusted associates around them but instead felt comfortable in building teams composed of the most talented individuals with differing views that made them somewhat uncomfortable.

During this time, we were running similar Action Coaching and Action Learning programs for companies such as Lilly, Novartis, Merck, Sprint, BellSouth, Avon Products, and PG&E, and we noticed the same phenomenon. It was not that the traditional leader had disappeared; there were still times and situations when a traditional leadership approach was effective. Nonetheless, a new type of leader and new types of leadership traits seemed to be emerging with amazing speed. This leadership sea change was a response to the rapidly changing business environment, one that had been turned upside down by e-commerce, diversity, global strategies, matrix and organic structures, downsizing, and many other factors.

Just as significant, management of other high-performing companies began noticing this same trend and directly or indirectly communicated to us the importance of developing leaders who possessed these new traits and could lead in a new and complicated business. All of these changes caused us to reassess our definition of leadership and attempt to identify the new characteristics of leaders. What we discovered was that these traits were often outside many executives' comfort zones. For instance, the ability to make right-versus-right decisions—that is, deciding between two equally good alternatives—was a challenge for many people. They had been trained to analyze the data and determine which choice was wrong and which one was right. To move forward without having a clear-cut right choice seemed odd to many of the leaders we talked to. They said they had been trained to make fast, analytical choices and not look back. It was counterintuitive to accept that there was no right choice and be sufficiently flexible so they could shift direction if circumstances changed.

One word that people kept using to refer to these new traits was *unnatural*. It struck us as the perfect word to describe this new type of leadership, just as *natural* described the old style of leadership. The best leaders commit unnatural leadership acts. They do things in the course of their daily activities that seem uncomfortable at first and not dictated by their experience or training. Yet these unnatural acts often are much more effective than natural approaches in confronting problems and opportunities.

Providing Theory and Practice

We have read many books and articles about leadership, and although many of them have important things to say, none recognizes this unnatural shift in leadership behaviors that is occurring in high-performing companies. While few would argue that the old command-and-control style of leadership is still viable, there is a widespread assumption that certain leadership traits are inviolate— that being authoritative, overly confident, decisive, and motivational are timeless leadership virtues. Underlying most of the previous writing on leadership are the following presumed truths:

- A leader should be a hero.
- A leader solves problems.
- A leader does it alone.
- A leader inspires.
- A leader controls his own destiny.

None of these truths is completely true today. Although there may be certain instances when heroic leadership is called for and an inspirational speech is necessary, new truths have emerged to supplant the old ones. Unfortunately, not many observers have noticed. This is due in part to the pervasive nature of the leadership stereotype. The media have reinforced this stereotype, especially through movies where leaders (from sheriffs to athletic team captains) display classic natural leadership traits. Just as significant, the business press tends to deify a handful of leaders such as General Electric's Jack Welch, creating the impression that their company's success is due to their charisma and singular brilliance.

Although these leaders may be charismatic and brilliant, their company's success frequently is due to many of their other leadership traits that reporters find difficult to identify or communicate. It is not easy, for instance, to explain how a leader's willingness to expose his or her shadow side—weaknesses or negative impulses—rather than project a flawless persona, tremendously improved communication and honesty within his or her organization.

One of our goals in writing this book therefore is to propose a new, provocative idea about leadership. In our earlier academic incarnations (David at the Universities of Michigan and Minnesota, Peter at Columbia University), we found the introduction of new leadership ideas a great catalyst for productive discussions. Too often, people in the business world take leadership for granted. It is what it is, and there is not much reason to give it much thought. In fact, leadership is an evolving concept, and it evolves particularly quickly during times of change. In the early 1980s, for example, leaders believed in the importance of limited "spans of control," organization designs with "staying power," and "when in charge, be in charge," among other truisms. To accept a fixed definition of leadership is to risk leading anachronistically. New leadership concepts shake things up, stimulating the type of debate that eventually translates into more effective leadership practice.

Given this last point, we should emphasize that this book is not written just to present a theory but to help readers put it into practice. In our work with some of the world's best-known companies in a variety of industries, we have enabled their leaders to commit unnatural acts to very positive effect. We have done so using our Action Learning and Action Coaching approaches, which rely on a variety of tools and techniques. Throughout this book, we share these tools and techniques with you. You will discover specific ways that leaders can make the transition from natural leadership to unnatural leadership behaviors. These methods are not designed to change people's personalities or magically transform a command-and-control leader overnight. Instead, they are created to help people increase their capacity for unnatural actions. Ideally, they will provide people with an increased repertoire of leadership skills so they can mix natural with unnatural behaviors.

We have organized the book in a reader-friendly way. As you will see, most of the book focuses on the ten key unnatural leadership traits we have identified, with a chapter devoted to each trait. We focus more on the soft or "people" side of leadership and organizations than the harder elements of strategy, structure, and measurement. We have worked with enough high-performing companies to know that outstanding leaders cannot ignore these business aspects and succeed. But our purpose is not to describe all aspects of business success—only those behaviors we are now observing in highly effective leaders across a variety of companies and industries. Although there are certainly other unnatural characteristics, we have picked the ten that we have found to be most valuable for leaders and their organizations. Chapters One through Three present our theory of the case, illustrating the contrast between natural and unnatural leadership traits and why unnatural traits have emerged. We set up the dichotomy of natural and unnatural leaders intentionally. We know that the contrast is not always as clear as we describe. Our purpose is to contrast a new way of leading with how many leaders have been trained and reinforced.

You will also find stories from the first chapter to the last about natural and unnatural leaders. Each of the stories is real and actually happened. Although we have disguised the names of some of these leaders we have worked with and their organizations, the drama, humor, and lessons of these stories still come through. You will read about the frustrations of talented executives who stubbornly rely on the approaches that brought them success in the past and discover (sometimes too late) that they are no longer as effective. Similarly, you will encounter executives who have become tremendous leaders but bear little resemblance to the leadership model most of us have in our minds. These are people who have taken risks by committing unnatural acts, sometimes going against the grain of their culture and their bosses.

How to Get the Most out of This Book

We have organized this book in four parts. Chapters Four through Seven deal with the self-aspects of unnatural leader. Chapters Eight through Ten address team leadership, and Chapters Eleven through Thirteen focus on enterprise or institutional leadership. Each chapter concludes with questions and exercises to help you develop your skills and ideas as an unnatural leader. As you first start reading about the ten unnatural acts, you may find yourself reacting with skepticism. We say this because it is exactly how we reacted when we first started seeing these unnatural behaviors emerge. For instance, we used to be convinced that leaders who revealed their vulnerabilities undermined confidence among followers. We assumed they would be perceived by others in their organization as weak, yet we discovered there were strong leaders who were very open about their vulnerabilities, because they were consistently willing to face reality, including their own limitations. Time after time, we ran into executives who were willing to say more than once, "I don't know." They admitted when they lacked the knowledge or skills to handle a situation. This admission, rather than branding them as a wishy-washy leader, prompted others to take initiative or demonstrate their competence. They appreciated their boss's honesty and openness and worked harder and more innovatively to deal with situations for which their boss lacked the answer. In a very real way, his expression of vulnerability mirrored the feelings they all had about a world where there is so much information coming at everyone so fast that it is difficult to know what to do all the time. When these leaders admitted that they did not know the answer, they helped their teams become more comfortable operating in this environment and acknowledge their own limitations or need to learn.

It took a number of coaching experiences with vulnerable leaders before we lost our skepticism. We hope it does not take you as long as it took us to believe in these unnatural traits. At the least, you have probably realized that the business world is becoming more, rather than less, complex, faster rather than slower, and more demanding and challenging rather than less. To succeed requires new ways of working, which we hope this book provides.

Your willingness to believe will depend in part on your position and your experiences. If you are an executive coach or you work in leadership development, you may have already discovered that the traditional model of leadership is no longer as viable as it once was. You may have learned that training people to become better decision makers or to plan, organize, measure, and control no longer has the same impact on their performance as it once did.

On the other hand, if you are a veteran executive who has enjoyed a successful career by being a natural leader, you may be more likely to resist the ideas in the following pages. If so, we hope you understand that we are not suggesting you make a 180-degree change in how you lead. We do not expect everyone to incorporate all ten unnatural leadership acts into their daily routine. Some may be too problematic for you to accept or implement; they may clash with your personality or your organizational culture to the point that it does not make any sense to adopt them. Given that some of our clients require intensive coaching before they adopt these unnatural acts, we do not have unrealistic goals for this book.

We believe, however, that everyone can benefit from it. At the very least, we hope it changes the way you view leadership by helping you broaden the definition so that it is no longer limited to purely natural acts. If you are in the human resource function of your company, we trust that this book will give you ideas about how to make your leadership development strategy more relevant to current organizational needs. If you are a younger executive, we think you will find that integrating some of these unnatural acts into your leadership style will strengthen your current performance and your future career. If you are a senior executive or a CEO, this book may give you the impetus and ideas to transform the leadership approach of your company.

We list these benefits knowing that even without this book, people will learn how to lead in unnatural ways. From CEOs to new M.B.A.s, leaders are skilled at adapting to their habitats. Sooner or later, everyone will realize that unnatural behaviors are critical given all the new issues and changes affecting the workplace. We think we are at the end of the "leader as heroic figure" era. We happened to have spotted this trend before most others only because we're at the nexus when it comes to leadership effectiveness in a changing environment. As executive coaches who work with the top leadership of the world's greatest companies, we are on the lookout for the best ways to develop leadership talent, and we identified these unnatural acts as much out of necessity as perspicacity. Nonetheless, we are certain that this discovery will provide leaders and their organizations with a great deal to think and talk about. If it also provides them with things to do, so much the better.

Part One

The Importance of Unnatural Leadership

| **Ten Unnatural Acts**

Unnatural leadership is not so much a rejection of the traditional leadership model as it is a recognition that leaders must behave in unnatural ways if they are going to be effective today. Certainly, there is still a need for decisive, pragmatic, results-oriented leaders. These and other natural leadership traits have been drummed into people's heads through formal education, training programs, media stories, and on-the-job observation, and there is a reason that they have become ingrained behaviors. We have all heard the stories about the indecisive CEO who could not make up his mind about committing his company's resources to that "new Internet thing" or the brainy senior executive who attempted to put what she thought was a breakthrough theory into practice and did not concern herself with results (and complained that no one was seeing the long-term picture even when her company declared bankruptcy).

As a result, certain leadership behaviors have become natural. They are almost intuitive; we have been taught how leaders behave and know there is logic behind why they behave this way. When we face a crisis, we do not close our eyes and cross our fingers. We quickly obtain information, assess, and act, as any other good leader would.

The problem, of course, is that the world has changed. Traditional leadership qualities, skills, and responses are no longer consistently effective. Highly effective and high-performing companies such as Intel, GE, Johnson & Johnson, Bank of America, Cisco, and many others have consciously and unconsciously changed the way work gets done, people are organized, and information is collected and disseminated. In the process, the way leaders must act in order to be effective has also changed.

What is effective today are unnatural acts: behaviors and attitudes that are not always described in classic leadership models and not recommended in leadership textbooks. Leaders need access to these unnatural acts; they need the option of expanding their natural leadership style and employing these untraditional and often counterintuitive responses when the situation demands it.

Before defining the ten traits of unnatural leadership, we'd like to give you a brief overview of how leadership requirements have evolved over time and to the point that a new leadership philosophy is necessary.

From the Great Man Theory to Chaos Theory

For the first two hundred years in the United States (and in many other countries as well), the prevailing notion was that great men are born, not made. The Great Man Theory posited that by virtue of their maleness, birthright, and social position, a small group of individuals were destined to be leaders, and the vast majority of people acknowledged this fact. Although an occasional maverick leader might emerge through entrepreneurship or some other means, most heads of major companies, politicians, and military officers emerged from the small circle of individuals whose destiny it was to lead.

During World War II, however, the demand for leaders exceeded the supply. Thus, the concept of leadership training was born and the gradual acceptance of the idea that leaders could be made rather than just born. The focus became defining what leaders must do and inculcating these traits during officer training. The hierarchical, bureaucratic manager became the norm for corporations after World War II.

Despite this training, the Great Man Theory did not disappear. In fact, biases about who is entitled to be a leader remained pervasive at least until the late 1980s or early 1990s and prevented many women and minorities from reaching top executive positions. Although few people today would admit to believing in the Great Man Theory, it still has an impact. Consciously or not, many organizations persist in selecting for their top spots middle-aged white males from backgrounds and colleges that are remarkably similar. In large corporations throughout the world, managers still act, dress, talk, and even think and decide in remarkably similar ways.

Over the years, a great deal of conventional wisdom about leadership has been gathered and dispensed. The $6 billion leadership development industry has provided training programs, seminars, books, tapes, and other tools designed to help people plug into the current leadership model. Companies hire consultants to define their own leadership model; we have helped more than a few companies do just that. When change is relatively slow, these leadership tools have served organizations well. The thinking goes as follows: if we study how the great leaders of the past (including our own) handled common situations, we can learn from and adopt their approaches and therefore handle these situations effectively. Reasoning from one set of circumstances to another similar set of circumstances is the basis for the case study method taught at many business schools and the competency models that drive many leadership development programs.

What happens, however, if the leadership situation you face is unlike anything leaders in the past faced? How do you deal with issues that are unique to your time and your business? How do you respond effectively as a leader when you are responding to constant, unpredictable change? How do you lead people who are unlike you, come from different backgrounds and experiences, and speak different languages?

As these questions suggest, conventional leadership wisdom is not always sufficient. More so than ever before, the word *organization* is a misnomer. *Organization* connotes an organized way of doing things, but as most organizational employees will attest, much of what they face each day is unexpected, unstructured, and unpredictable. Random events outside the organization, such as the invention of a new technology, a Third World country's entry into the market, terrorism and security concerns, or a sudden change in customer taste, are impossible to anticipate. They are especially difficult to anticipate when they take place all the time. Thus, leaders who undertake to replicate their predecessor or even emulate today's leadership heroes are destined to failure. The business world is moving too fast.

According to most leadership theories, a logical set of responses exists that corresponds to a rational set of challenges or conditions. Unnatural leadership is a response to an irrational, chaotic, unpredictable universe. Think for a moment about this universe. People are faced with constantly increasing pressure for performance with fewer resources, changing organizational requirements, paradoxical pressures for both long- and short-term results, global and local customer and market requirements, mandates for diversity, and needs for consensus—and the list goes on and on. Certainly, there are moments of lucidity and logic within every working day, and during these moments, traditional leadership traits and approaches are quite effective. At times, a leader can respond quickly to a problem and focus on the most results-oriented solution, and everything will work out well. Other times, however, this approach will not work because of the ambiguity surrounding the problem or the need to satisfy multiple stakeholder groups (with conflicting needs) such as other functions or business units, and lack of complete information.

Leaders today are grappling with conflicts and contradictions, which are preventing them from relying on a single right leadership answer since that no longer seems to exist. For instance, a senior executive at Bank of America has been attempting to align himself with the bank's strategy: bringing together all the various services the bank offers and leveraging the customer (that is, selling the customer new investment products). The concept is to broaden and deepen the customer relationship or "share of the wallet."

This executive is in the commercial banking group, and although he understands and appreciates the leverage strategy, he also is aware that his success in selling noncommercial services is difficult to measure. More important, this executive is reluctant to share his own clients with his colleagues from other service areas for some very good reasons. As much as he likes and trusts his colleagues, he does not want to give up control; he worries that one of his colleagues might unintentionally disappoint or alienate a client, leaving him in a less advantaged position. Most important of all, Bank of America does not pay him for introducing new services to a client; his compensation is linked to his results selling commercial products.

If this executive follows a leadership path based on how he is measured and rewarded and that makes him feel comfortable and in control, he will largely ignore implementing the leveraged strategy important to the bank's success. As a result, he is likely to receive praise and maybe even a promotion. Nevertheless, he agrees with the new strategy and believes it is the right course for the company. Still, it is only natural that this executive will choose the path of least resistance. The Bank of America is like most other companies grappling with this complex issue: what is right in the long term may not be right for dispensing short-term rewards.

High-performing companies are learning to provide their leaders with the option of acting unnaturally when appropriate. Unfortunately, some companies insist on rules that are increasingly irrelevant. While they encourage their leadership to deliver results, they unconsciously reward them for doing so in a way that is consistent with past thinking. They sustain cultures where leaders are implicitly expected to have all the answers, closely monitor and direct the activities of the people who work for them, and control the destiny of everyone and everything.

We are currently working with a midsize consumer products company that has made a strong effort to move away from its traditional leadership culture and instead formally and informally motivate managers to pursue unnatural leadership behaviors when appropriate. For instance, the company decided to pursue a new market segment through an Internet strategy. Some of its top executives wanted to own this new business wholly and retain all the returns on their investment. Another segment of management, however, had listened well to the company's message that sometimes unnatural behaviors are called for. They reasoned that the wholly owned version of the strategy would be too costly and take valuable resources away from other areas. They advocated partnering with one or two Silicon Valley dot-com companies, reducing the size of their initial investment and increasing the speed with which they entered this new market. Although this type of partnership ran counter to the company's past practices and some senior executives attacked this plan as foolhardy, claiming it would necessitate sharing proprietary information with outsiders, the company decided to pursue these partnerships. As of this writing, the strategy has been beneficial for all the parties.

The top executives in this company exhibited a willingness to connect rather than create, one of the ten unnatural leadership qualities.

Ten Unnatural Acts

Unnatural leadership behaviors are not limited to the ten we focus on here; in fact, there are probably two or three times that number. We thought long and hard about how to winnow our list down to a reasonable number. Ultimately, we chose the unnatural behaviors that combined effectiveness with degree of difficulty. In other words, we have found these ten behaviors to be to be what effective leaders actually do, and we have also learned that many managers have difficulty putting them into practice because they go against the grain of what they have been taught or because other behaviors have become second nature to them.

The following overview of the ten unnatural acts is organized according to the domain in which they are important. The first domain is the personal challenges a leader must face: how to manage oneself as a leader and as a human being. The second domain is the leadership behavior in working with a team. The third domain consists of the organizational challenges and opportunities with which an unnatural leader must contend. Although each of the unnatural acts applies to all of three domains, these simple categories provide an easy way to understand them.

Personal Challenges for the Unnatural Leader

People who aspire to lead others must continually challenge themselves. The following are the personal unnatural acts for leaders.

1. Refuse to Be a Prisoner of Experience

Leaders get in an experience rut. They do the same things the same way because it worked in the past, they don't have the time to change, or it has contributed to their current success. Rather than analyzing whether a new idea or approach might work better, they reflexively rely on standard operating procedure. The wide-eyed, blue-sky thinking that many young entrepreneurs have practiced was possible because they were not prisoners of their experiences. Their unwillingness to rely on the usual case histories helped them create new industries and companies.

When companies select leaders, two of the first questions they ask are, "Has he done anything like this before?" "What is his track record?" We assume that if that person has done it before (and done it well), he can do it again. Experience is still important for leaders, and there are times when it is the most effective predictor of future success. The problem, however, is that because of constantly improving technology, processes, and best practices in a world that is constantly changing and where success is being continually redefined, experience can be a handicap. Today, leaders must discipline themselves to look at problems and opportunities with a fresh eye. This is difficult because people naturally want to repeat an approach that worked in a similar situation. It is a challenge to consider an alternative to what brought you success in the past or to your current position in the present.

Several years ago as part of a top level Action Learning program, we helped challenge the senior leadership of a large pharmaceutical company to explore Internet strategies to develop their business. This ran counter to their traditional expansion strategies; they had a number of strategies that worked before and seemed likely to work again. They were in the classic innovator's dilemma: How much would the future look like their past? Still, they agreed at least to explore Internet possibilities, and as part of this exploration, they visited a number of dot-com companies. This groundwork helped them start thinking about effective ways of redefining their business, and it exposed them to new management practices. As a result, they started to refashion their business environment in ways that would attract a new generation of technology workers—people who would be crucial to implementing their on-line business delivery strategy.

2. Expose Your Vulnerabilities

Confidence, decisiveness, and certainty are hallmarks of leaders. Even neophyte managers recognize that the people who are placed on the fast track are those who seem to have all the answers. Conversely, managers who appear confused or uncertain are the ones who get sidetracked. The media are filled with CEOs who have all the answers, are on top of the situation, and confidently predict what the next quarter or year will bring.

Yet we have seen a number of senior executives who have made critical mistakes because they refused to admit that there was a gap in their knowledge or that they did not know how to deal with a problem. They believed that leaders must know a lot—or they must *seem* to know a lot. In their heart of hearts, they believed, "When in charge, be in charge," even when they did not know what to do. Some of these leaders were CEOs or top-level executives, and their feigned certainty invited a conspiracy of ignorance. When they said what the answer was, everyone nodded and agreed that that must be the answer.

In an environment where information is vast, overwhelming, and constantly changing, it is important for leaders to have a strong point of view but also to be open enough to say, "I don't know," and admit that their skill set or background has not prepared them to deal with a particular issue. Leaders face so much ambiguity, complexity, and uncertainty that they cannot possibly know all the answers. At times, the appropriate response is to be perplexed. We know that this confused response is tremendously uncomfortable for some people. But every so often, it's important to admit that you are uninformed about a subject or a situation is so convoluted that you cannot grasp it. Leaders who are certain and knowledgeable in other areas will motivate others with their honesty. Today, direct reports, team members, and others respect managers who can admit their shortcomings without whining or pretending.

It is also important for leaders to be learners, and this requires a number of unnatural behaviors, including asking numerous questions, saying, "I don't know," frequently, and scheduling time for learning activities such as talking to experts, benchmarking, and training.

3. Acknowledge Your Shadow Side

Most of us have behavioral traits or attitudes that surface at inopportune moments and sabotage our efforts. Mike Lombardo and Morgan McCall, authors of *The Lessons of Experience,* have termed these traits "derailers," referring to how they derail us from our goals. We refer to them as the *shadow side*. The shadow side of a powerful leader may be to get caught up in his power and become arrogant. For others, fear of failure can create paralyzing anxiety about doing the wrong thing.

The notion of the perfect leader should be a thing of the past, but many executives today still strive for perfection. They are unwilling to admit or unable to see their flaws. Years ago, there was a much greater margin for the errors produced by trying to be perfect. An arrogant CEO of a successful company had a much more difficult time derailing his career and his company.

Today, unacknowledged shadow sides get many otherwise fine leaders in trouble. Talented people leave a company rather than tolerate working for someone with a hot temper and sharp tongue. Discrimination suits are filed against managers who are biased against women, seniors, or minorities. Teams discuss a leader's shortcomings openly and strategize about how to manage around a manager's volatility or perfectionism.

Gina, on the other hand, is a well-known top executive we have worked with in a major global corporation who readily acknowledges her shadow side. She is very open about her tendency to avoid conflict and wanting people to like her. Her openness helps her direct reports and team members work more effectively with her—they refuse to let her steer them toward consensus when they are not ready for it—and helps her be aware of her tendency. Her shadow side does not disappear, but she is in a better position to manage it.

Recently, we facilitated a leadership program for the top five hundred leaders of Sprint. Bill Esrey, the chairman and CEO, and his direct reports participated in a panel discussion in which they all openly discussed their 360-degree feedback survey results, shadow side tendencies, and development needs. Their courageous example gives permission to each senior leader to do the same.

4. Develop a Right-Versus-Right Decision-Making Mentality

In his book *Defining Moments: Choosing Between Right and Right,* Harvard Business School professor Joseph Badaracco argues that leaders are no longer rewarded for making choices between what's right and what's wrong; those are too easy today. Increasingly, the most important choices are between what's right and what's right. In other words, the decision is between two positive outcomes, and no amount of information or analysis will yield a single correct answer.

Natural leaders want correct answers. They are comfortable viewing situations as having a right course of action and a wrong one. Certainly they realize that sometimes tough decisions are required, but they make these decisions by researching the issues, gathering information from others, and then deciding based on the evidence.

Today, however, no amount of analysis and research will yield a correct answer in certain situations. For instance, many companies are faced with choices involving local interests versus the need to be globally competitive. Companies have to continue to meet the requirements of local markets, but at the same time they must achieve efficiencies and economies of scale to compete globally. As you probably know all too well, numerous right versus right decisions emanate from these two requirements and confound leaders who have been raised to see issues in black and white terms. Similarly, many companies are struggling with Wall Street's expectations to raise the bar on performance and make people accountable for results, and at the same time create a work climate where people feel trust and respect and are being developed as professionals. Sometimes, given limited time and money, leaders see this as an either-or choice and start analyzing it accordingly. They grapple with whether it is better to make demands on people that may increase performance but negatively affect the work environment or to ease up on these demands in order to make people feel valued (and to ensure that they will not leave the company in search of better work environments).

The unnatural act, therefore, is to be willing to accept that there is no one right solution, freeing yourself to consider a range of solutions. You may opt for one approach now but remain open to switching to another approach as circumstances change. Many times, the unnatural behavior is to make decisions based not just on facts but on values. Instead of weighing all the evidence and seeing which way the scales tip, leaders need to consider the organization's values and which action is most likely to dovetail with these values

Leading Teams as an Unnatural Leader

In addition to developing oneself, a leader must bring people together in teams and groups to accomplish an outcome. We have identified unnatural acts that leaders must perform to build strong teams.

5. Create Teams That Create Discomfort

It is a natural tendency to surround yourself with trusted others. The logic is that you can trust your team and can count on them to make decisions and move forward quickly. You want the people you rely on to think like you and to have delivered for you in the past. Many companies rely on relationship networks for choosing leaders. Senior leaders ask each other who is good and who can be trusted. The result is a remarkable homogeneity of the leadership talent pool.

How many leaders are willing to choose team members whose thinking they view as radical, untraditional, or unusual? How many leaders pick people who have fought with them on issues in the past or have viewpoints that are at odds with their own? Not many. This is not to say that you should purposely pick only individuals who are contentious or iconoclastic; there is a difference between people who are willing to disagree with you and those who are disagreeable.

Teams can easily lapse into predictable thinking patterns, and today's environment undercuts predictable decision making. More so than ever before, opportunities as well as competitive threats and problems are coming from unexpected places, and you need a team made up of members who will push you hard enough to spot them. It's uncomfortable when someone asks you why you are taking a certain action, and it's even more uncomfortable when that person refuses to accept a variation on the typical answer: "We've always done it that way." But if you can create conditions that invite open dissent and challenge and encourage strong points of view in addition to your own, you are likely to come up with more alternatives and a wider range of potential strategies.

The general manager of the Latin American division of a large consumer products company put together a team of people with whom he had worked as a general manager of an Argentinean company. He did so knowing that he could count on his team for support in a tough new job. What he could not count on them for was challenging his standard operating procedure and pushing him to think more creatively about the issues his company was facing. As a result, he tried to tackle some big problems in the same way as his predecessor had, and with the same lack of results. Just as significant, this general manager became known as someone who demonstrated favoritism toward his cronies and that all his decisions would also favor Argentinean markets. The result was almost predictable disaster.

Leaders need to recruit at least some team members who have different perspectives and are willing to stimulate debate and challenge. This can mean everything from hiring someone from the outside to picking younger, high-potential managers or mavericks.

6. Trust Others Before They Earn It

Conventional wisdom holds that people must earn rather than be given trust. In many organizations, bosses expected others to demonstrate loyalty and results before they put any faith in them. Leaders often (unintentionally) have an implicit distrust of people who have not yet proven themselves or behave or act differently than they would in the same situation and while acting open actually extend their trust slowly and reluctantly.

Intuitively, it may make sense to withhold trust until you get to know someone better. But the counterintuitive opposite is not as naive as it might seem. In reality, it is pragmatic. There often is no time to build trust. Mergers, acquisitions, and alliances throw people together quickly. Yesterday's fierce competitor is today's colleague in the next cubicle, and the imperative is often for these new groups to move quickly. High-performing companies often form temporary project teams because of an opportunity that must be acted on immediately. Similarly, organizations have become much more transitory places than they were before, and if a manager waits a few months or years until she fully trusts a direct report, she might find that she has waited too long; the direct report has already secured a job with another company (or another group within the company).

We do not advocate blindly trusting everyone, but we are suggesting that when appropriate, leaders today need to trust first and ask questions later. Put another way, they must take the optimistic view that most people can be trusted (versus the cynical perspective that most people cannot). We have found that one of the best ways to produce trustworthy employees is by "going first" with trust;

when people see that you trust them, they respond in kind. Hugh McColl, former chairman of the Bank of America, once gave a powerful speech to a thousand of his top executives when his company, NationsBank, was merging with Bank of America. He stated that the executives of the newly formed bank must immediately extend trust to the people who report to them, including any new people on their team. His point was that given the pace of change in the banking industry and to make a huge merger successful, they must take a leap of faith and extend their trust so that programs can move forward with great speed.

7. Coach and Teach Rather Than Lead and Inspire

More than some of the other unnatural acts, this is one that some executives may acknowledge as important. Unfortunately, this recognition does not translate into action. They may acknowledge the importance of leaders as coaches but feel they lack the skills or time to coach and teach. They prefer the traditional leadership posture of developing an inspiring vision that will motivate others or relying on their personal example as sufficient inspiration. "Coaching is what my team needs to do with their team" is the underlying attitude of many leaders.

Direct reports today expect to be developed. They also expect a closer relationship with their bosses, appropriate guidance, and feedback. In an ambiguous business world, with customer, product, service, and process choices and changes, people can feel more confused about work and career issues than ever before, and they look to leaders to provide advice about how to navigate a rapidly changing, complex organization and uncertain political terrain. Improving the performance of others requires feedback and coaching.

The intimacy of coaching and the time it requires are foreign to many leaders. They grow uneasy when someone comes to them seeking honest feedback or opens up and starts talking emotionally about the work issues they are facing and the feelings that result. They often do not feel capable of giving good feedback, ducking opportunities to provide their honest reactions, or are reluctant to do so; they do not feel qualified to give advice that will affect an individual's career and life.

Leading the Organization as an Unnatural Leader

At the enterprise level, leading "teams of teams," an unnatural leader must act in the following ways.

8. Connect Instead of Create

This unnatural behavior is more than untraditional; it can seem disloyal to the company or country. In the past, leaders have been proud of their own innovations and home-grown ideas. Many of them have difficulty embracing not-invented-here concepts. In an Internet-connected, fast-moving world, however, it's not always possible to create solutions, and now management best practices occur constantly, everywhere, and in the most unlikely places.

Forming alliances with unlikely partners, including competitors, is an increasingly common experience for leaders. Many times, it takes longer to create something on your own than to acquire it through a coalition. No company today has sufficient resources internally to keep up with market and technological developments popping up all over the globe. For this reason, companies must build networks with other businesses, educational institutions, professional organizations, and even regulatory agencies; they may need to partner with companies that are much smaller or larger than they are or that are located on the other side of the planet.

Within companies, boundarylessness, first pioneered by GE, is today a standard for high performance. Managers need to become like plagiarists in ferreting out new ideas and best practices and then rapidly borrowing them for their own team or business unit. This leadership behavior takes advantage of a company's intellectual capital and increases competitiveness. But many leaders still want only their name on an idea or project, and so go it alone.

Admitting that they need outside help feels wrong to many leaders. They also are wary of exchanging potentially proprietary information with outsiders, especially competitors, and so draw the boundary narrowly around what they disclose or import. Connecting instead of creating, however, greatly widens a company's access to information and ideas. While pride of ownership is great, leaders need to learn how to borrow and trade, because in a fast-moving world, ideas increasingly are becoming available to all.

9. Give Up Some Control

Today's organizations look down on a controlling leader, yet natural leaders have a strong need for control. It feels unnatural to let go. These leaders are naturally trying to control because of the intense pressure for results, as well as the high volatility of the marketplace. And some leaders get ahead early in their career because they learn to control situations and people. As they move up the organization, they unconsciously keep trying to control increasingly larger groups and business units.

We are not suggesting that leaders give up all control, just some. An unnatural leader must find the right balance between control and autonomy. Although there are different types of control that a leader must deal with, we are primarily talking about the control of people. For instance, instead of restricting employee behaviors, an unnatural leader would establish an environment of performance accountability where everyone is aware and committed to meeting certain standards. General Electric, for example, has encouraged leaders to have twenty or more direct reports. The logic is that a manager with many direct reports is less likely to spend time controlling and monitoring them.

Control may be part of a leader's personality, and control must also be looked at case by case. Unnatural leaders must be aware of the various situations and parts of their personality that may have an impact on their need for control. Controlling acts are sometimes hard to identify because they are subtle and occur over time. However, a leader can learn how to give up control and find a midpoint.

10. Challenge the Conventional Wisdom

Unnatural leaders must be willing to take a risk and challenge the conventional wisdom yet simultaneously preserve the culture's strengths. They must seek to reshape the organization, not tear it down.

Conventional wisdom in most companies today is an unwritten code about how to behave and how to do business ("how we do things around here"). It is based on past experience rather than current realities. Many times, conventional wisdom is not spelled out in policy manuals but is observed and intuited. This wisdom is followed unconsciously.

Companies with strong cultures are especially prone to conventional wisdom. It can have a positive effect by helping to acculturate employees, but it can also be negative because it can lead to stifling bureaucracy when the implicit rules become too ingrained and rigid. This leads to controlling practices and processes and makes it very difficult for organizations to make substantive change, even though they may embark on well-publicized change programs.

When going up against accepted policies and practices, unnatural leaders face many obstacles. When they challenge conventional wisdom, they seek new perspectives on the business and enroll others in the process of analyzing the conventional wisdom. Challenging conventional wisdom is not done alone and is not done is one fell swoop; instead, it takes the strategic help of others and a continuing questioning of basic assumptions. Unnatural leaders are permanent change agents who also know when to protect the status quo.

Overcoming Your Reluctance to Do Something Unnatural

The concept we are asking you to embrace is not easy. These ten unnatural acts mat not only seem like heresy intellectually, but they probably feel wrong in your company. When you attempt to connect instead of create or when you expose your vulnerabilities, a voice inside your head may whisper, "Are you crazy?" To understand how ingrained natural leadership behaviors are and how reinforced they are by the modern age of media business heroes, consider the following story.

A few years ago, we ran a management simulation game for a group of M.B.A. students. Each student was assigned a role—CEO, chief operating officer (COO), divisional vice presidents, and so on. After the students studied for their roles, they broke up into separate offices and began the simulation (they could communicate with each other by telephone and e-mail as problems were introduced). Most of these students were in their early twenties and had not worked long in corporations, if at all.

Within five minutes, the woman portraying the CEO was in her office issuing orders to her team. The executive vice presidents were barking orders into the telephone, demanding meetings, summoning direct reports, and trying to control every aspect of the simulation. During the debriefing, the woman playing the CEO explained her behavior as being in the interest of speed and prompted by the urgency of the situation we presented; she talked about what she had read about GE's Jack Welch and other leaders and how she was using them as models. Just about all the other students felt that they needed to be decisive and take control in order to beat the competition. They wanted to demonstrate edge and energize their troops. If this is what students believe, you can well imagine how older, veteran executives are thoroughly indoctrinated in these traditional leadership principles.

On top of that, the intense demands of the workplace often short-circuit unnatural responses and connect immediately with natural ones. Tight deadlines and pressure for improved performance can drive people away from unfamiliar, unnatural acts and toward more familiar behaviors. Let's say it's October, and the year-end numbers are looking rather dismal. Most leaders will respond by applying pressure, reverting to command-and-control mind-sets, and start squeezing out performance from people in order to obtain better results. Anxiety, insufficient time to respond, and unyielding requirements or expectations cause people to fall back on comfortable, well-practiced leadership behaviors. In our experience, even knowing that piling on the pressure does not work, most managers keep doing so.

To keep unnatural behavior options open, high-performing leaders must remember that there is more than one way to do things. There is an alternative for producing improved results under deadline pressure. Creating a dialogue, facing reality, and seeking understanding and involvement can also achieve results. We have worked with many leaders who have moved from a position of control and compliance to one of openness and involvement with great success. This does not mean that they suddenly stop asking people to do things, hold the performance standards high and firm, or refrain from holding people accountable for goals. Instead, they do so by creating environments in which people can be open with each other and communicate clearly and continuously.

Perhaps more than any other factor, trust helps leaders overcome their natural tendencies and use unnatural leadership traits when appropriate. When executives understand that mutual and widespread trust is crucial for getting things done in the current environment, they are much more likely to reconsider their traditional responses. When they understand that they give trust but must earn it from others, they begin to change their behavior. Typically, they become aware of the historical perspective we described earlier and recognize that in the past, information could be coded, procedures could be defined, the pace could be slow, the boundaries were clear, the surprises were few. They then contrast this past with the chaotic, uncertain, ambiguous present and realize that trust is crucial. At a time when people are partnering with competitors, working closely with peers in offices thousands of miles away, and attempting to transact business in cyberspace, it is difficult, if not impossible, to hold everything together through rules and orders alone. Trust is the cement, as unnatural as it might seem.

To help you understand the need for unnatural behaviors in your workplace, let's look at the environmental factors that have emerged and rendered the traits of natural leaders ineffective in many situations.

Assessing Your Unnatural Leadership

Reflect on your leadership effectiveness. On a scale of 1 to 5, indicate how much you practice each of the ten unnatural leadership behaviors.

Act of Unnatural Leadership	Your Rating
Refuse to be a prisoner of experience.	1 2 3 4 5 Rarely Always
Expose your vulnerabilities.	1 2 3 4 5 Rarely Always
Acknowledge your shadow side.	1 2 3 4 5 Rarely Always
Develop a right-versus-right decision-making mentality.	1 2 3 4 5 Rarely Always
Create teams that create discomfort.	1 2 3 4 5 Rarely Always
Trust others before they earn it.	1 2 3 4 5 Rarely Always
Coach and teach rather than lead and inspire.	1 2 3 4 5 Rarely Always
Connect instead of create.	1 2 3 4 5 Rarely Always
Give up some control.	1 2 3 4 5 Rarely Always
Challenge the conventional wisdom.	1 2 3 4 5 Rarely Always

What leadership skills are required today in your organization?

What unnatural leadership acts would increase your effectiveness the most?

Chapter Two

Adapting to an Increasingly Unnatural Environment

The forces compelling high-performing leaders to commit unnatural acts can be complex and confusing. Some executives we have interviewed about this subject have protested that it's risky to extend trust before it's earned or that *their* organizations would not be receptive to leaders who acknowledge their shadow side. They maintain that although the world might be changing, the company they work for is not.

We present some compelling evidence that everyone needs to provide themselves with the option of committing unnatural acts— and that if you are attuned only to the current reality in your company, you may be missing the larger forces around you. Whether you are in the most tradition-bound Fortune 100 organization or part of an entrepreneurial, closely held business, adding unnatural leadership behaviors to your leadership style is a wise move.

Most of us are aware that major changes taking place in the world affect how we lead and work, but we see these changes through the distorting prism of our jobs and companies. We filter our observations through the context of what we do each day and what our organizations require us to do. We absorb implicit messages about how to act and how to lead. Thus, we are not always able to see the emerging environmental forces with clarity. We may know intellectually that the Internet is a powerful force reshaping the way business is conducted, but if our company is slow to invest in e-learning or e-commerce or is now pulling back in the wake of dot-com failures, we may not be fully aware of all the ramifications of this continuing business shift, which is not going away.

The problem may also be that a company acknowledges and embraces the forces that demand unnatural leadership behaviors but continues to measure people based on traditional leadership actions. Martha, for instance, is a country manager for a well-known cosmetics company. Her company has embarked on a global product strategy, and as a result Martha has both global product and country market objectives. Because she is measured and rewarded primarily on how her country performs, her country goals take precedence over her global ones. At the same time, Martha recognizes that her company probably does not want to emphasize these suboptimized country priorities, although its reward system continues to reflect them. In addition, Martha is well aware that the future of the company, as well as her long-term success, is dependent on achieving global goals. As a country leader, it would be unnatural for Martha to focus her attention on global issues. At the same time, it would be the right thing to do.

Leaders face these conundrums every day. In our Action Coaching relationships, we work with leaders who must look beyond the reward and measurement cues provided by the organization and determine the right thing to do. Let's take a closer look at the forces behind these confusing choices and how unnatural acts can often be the right response.

Powerful Forces

The forces we describe represent an unusual confluence of workplace events and requirements. Unlike the big-issue trends we discuss in the next section, these forces directly affect how leaders get things done each day. Some have been around for a while and have recently gained momentum, and others are just starting to emerge. All of them, however, are affecting leadership in significant ways and mandating that leaders arm themselves with unnatural as well as natural leadership capabilities. Individual companies such as GE, Intel, and Johnson & Johnson that we work with are responding with new management practices and organizational structures. But the following main forces are reshaping day-to-day leadership in almost every company in every industry.

The Need for Agility

Chris Meyer, author of *Fast Cycle Time: How to Align Purpose, Strategy, and Structure for Speed,* uses a metaphor that captures the need for business agility. In the past, Meyers says, leading a big bureaucracy was like driving a truck filled with cartons of vegetables down a winding mountain road. You drove slowly and carefully, and if a carton fell off, you stopped, backed up, and picked up the carton. The goal was to arrive at a destination with the vegetables in perfect condition. Today, you are careening down that same road, and it's acceptable if some of the cartons fall off. Because only one or two cartons are essential and getting to your destination before your competitors is essential, you can tear down the road without stopping as long as those one or two critical cartons remain on board. Some chaos, some spillage, and some mess are acceptable as long as the goal is met.

The agility to take turns quickly and not become frustrated when a few cartons spin off the truck on a turn is crucial. We need more than speed in getting there before the competition; we also need the business agility that allows us to operate effectively at increased speed. We are not going to belabor the obvious—everyone knows that speed is crucial in a global economy. What is not so obvious, however, are the accompanying agility and alignment. Silicon Valley companies like Electronic Arts, Cisco, and Palm have learned to stop on a dime and change directions overnight: freezing investments, redeploying teams, hiring scores of new people, and completing huge projects in a figurative nanosecond. And as fast as they move, they remain able to keep most parts of their organizations synchronized.

Unnatural acts on the part of leadership facilitate this agility. Unnatural leaders connect with others inside and outside their company, instead of create, and the elasticity of multiple relationships creates flexibility in the organization's strategy and execution. Multiple relationships offer more resources (more information and more ideas, for example) that open up alternative ideas and strategic paths when companies hit roadblocks. Similarly, their willingness to extend trust easily discourages name calling and pointed fingers when a crate falls off the truck. Rather than blaming someone or agonizing over and researching what went wrong, these leaders are willing to adapt, focus on what is next, and keep moving. In other words, they can adjust to minor mistakes.

New Work Styles

Working on-line, flex-time schedules, teleconferencing, dual careers, spiral career paths, continuous learning, and global competition are changing traditional notions of how work gets done. One of the companies we have worked with, Electronic Arts, is an entertainment and software business. It makes creative and challenging electronic games that are fun for people of all ages. Many of the design staff arrive at the office at noon, work until late at night, and skip work a day here and there to surf, pursue some other activity, or otherwise energize their personal creativity. Sofas and couches are scattered around the office so people can take naps, and televisions are everywhere for people to watch. The company has arrived at a work style and business that emphasizes its key success factor: creativity.

In another form of creative management, Cisco Systems now does all its human resource transactions electronically: recruiting, compensation, appraisal, training, and orientation. New Cisco employees complete benefits enrollments and go through orientation on-line before they even begin work. In many other companies today, people who type in the appropriate password can access all company information about themselves on-line. Through Yahoo! chat boards, they can also learn what others in and out of the company are saying about the business, management, and the veracity of official communication at any time. Groups and teams of employees now appraise themselves and each other on-line. Work assignments are handed out, decided and delegated, and even measured through an interactive network of decision making. We have met people who are successfully performing their jobs yet have not met with their supervisor or colleagues in many months.

In short, the notion of a supervisor becomes old-fashioned or even quaint. How do you supervise someone who is not working in the same office as you are or is even on another continent? How do you do a performance review of someone you work with only on-line or by telephone or see in person only every six months?

We are working with a senior executive who was promoted to manage a new team, but no one on his team was located in his office; they were in San Francisco, London, Miami, Chicago, Seattle, and Los Angeles. One of his first acts was to travel to meet them. If he tries to manage this team using only natural leadership skills, he will fail. He cannot motivate and develop members of his virtual team the way he motivated and developed members of his on-site team in the past.

An unnatural leadership act like coaching and teaching instead of leading and inspiring is very useful to this virtual team leader. To keep people in diverse locations committed and engaged, he needs to find ways to coach and teach them so they feel involved in the team and its purpose. In fact, in the current world of work, one of the main requirements of unnatural leadership is to build what not-for-profit organizations refer to as communities of concern. A not-for-profit group manages voluntary associations of people who believe in a common mission or cause and commit themselves to the work because of this belief. They link together because they share a purpose rather than procedures and processes. Today's environment of virtual workforces, complex team structures, and constantly changing requirements requires a leader who can engage people through a community of concern. The ten unnatural acts can help leaders engage and include people so that they believe in the organization and want to stay involved.

Constant Conversation

It's not unusual for middle management leaders we work with to receive five hundred e-mails daily. Most leaders now begin and end their day on-line, sorting through endless streams of information flowing their way. In most organizations, feedback is instantly and continuously available from customers, employees, and others. There is a constant back-and-forth flow of information, resulting in an interacting web of people. The result is a large, organic, interactive community that is constantly shifting and moving toward organizational goals and in a strategic direction. High-performing leaders must listen, absorb, and respond to all this information and participate in multiple dialogues. At the same time, leaders can easily become overwhelmed by all the data or lose their ability to discern what's important and what's not.

To gain some perspective on what is relevant and important and what is useless noise requires detaching yourself so that you can reflect and gain perspective on all the voices you are hearing. Rather than reacting quickly and decisively to every message and trying to gain a corner on the information market (as a natural leader would), you need to be willing to step back and contemplate. Not reacting immediately takes a certain amount of courage since there is so much information sloshing around companies these days, and a common fear is that if you step back, you might miss something important. Nevertheless, it's better to miss something than to become overwhelmed by data and lose all sense of perspective. In our Action Coaching relationships with senior executives, one of the most important outcomes we work on is choosing to lead rather than continuing to react.

Constantly Changing Competition

Because the barriers to entry are so low in many information-intensive industries, new competitors can appear overnight. Rather than vertically integrate all functions, many new companies can suddenly appear that outsource most of their internal operations and focus on brand and positioning. In traditional service industries, providers such as travel agents, financial advisers, and even lawyers and doctors are being replaced by well-informed customers who choose to deal directly with suppliers. As a result, new business models are being created based on information availability. Sources of business value are thereby being redefined. Companies are now questioning how to make money and create if customers can bypass them.

Similarly, resource allocation in response to or in anticipation of competition has radically changed. In the old days of strategic planning, companies decided in advance where to allocate resources and then implemented a plan. Three-year strategic plans, for example, were built through endless meeting and presentations, resulting in a thick document that grandly defined the future. Today, customers (rather than companies) dictate resource allocation. Many companies such as Microsoft, Oracle, Dell, AOL Time Warner, and Sun are racing to create a strategy that is being defined by increasing customer usage of the Internet.

We are also seeing companies that are competing in the morning and partnering in the afternoon. Merck and Johnson & Johnson, for example, are competitors in several drug categories but have undertaken a successful joint venture in which employees and information move freely back and forth. Marketing and manufacturing joint ventures between fierce competitors have become commonplace.

Natural competition has become unnatural. Here is an area where Unnatural Act 1—refuse to be a prisoner of experience—comes in handy. Leaders will need to challenge their competitive assumptions. In high-performing companies such as GE and Intel, most leaders have learned to be paranoid and afraid of the future, no matter how much the media or Wall Street congratulates them. They have learned, often the hard way, that just because the company dominates a market or product or technology today means nothing about tomorrow. In fact, just thinking about your competitive framework is difficult if you rely on your traditional team, because teams can easily become invested in viewing the future through the status quo. Developing teams that create discomfort can ensure multiple insights about what is really happening or could happen. Maintaining a product or service differentiation in the customer's eyes makes it imperative to scan the environment with your own eyes and mind wide open, and a team whose members represent a variety of backgrounds and skills and speak their mind will serve competitive thinking well.

Self-Management Expectations

Increasingly, employees resent being told what to do and how to do it because they now know so much about so many things. They want the freedom to use their own initiative to achieve results, and they want their employers to respect their ability to manage themselves. The whole notion of accountability thereby moves out of the context of roles, positions, or formal authority. Many companies such as Cisco, Oracle, and smaller high-tech organizations emphasize and expect self-management. When a company emphasizes a self-management philosophy, the management practice is to encourage and allow employees to take accountability for solving a customer problem and to take ownership for the problem and solution no matter what department they are in or where they are in the hierarchy. They have the authority to seek help if they need it and gather information if they do not have it. Self-management is highly pragmatic; the "how" of it is not as important as obtaining the desired results. This means that someone can sometimes even violate policies and procedures—perhaps create an alliance with a competitor or ask to see sensitive information—in order to arrive at a solution.

As you might imagine, self-management and natural leadership do not always mix well. Certainly, a leadership style of controlling, monitoring, and measuring is ineffective. But even traditional notions of team management and strategic planning can thwart expectations for self-management. Especially in Silicon Valley and Silicon Alley, we have seen bright, talented people who want their bosses to act like anything but traditional leaders. They respect leaders who can show their shadow side and expose their vulnerabilities; they respond best to leaders who understand the complexity and ambiguity they face and aren't hung up on right-versus-wrong decisions.

The Big Trends

Besides these daily workplace forces, larger social, economic, and technological trends are rendering exclusively natural leadership obsolete. One inescapable force, for instance, is the rapidly accelerating rate and volatility of change. In just about every industry, people are struggling to keep up. For this reason, it sometimes makes sense to rely on an unnatural act such as giving up control. Collective rather than conventional wisdom often provides answers during periods of rapid change. At some point in the past, leaders' decision making could keep up with the pace of change. Now, the goal should be to step back so that the requirements for continuous innovation can be viewed with perspective and multiple inputs.

Similarly, the push for performance requires people to do more faster and with greater innovation than ever before. Every leader we are coaching is faced with reducing budgets while increasing performance. Because there are fewer people to do the work, they have to be much more productive. Leaders can push only so hard, and many companies we work with that have pushed for lean workforces with stretch targets have discovered their limits. Leaders need to understand the complexity of motivation and develop more indirect motivational strategies that foster work involvement and make risk-taking mistakes acceptable. The leader who is willing to coach and teach is much better suited to this performance environment than the natural leader who relies on more direct motivational methods.

When there is an extraordinary push for performance, stress is inevitable. Just about everyone in a position of responsibility is under pressure to do better and come up with breakthrough ideas. Leaders used to crow, "I don't get ulcers; I give them." Today, the best managers reduce the impact of stress on others in many unnatural ways, from acknowledging their shadow side (such as admitting that they have a tendency to be overly critical) to extending great trust (rather than making their staff feel as if they can't quite get it right). Leaders deal with their own stress by pacing and taking care of themselves; they do not become workaholics and set unrealistic performance standards for themselves. In coaching executives, one of our first questions is, "How much and how hard do you work?" Those who are trying to do it all themselves have not figured out how to lead.

Diversity is another significant trend that has made it difficult for managers to rely on traditional leadership models. One size no longer fits all or even a few. Inclusion rather than exclusion is critical in most matrix or global companies, and this means that leaders must learn to acknowledge the reality of people as individuals rather than as a homogeneous group. This takes emotional intelligence and extra effort.

We have worked with senior executives who have had subtle problems adapting their management style to women, arrogant CEOs in training, aggressive M.B.A.s, young technogeeks, ethnic minorities, and others. "Why do I have to adapt to them when they must learn the importance of adapting to me?" is a question we have heard more than once. It may feel unnatural to be a trusting, connecting, flexible leader. We have worked with many young command-and-control managers who persist in believing that the leader's role should set the course and everyone else must follow or get left behind. Most leaders today, however, do not have the luxury of a homogeneous group of direct reports who share the same experiences, hold the same beliefs, and approach their work and their careers in a similar manner. Sometimes, in an era of political correctness, leaders like to pretend that everyone is the same and should be treated as if they are the same. To accommodate the diversity of people in just about every company—and to take advantage of the synergies such diversity can produce—leaders must be willing to deal with people in ways their own mentors and bosses would never have countenanced.

Although there are many significant trends like globalization, Six Sigma, and the War for Talent and new research and manufacturing technologies such as biogenetics and genome research that require new team and leadership methods, we think the most significant impact on leadership today is the growing impact of the Internet. We have already alluded to some of the ways the Internet has created unnatural leadership and now will spotlight a few of them.

First, the Internet has made it difficult for leaders to position themselves as confident visionaries. Despite recent setbacks with dot-com implosions, the Internet continues to affect every company in just about every industry. Companies are learning how to communicate differently with customers, suppliers, vendors, and potential and current employees by establishing ongoing two-way relationships. Many pharmaceutical companies, for instance, are working to adapt to a new marketing and selling environment. Patients are much better informed than in the past, they communicate with each other on-line in chatrooms, and the role of the doctor is changing from expert to intermediary. Pharmaceutical companies are using television direct response advertising and other tools to get people to request a specific brand of drug from their doctor rather than waiting for the doctor to prescribe it.

They are also working through on-line pharmacies, some of them owned or managed by competitors. One pharmaceutical executive admitted to us that he did not know if the window of opportunity was open or closed for his company in terms of Internet sales and that he was unsure which strategic course to pursue. One course could require massive investment today to be ready for a future that may not materialize. One of the unnatural aspects of e-commerce is understanding that there is not a right-versus-wrong direction. In the recent past, traditional companies debated whether to junk their traditional distribution network and convert it completely to Internet sales, which has turned out to be a silly question. As with most other business opportunities, e-commerce presents a right-versus-right decision, and it's sometimes difficult for traditionally confident, visionary leaders to come around to this point of view.

Second, the Internet has created a generation of young employees who feel more comfortable with and are more proficient at on-line activities than the leaders of their organizations. As a result, executives in their forties, fifties, and sixties must reverse roles with these "kids" and adopt the role of learner. More to the point, they must expose their technological vulnerabilities, a very unnatural thing to do, especially for senior executives dealing with employees thirty years their junior. The uncomfortable question people are asking is: How do I lead someone who knows much more than I do about an increasingly critical part of our business?

Along the same line, leaders must recognize that they are vulnerable in ways they never were before. Even the biggest and best companies can quickly lose market share in an Internet-driven marketplace. The connectivity of the Internet facilitates fast alliances between unusual partners (for instance, a midsize Pacific Rim company and a small company in Dubuque) that can take customers away from larger organizations. AT&T focused on traditional competitors like MCI and Sprint, but the real threat to its long-distance business has come from smaller niche players as well. The point is that leaders will benefit from admitting their vulnerabilities not only as individuals but as organizations. The aggressive confidence (some might call it arrogance) of large, long-dominant companies is misplaced in an Internet world where things change quickly. Leaders who are willing to look for and talk about their vulnerabilities are facing reality, and they will be much more effective than leaders who believe their organizations and themselves are invulnerable.

Breaking the Rules of Natural Leadership

When you consider the various forces and trends shaping the business environment today, you realize why people relying on traditional leadership practices feel uncomfortable in the current environment and why they talk about being old-fashioned leaders or wonder if their management style no longer is a good fit for their companies. For many years, natural leadership behaviors grew out of a relatively stable, homogeneous, predictable work context; these behaviors were ideally suited to the trends and workplace forces of the day. Now, there is often a disconnect between these behaviors and the environment. That is not to say that acts of natural leadership have become irrelevant. In certain situations, companies need natural leadership approaches to solve problems and capitalize on opportunities. In other situations, however, they need access to an unnatural focus.

Nothing makes this point better than a review of five rules of natural leadership. We describe these as guidelines to the leadership style we think is fast fading. Let's look at these rules and how they can come into conflict with the forces and trends just discussed.

Natural Leadership Rule 1: Leaders Are Heroic

The natural leader mirrors the heroes of our culture—generals, astronauts, athletes, and so on. These heroes are cool and collected, decisive and demanding—fine qualities for any leader that nevertheless clash with business realities. Sometimes, leaders who maintain a heroic front in the face of roiling change and chaotic conditions appear out of touch with reality. When a leader openly states, "I am in charge here," in solving organizational problems, we wonder if he understands the importance of other people. And yet many leaders continue to behave this way, and the media like to celebrate this type of charisma. Leaders may gain credibility if they are honest and admit they are confused and worried about e-commerce competitive threats or acknowledge their indecisiveness about revealing possible downsides for the business. Although no one wants a leader who always says, "I don't know," or walks about in a state of perpetual confusion, the current environment suggests that leaders should leaven their heroic pose with openness about their fears and doubts. We live in a time in which cynicism is common, and the leader as hero is frequently a target. Unfortunately, many business leaders surrounded by prestige and perks believe they actually are (or need to be) heroes.

Natural Leadership Rule 2: Leaders Favor Results over Values

Organizations may dispute that leaders favor results over values—especially given the ubiquitous nature of value statements and pronouncements about corporate commitments to a higher purpose—but results remain the legacy of post–World War II leadership. In recent years, short-term results have become the leader's mantra because of pressure from financial analysts and shareholders.

Unnatural leadership does not mean that values count more than results but that they are given equal consideration. This can be extraordinarily difficult for an organization to do, even when it formally measures leaders with a two-by-two matrix with performance on one axis and values on the other. If you think about the four quadrants of such a matrix, you know that people who occupy the quadrant of "demonstrates values but not results" are often given a second chance but ultimately terminated. People who occupy the quadrant of "demonstrates results but not values" are often given unlimited second chances. No other single act demonstrates a company's commitment to its values than by removing a leader who has produced extraordinary business results but in a manner that violates the company's values or spirit.

Companies with a results-first culture, however, can easily alienate employees, potential alliance partners, and others, and many discover this when the company's fortunes turn down. Unfortunately, Wall Street is rarely interested in a company's values, and the financial media and commentators give this issue little attention. Leaders pick up this reality and adapt their behavior accordingly.

Values-driven companies foster cultures of inclusion; they attract and retain highly transient, highly marketable employees to stay with an organization; they attract and motivate people who desire a specific work style and engage people in a sense of purpose. As crucial as results are, leaders need to fight their "results reflex" at times and strive to balance results and values.

Natural Leadership Rule 3: Leaders Are Practical and Present Oriented

Practical and present-oriented leaders run meetings with clear agendas; approach problems in straight lines; rely on traditional business methodologies such as planning charts, process mapping, and budget forecasts as a basis for leadership; and apply logic and step-by-step analysis to problems, opportunities, and people. If they spend too much time with blue-sky thinking or are overly conceptual and futuristic in their approach, they are considered soft. Both-feet-on-the-ground cultures frown on leaps of logic and imaginative jumps.

If you recall our analogy of going down a hill in a truck and allowing certain cartons to bounce off without stopping to pick them up, you'll understand the danger of leadership that must stop and pick up every spilled box. The tremendous need for agility sometimes requires leaders to cut corners or solve problems with imagination and intuition rather than always using fact-based analysis. In certain ways, the world of the Internet rewards fuzzy logic. In short, successful leaders combine hard and soft qualities, who can do short-term analysis but can also be futuristic and play hunches.

Natural Leadership Rule 4: Leaders Are Powerful

Leaders who sit on top of a hierarchy—especially one that is vast and far reaching—are deemed powerful. To control their mini-universe, they must appear powerful and exercise their power. Unnatural leaders, however, have also learned the value of empowering other people as well as systems, and they have learned that humility may be warranted in an era in which businesses can reverse quickly. Given the importance of talent and knowledge within organizations, the vulnerability of even the largest corporations, changing work styles, and information flow, personal leadership power and position power have far less impact than in the past. Effective leaders are much more willing to invest real power in others in order to get something done, to invite their direct reports to push back, and push back again if they believe the leader's course of action is wrong. In a very real sense, they invite challenges to their power.

Natural Leadership Rule 5: Leaders Do Not Fail

Natural leaders cultivated this rule and were often able to sustain it by hiding their mistakes or never taking the risks that would result in failure. Somehow, some leaders must regularly relearn that a cover-up is almost always worse than the initial mistake. In an environment where it's crucial for leadership to take risks, a certain amount of failure will happen. We also need leaders who can relate to a diverse group of people and can communicate honestly and openly about themselves in order to build trust. An individual who steadfastly refuses to admit mistakes or avoids situations where she might make them is someone who will struggle in the current environment.

Charles Handy, a management writer, put it best when he noted in *The Hungry Spirit* that it is time for us to "acknowledge that there are over forty million learners who aren't in school any more and who need to urgently discover their strength through failings."

The New Challenge of Leadership

Leaders who rely exclusively on power, heroism, and pragmatism in today's business organizations will be ineffective. The environment we have described, which most people experience, is too complex, variable, and unpredictable for natural leadership rules to prevail, and yet we continue to see companies promote and regard this style of leading. In certain circumstances, empowering, reflective, and self-critical actions are called for. Leaders need access to responses that may feel wrong but will serve them well. They need to get past their initial reluctance to listen rather than speak or to be open instead of closed off. The real challenge of leadership is doing what comes unnaturally, and as we'll see, a number of highly successful leaders have met this challenge.

Breaking the Rules of Natural Leadership

Which of the rules of natural leadership create the biggest problems in your organization? Check all that apply.

_____ Leaders are heroic.

_____ Leaders favor results over values.

_____ Leaders are practical and present oriented.

_____ Leaders are powerful.

_____ Leaders do not fail.

Describe how these rules create problems for you or your organization.

Give some examples of how you are breaking the rules of natural leadership and the impact on your organization:

Being open about fears and doubts (rather than trying to be heroic)

Balancing results and values (rather than focusing only on results)

Solving tomorrow's problems with imagination and vision (rather than looking only at today's issues in the same old way)

Sharing power and engaging others (rather than trying to control everything yourself)

Admitting your mistakes (rather than pretending they never occurred)

Chapter Three

| Resistance Factors

Contrary to what you might expect, many executives buy into the concept of adopting unnatural leadership behaviors. When we talk to executives about their leadership style and the need to incorporate unnatural traits in order to improve performance, they often nod their heads vigorously and are enthusiastic about making the changes required. Rather than become defensive and attempt to justify their natural leadership roles, they frequently agree that unnatural traits are just what they and their employees need to drive business performance.

Yet we have found a gap between word and deed. No matter what people say or think, they often have difficulty translating intellectual agreement into action. Part of the problem is the same challenge that dogs people who are trying to diet, stop smoking, and start exercising. Changing long-term ingrained behaviors is difficult, and leadership behavior is no exception. It's even more difficult when these behaviors are largely unconscious, as many leadership behaviors are. On top of that, strong leadership cultures teach people specific lessons about how to lead that become dogma over time. Even with the support of management, it can be difficult to get people to preserve certain positive aspects of their company culture and at the same time embrace new leadership approaches.

We are working with a well-known company that wants to emphasize business process improvement and reduce cycle time. Although the CEO and senior leaders have embraced the Six Sigma methodology of minimizing mistakes or defects, their leadership style and implicit cultural rules emphasize individualistic, entrepreneurial leadership. They went so far as to hire a senior executive from the outside who embodied the needed process skills. But six months later, everyone was grousing that the new leader "just didn't fit in around here."

For these and other reasons, overcoming resistance to unnatural leadership can be challenging. We have found that being aware of resistance points can help people meet this challenge. By understanding why managers shy away from unnatural leadership acts, companies can facilitate both their own and others' ability to take on new and different ways of leading.

Points of Resistance

Some otherwise bright and talented executives find themselves unable to extend trust before people earn it despite being encouraged to do so by their bosses and the demands of their business. Their personality prevents them. Others struggle with acknowledging, much less exposing, their vulnerabilities, though when asked what they are afraid of, they often cannot identify anything. And there are those who are prisoners of their experience, even though they know they could advance their careers if they were to escape from that prison.

Resistance to unnatural leadership is not always logical, rational, or explicable. At first, the source of this resistance may be difficult to identify. Over the years, we have worked with many executive teams and have encountered acute and subtle resistance to change. We have explored these sources and created a list of resistance points to unnatural leadership.

Counterintuitivity

"It doesn't feel right" or "It makes me uncomfortable" are ways of expressing the counterintuitive nature of certain unnatural leadership traits. Most people "feel" that they should recruit team members with whom they have worked before or whom they deem trustworthy. Adding as a team member someone they have clashed with in the past or someone they do not know well seems to go against every one of their leadership instincts. A small voice inside of them protests that they are about to do something a real leader would never do. But they do not bother to analyze what fresh opinions might add to a team or how dissenting voices might help the team deal with new and unfamiliar problems. As natural leaders, they feel compelled to surround themselves with an inner circle of people they know well.

We are consulting to a large global corporation that has acknowledged that senior-level executive selections usually are based on who knows whom—despite a world-class succession planning system and a leadership bench filled with hundreds of talented people. When a senior executive in this company is about to fill a key position, she examines the slate and picks someone she knows. An executive who does not know anyone on the slate calls someone she trusts and asks that person whom he would pick. Leadership planning systems seem ineffectual when confronted with cultural reality.

The Lack of a Singular, Personal Point of View on Leadership

Surprisingly, many leaders cannot articulate their own view of effective leadership and have no time to read leadership books. They are too busy doing to think about how and why they are doing it. We run senior leadership Action Learning programs in many global companies in which we ask leaders to articulate their view of leadership and explain their personal theory of motivation and rewards. Yet often they are unable to verbalize their perspective—or they do not have one. Highly effective executives rarely reflect on their leadership philosophy, and as a result, they reflexively follow their education and instincts about how to lead. For many, an Action Learning program forces them to reflect on what they do and who they are, something they do not do on the job. They resist unnatural leadership traits because they are not used to stopping the action long enough to think about new leadership ideas and whether they fit with their personal viewpoint. Another way of stating this resistance point is that they lack a theory of the case. Because they cannot explain why they lead the way they do, new ideas about leadership are threatening to them. They lack the anchor that a personal vision of leadership provides.

Real or Perceived Organizational Sanctions

We have found that many people blame their organizations or senior leadership for their resistance to unnatural acts. In some instances, they are right to blame them. For instance, senior leaders in one well-known company we have worked with has constructed a new leadership model for the company emphasizing creativity, entrepreneurship, and empowerment. They want people to challenge their bosses and take responsibility for making decisions up and down the line. In reality, though, everyone knows that in this company's strong execution-oriented culture, anyone who crosses the boss is considered not on the team. Despite the explicit emphasis given to an environment open to certain unnatural leadership behaviors, the implicit reality is that people are still spending time trying to figure out what the boss wants (and figuring out ways to meet the boss's needs). Frequently, we notice this in jokes and other humor when a group of subordinates decides who among them is going to tell the boss bad news, a change in plans, or a fundamental disagreement with a strongly held opinion. In most companies, senior leadership is unwilling to take meaningful steps to demonstrate that the old culture is no longer acceptable and more unnatural acts are required.

Sometimes, however, management is sincere about changing a company and creating a culture receptive to unnatural acts. Unfortunately, the old culture is so powerful that no matter what leaders say or do, no one believes them. One company undertook a major initiative to convince its leaders to adopt unnatural leadership practices such as connecting instead of creating, and coaching and teaching as well as leading and inspiring. From communicating this initiative verbally and in writing, to holding seminars and training programs designed to help leaders become more effective, the senior leaders made an effort to motivate people to shift their leadership behaviors. Nonetheless, most managers did not believe they could trust the explicit messages they were receiving and fell back on natural leadership behaviors.

Success Patterns

This resistance factor is a bit more subtle than the others but no less insidious. Some companies believe that there is no point investing in leadership development because the current leadership practices work just fine. They fear tampering with their successful formula and see no need to endorse new and unusual practices that do not fit that formula.

We have worked with a number of companies at the top of their market and technology curves that could not accept how the future may look different from the present. Although the senior leaders were sophisticated and very aware about how companies like Daimler-Benz, Ford, Compaq, Gateway, Lucent, and others did not adapt to a fast-changing marketplace, they have trouble translating that awareness into unnatural leadership behaviors. They fear doing anything that might compromise their current performance and results. It is a major irony of business that the seeds of destruction are often sown at the pinnacle of success. Creating diverse teams that may struggle to agree on business direction or coaching people rather than motivating and directing them seem like actions that do not fit the company's success pattern.

Even moderately successful companies rationalize why they must stick with their current culture. Consider a company that has been struggling for years with unpredictable financial performance. Because it has difficulty forecasting accurate financial results, it often experiences eleventh-hour crises when it has not met targets and goes through a mad scramble (cutting costs, accelerating sales programs) to avoid disappointing Wall Street analysts. As you might imagine, this crisis mentality puts tremendous pressure on people, creates turmoil, and encourages some degree of deception in the ranks. At the same time, this annual firefighting usually works. Each year, the company manages to make its projected numbers, drain the orders pipeline, and backfill the fourth quarter, and as a result, management sees no need to change. Getting ahead of the game seems unnecessary, and the last few months of the year are planned to achieve extraordinary results compared to what had been accomplished before. Leaders who exhibit unnatural behaviors are frowned on and viewed as veering away from "the way we do things around here." Resistance therefore is based on the mistaken notion that success is predicated on preserving past practices. What senior leaders do not see is that they are maintaining only marginal success that is nowhere near what it could be.

The Fear of Giving Up Power and Control

Many of the unnatural acts we have discussed entail giving up a certain amount of power and control. Working in a matrix, acknowledging personal vulnerabilities, extending trust before it is earned, or revealing a shadow side all require leaders to cede some of their traditional power over others. We coach many executives who believe in the core of their being that if they are responsible for results, they better make sure they retain control over everything that affects those results. Companies reinforce this belief through senior management meetings in which people are grilled about their numbers and organizations and embarrassed if something unexpected has occurred on their watch. Performance measurement and reward systems measure people on and reward them for meeting traditional leadership criteria (such as achieving individual objectives and business unit performance).

We recently ran an executive committee team-building session in which opportunities for better alignment were endlessly discussed. Midway through the meeting, the CEO announced he was changing the reward system to reflect group performance immediately. At that moment, behaviors changed. "What do I need to do in order to prevail over you?" became "How can I help you right now?"

Some companies tacitly endorse the search for perfection and the avoidance of mistakes. Power and control are crucial if mistakes are to be avoided, the reasoning goes. In some industries, such as accounting, pharmaceutical research, and silicon wafer manufacturing, perfection is an absolute requirement, and leaders raised in this context often transfer the need for perfection to every aspect of their leadership style. Quite often, they cannot see when an 80 percent solution may be just as viable as (and maybe more so than) a 100 percent solution. What you give up in perfection, you more than make up for in speed, more inclusive decision making, and so on. To apply Six Sigma standards to the messy, imperfect process of leading human beings may be a signal that someone is afraid of loosening his grip on the reins.

The "Trust No One" Mind-Set

It is astonishing that leadership in organizations still subscribes to the World War II slogan, "Loose lips sink ships." Although few leaders will admit that they do not trust their staff, they nevertheless communicate distrust by refusing to discuss with them the future of a product, the need for a company to retool, or the loss of significant business. In high-performing organizations such as GE and Intel, the trend, however, is toward much more transparency.

A very successful CEO once asked us, "How can I motivate people unless I accentuate the positive and give them reason to hope?" While extending trust to those who have not yet earned it is one of our unnatural acts, all the acts require some degree of trust. Leaders must get past the idea that people cannot handle the truth or that they will flee en masse at a whiff of bad news. The remnants of paternalistic management are best seen in how companies handle information. Most people are surprisingly resilient and respond better to leaders who tell them the truth, even if it is about potential difficulties. Nonetheless, we have seen many outstanding leaders acknowledge a truth to themselves but refuse to help others deal with the same reality. These leaders refuse to tell their employees that they have to do things differently—perhaps learn a new technology, increase sales, reduce errors, or find new ways to get work done—fearing that they might take offense and leave. In fact, if people cannot handle the truth and do not appreciate the trust a leader invests in them, perhaps they should leave.

A Rejection of the Trickster

Given the unpredictable, volatile nature of today's work environment, we need to accept the disconcerting surprises that have become a routine part of this environment. Ancient cultures acknowledged the role of an unseen trickster who makes a sudden appearance and changes things in unexpected (and sometimes humorous or ironic) ways. Rather than trying to eliminate the trickster from corporate life or complaining about his capricious nature, leaders need to accept this creature and learn how to capitalize on the changes he introduces.

Technical glitches, unexpected events, and missed opportunities are some of the things that can only be explained by the trickster. An e-mail intended for Customer A will occasionally wind up in the hands of Customer B. A company may find itself without a key supplier because the country where one of its manufacturers is located has just nationalized its factories. Right-versus-right choices, in fact, are classic trickster stuff. Rather than being paralyzed by a decision between cutting costs or increasing marketing to pull out of a product forecast decline, leaders must learn to accept the absurdity of the choice and make the best decision possible under the circumstances. Resisting this unnatural act because you do not like the tricks the trickster plays is a no-win position. Appreciating the trickster's ways is a much more productive (if unnatural) way to go.

Examples of Resistance at Work

On the surface, it would seem that people could easily get past these resistance factors through an open conversation with a boss or through coaching. Within most companies, however, it often takes a more concerted effort to overcome these factors and learn to embrace unnatural acts. To grasp the difficulty of overcoming these factors, we'd like to tell you the stories of Ron and Len.

Ron is a very strong senior leader in a highly competitive and globally successful organization. It would be fair to describe its culture as Darwinian and Ron as the embodiment of this culture. After joining the company right after he graduated from college, Ron received promotion after promotion by outmaneuvering his internal competition through a series of "land grabs"; he has made convincing arguments to his various bosses that he can manage projects, people, and resources better than his peers, and he has backed up his arguments with results. In essence, Ron followed the prescribed route to the top in his organization, one that condoned his aggressive posture. Over the years, he became the classic motivational, take-charge leader, stepping on some toes along the way but more than compensating with his performance. Although Ron is viewed as a potential CEO successor in his company, his boss called us in to coach him. The reason, he said, is that although Ron "is bright, talented, and gets things done, I don't trust him." Other people told us that although Ron is a strong leader, he had serious problems getting along with others.

To be a CEO in this company today requires different leadership skills from those required even three years ago. Unnatural leadership acts like connecting instead of creating and extending trust before it's earned are foreign to Ron. Yet these and other traits are crucial for the company. Global project teams require interdependence and constant coordination, marketing must work with development and manufacturing, and the company is a much more diverse place in a much different competitive environment than the one Ron joined many years ago.

The problem is that Ron is being asked to move away from the very behaviors for which the company has rewarded him over the years. Not only that, but senior leaders do not want him to make a 180-degree change, since they still value his results-producing skills, and he knows it. What is confusing to Ron is that he needs to integrate new behaviors into his repertoire that seem at odds with the traits he has honed to perfection over the past seventeen years. Although Ron is acutely aware of the changes he must make if he wants to be a serious CEO candidate, he is uncertain how to make them and wonders if they are really worth making. He is considering leaving the company because it is changing in ways he does not like and there are other companies that will appreciate what he brings to the table, especially given the globally recognized brand he now represents. Ron has a serious dilemma. Is the company serious about the messages he is suddenly receiving? Should he leave or recommit to the company and take the hard steps of changing his leadership behaviors? Some days he prefers to rationalize why he shouldn't change, and others he prefers to get on with it.

Len is a top manager in a beleaguered company. Facing significant financial pressure to meet analyst and investor expectations, Len worried whether he would be able to maintain the company's level of performance in the face of changing distribution networks and a new business model. Len knew only one way to get through a crisis, and that was to throw himself into it with a hero-like intensity. For months, his every waking moment was consumed by the company's woes. Despite his energy and effort, Len was unable to resolve the crisis. Still, he persisted in working long hours, as if his mere presence in the company's headquarters might be enough to see the company through.

During this period, Len dramatically changed his personal routine. A devoted exerciser, Len stopped working out, claiming he no longer had time to go to his health club. He canceled two vacations he had planned with his family and frequently stayed so late at the office that he did not eat dinner at home. He suffered from insomnia and used it as an excuse to get up in the middle of the night and work on the computer.

Len began to look noticeably pale and haggard. Just as disturbing were his personality changes. There were times when he would uncharacteristically snap at others, and other instances when he would withdraw from the action and hunker down in his office with the door closed for hours. One day, Len told his inner circle that he did not know if he was up to the job and was highly self-critical of his performance and the company's future. His staff was devastated. They knew that Len was not being realistic—the company was in the doldrums, not in bankruptcy—and he was behaving like a fallen hero. Len had skipped the unnatural step of revealing his vulnerabilities and was simply wallowing in self-pity and confessing to crimes he did not commit. He resisted the unnatural act of keeping himself in good shape because it seemed to be a luxury a true leader would not afford himself.

Later in the chapter, we'll return to Len and Ron and how they dealt with their respective resistance factors. First, however, we focus on the tools and techniques that we have found to be effective in overcoming this resistance.

An Arsenal of Resistance Fighters

It is impossible to teach people unnatural leadership skills by sending them to one training program or giving them an instruction manual. In fact, these are the worst ways to impart these skills for many reasons, not the least of which is that they do not address the resistance factors.

When we work with our clients, we use Action Learning or Action Coaching methods to help people make the transition to new leadership behaviors. Both revolve around assignments that are crucial to the organization and that wrap learning around real work. In this way, people engage emotionally as well as intellectually and respond on a deep level to what they learn. By receiving feedback about who they are in a work setting (rather than just about what they do) and having the opportunity to reflect on what they learn, people experience personal and professional growth. This learning context enables them to get past resistance factors such as fear of giving up power and control. Whereas they might not be willing to give up power and control in a typical work setting, they will be more likely to do so in a hybrid environment of learning and work. Leaders become part of a team of other high-powered learners and work collaboratively on a business project. They often do this while undertaking their regular full-time job—and so must give up some of their routine and part of their control to others who carry on back on the job. An intense Action Learning program might not only throw them together with others on a demanding assignment that they cannot personally drive, but also give them opportunities to deal with their feelings in this challenging environment. In this way, they get beyond the purely cognitive awareness to something deeper.

Action Techniques

There are many techniques that are part of this action approach. Let's look at some of the ones that we have found to be highly effective and that we use to reduce resistance to unnatural leadership.

Refocusing Attention on the Big Picture

Leaders become mired in the details of their daily to-do list. Many times, they do not see how it's possible to acknowledge their shadow side even while it works to reduce their effectiveness. They look for the single right answer to a business issue rather than develop a right-versus-right mentality until they become aware of what is taking place outside their teams, departments, divisions, and organizations. When they become aware of a larger context or best practices in their own company or see what's going on in other organizations, however, they sometimes gain the impetus to fight their natural inclination to resist. Sometimes in Action Learning and Action Coaching programs, the first step is simply to build a context of how the world has changed. When people realize that their leadership behaviors may impede their business results but can improve their behaviors, they are much more willing to change.

We conducted a senior-level Action Learning program at a large pharmaceutical company designed to help senior executives look at the implications of the Internet economy on their business. We arranged for them to visit a number of high-tech and dot-com companies with a significantly different management style. They were profoundly affected not just in terms of the Internet's effect on their business but culturally as well. They witnessed a very different style of leadership at a number of Silicon Valley companies, and although they were not ready to adopt everything, they saw the relevance of certain unnatural practices for their own company and broadened their context.

Acknowledging the Paradox and Chaos Facing Leaders Today

Companies routinely issue strategic plans even though the future is increasingly unpredictable and volatile. They blithely guarantee the benefits of a merger, only to report in twelve months that the expected benefits will "take longer than expected." Through everything from meeting schedules to calendars, routines, travel plans, and events, senior management often acts as if their world is an orderly, logical place. Many executive rows in top companies convey the impression that everything is completely quiet and totally under control. One senior executive we have coached has his calendar almost completely filled for the next twelve months with management routines.

Unfortunately, the business world is an increasingly chaotic and random place. Consider that CEO tenure now averages three years (down from seven), two missed quarters constitute failure, a missed technology bet can reduce a company's market advantage overnight, and merged organizations redefine long-standing cultures almost as quickly. Senior management may need to communicate that ambiguity and unpredictability are the norms. We have worked with many executive committees that confidently discuss the future and courses of action. Privately, individuals confide to us that they have never seen anything like the current situation before but are unwilling to disclose their concern to others. When they open up, leaders discover it is much easier not to be prisoners of past success and accept the trickster as part of work life.

Encouraging and Catalyzing Self-Awareness

Leaders may need some impetus to overcome their resistance to exploring alternative leadership approaches. Coaching, open dialogue with other leaders, and various feedback processes can provide that impetus, helping leaders recognize the consequences of their natural leadership traits. It is only when someone is told that his direct reports find his controlling personality and tendency to issue directives off-putting that he is willing to consider alternatives. The higher an executive ascends in the corporate hierarchy, the harder it is to obtain this type of feedback.

Just about every Fortune 500 company has a chatroom in which the senior executives are openly discussed. These bulletin boards are often brutally honest and sometimes painful for leaders to read; many executives deny reading them. Nevertheless, they offer senior leaders unique insights into how their leadership is being received and into the moods and grievances of those motivated to write.

Challenging Assumptions

This technique works together with developing self-awareness. People resist unnatural leadership acts because they hold certain false assumptions or because they have never really examined the assumptions underlying their actions. For instance, one leader we work with operated on the unconscious assumption that his direct reports wanted strong, clear direction; in fact, they were not comfortable being told explicitly what to do. For this particular executive, the assumption grew out of the corporate culture in which he had advanced, as well as the home in which he was raised. As coaches, we challenged his assumptions, getting him to consider whether his direct reports might have their own ideas about how to deal with customers, especially because they were closer to customers than he was. After talking with us as well as his team, he was willing to test his assumptions and experiment with unnatural leadership behaviors. For the first time in his career, he recognized that his highly controlling style might not serve his direct reports or his organization as well as a less controlling style might.

Starting with Small, Unnatural Steps

Resistance is often a more attractive alternative than making a sharp change in leadership behaviors. Faced with the daunting task of embarking on any significant personal change program, most people resist. For some leaders, implementing any of the ten unnatural acts is intimidating. What can facilitate implementation, however, is allowing people to make a smaller-scale change in a safe area, such as behavior in meetings. As part of our Action Coaching programs, we often ask a leader to pick a project or task that can serve as a laboratory for controlled experiments with new behaviors. One senior executive opted to experiment with a new project team he needed to choose. Because the team was not involved in a critical area and its mission was not tied to a deadline, this executive felt comfortable changing his approach. We encouraged him to choose at least some members for the team whom he did not know but who represented a greater diversity of ideas and expertise than he was used to. We also had him anticipate and rehearse how he might manage the team differently. Ultimately, he found that his work with this team was more productive and more satisfying than any of his team projects in the past. With this small leadership accomplishment under his belt, he was willing to commit another unnatural act with a project team that had a more prominent role to play.

With another executive who ran his senior leadership meetings like a juggernaut with rigid agendas and predictable outcomes, we encouraged him to introduce five minutes of blue-sky discussion and brainstorming after each two hours of planned interaction. It was an intimidating possibility, but he began to develop his flexible and creative capacity.

Tools for Overcoming Resistance

Within the framework of these techniques, specific tools can help overcome pockets of resistance to unnatural acts. Following is a sampling of the ones we have found to be particularly effective.

Designating Experimentation Zones

Designate times and places where people are encouraged to test new ideas. It may be as simple as setting aside a specific time for a team of leaders to talk about an issue without adhering to written and unwritten policies about how a given issue is traditionally handled. Arthur Andersen in London created a "chaos zone" where leaders spend time thinking about what they do in different ways so that they are not bound by traditional views of how the business is run. Experimentation zones give people the opportunity to take small unnatural steps without fear of sanction.

Using Peer Coaching, Peer Review, and 360-Degree Feedback Surveys

Resistance factors flourish in isolating environments and dissolve in open, feedback-rich ones. For leaders to be willing to expose their vulnerabilities and reveal their shadow sides, sometimes it takes the jolt that peer coaching, peer review, and 360-degree feedback can provide.

CDR International Leadership Derailers

Psychologist Robert Hogan has developed psychological tools for CDR International to help leaders understand their vulnerabilities under stress; we have found that these tools also can help them become more receptive to unnatural acts. Leaders who use these tools develop a heightened self-awareness and think about their own long-standing behaviors that may not be as productive as they assumed. For instance, some people who are usually self-confident can become arrogant under stress and reject the advice of others, and perfectionist tendencies might translate into micromanagement when the pressure is on.

When leaders know what their personal vulnerabilities are, they can often prevent them from becoming career or performance derailers. Many times, leaders end up relying on natural leadership behaviors under stress; they become more authoritarian, more controlling, and more unwilling to listen to anyone outside their inner circle. Recognizing this tendency and the harm it can do helps leaders consider unnatural acts even under stressful conditions.

Reflecting on Consequences of Actions

As simple as reflection is, it is often difficult to get people to take time out from doing and just think about the consequences of their actions. Specifically, we ask leaders to think long and hard about their leadership acts and assumptions. We have found that it's useful to ask people to translate their reflections into a personal vision that describes the type of leader they want to be. In Action Learning programs, participants begin each day with organized reflection about what is happening to them, what they are learning, and their reactions. For many, this is their only opportunity to step back from the action of their job and gauge their own reactions.

People do not change without serious contemplation of who they are and what they have done. Resistance to unnatural behaviors is easy when little thought is given to a personal leadership approach; managers do not give themselves the time and space to question that approach. When they reflect on it, however, they're much more likely to see what has not worked and consider alternatives.

Using Transition Teaching

We have found that leaders are frequently most open to learning unnatural leadership skills during periods of transition. These periods may entail a promotion—from a manager to a manager of managers, for instance—or a horizontal transition, such as assuming responsibility for a new project team or working on a new client engagement. Typically, people attempt to transfer their old leadership approach to their new situation, and it is not always effective. When they fail in some way, a teachable moment materializes. Many companies now attempt to capitalize on these moments by introducing leaders to unnatural leadership skills, providing coaching and other training that encourages them to consider these alternatives in their new situations. At Johnson & Johnson, for example, leaders in transition to new senior assignments are given coaching and new information to handle their new assignment more effectively.

Personality Issues

Engaging in unnatural acts takes a certain amount of risk, and some people are more inclined than others to take these risks. Resistance therefore may be more a matter of personality than of culture. As much as an organization's culture might encourage adoption of unnatural acts and as many tools as it might provide to facilitate this adoption, whether a leader embraces unnatural acts can come down to personality. An inherently distrustful executive, for example, may be unwilling to risk extending trust to others before it is earned. A leader who is an inveterate pleaser may refuse to assemble a diverse team that may engage in sometimes acrimonious debate. Therefore, consider your own personality or the personality of those you are coaching when you attempt to encourage unnatural leadership. A small minority of people are probably inherently unable to embrace these unnatural behaviors. We have found, however, that most leaders are capable of embracing them if they receive sufficient support from their organizations. With proper coaching, a system that rewards unnatural acts, and a culture that makes it possible to test these acts, even "control freaks" can learn to democratize and decelerate decision making.

Some people do not overcome their resistance to unnatural acts until they are confronted with a crisis. Until that crisis point, they sincerely believe they are doing the right things and refuse to challenge these beliefs until their everyday reality dramatically suggests otherwise. Mark, for instance, had a propensity for restructuring companies that left investors pleased but the surviving employees devastated. In midcareer, his methods failed miserably. Not only did a downsizing he orchestrated fail to deliver the expected financial results, but it left him open to harsh criticism from both his own workforce and outsiders. Only on receiving and reflecting on this criticism was Mark ready and able to consider making some unnatural changes in his leadership style.

Overcoming resistance sometimes requires a personalized approach. If you'll recall our earlier example of Ron (the senior leader in a Darwinian culture), he responded to continuous and pointed feedback. As political a creature as he was, he also was sensitive to what others thought of him. We found one direct report who genuinely loved Ron and was unusually perceptive about Ron's leadership style. We asked Ron to listen to this direct report and his belief that Ron's manipulative style and disregard for other people's ideas made people think he could not be trusted. This individual belonged to the same church as Ron (Ron had a strong spiritual side that he kept well hidden from others at the company), and although he was reluctant to listen to him at first, we facilitated some meetings that helped Ron open up and begin a real process of transformation. Ron now possesses a number of unnatural leadership traits that he has put to good use. Not only is he more effective in his job and more likely to be a good CEO candidate, but he is energized by his unnatural acts. It's difficult to perform at your peak when you are leaving angry, unhappy direct reports in your wake, and Ron is no longer creating that hostility in people he works with.

Len, the fallen hero who was failing to take care of himself, required a different type of intervention. He did not grasp the connection between his physical exhaustion and his morale-lowering behaviors with his team. He just could not admit to himself that his physical and emotional exhaustion was having an impact on his work performance. As outside coaches, we were able to help him see this connection. Len was able to admit to us (as he was not able to admit to others) that he had not been taking care of himself. We helped him realize that there was nothing irresponsible about taking the time to exercise when the company was in trouble. Once he accepted this fact and started exercising, he was able to shore up the confidence in his leadership that had begun to erode. He began feeling better about himself when he got in shape, and that feeling was communicated through his body language and attitude to the people who worked with him.

Setting a Good Example

CEOs and other members of senior management teams can reduce resistance to unnatural leadership in a number of ways. We have discussed some of the actions they can take, such as creating formal and informal rewards that encourage rather than discourage unnatural acts and institutionalizing coaching, feedback, and other self-awareness generating tools. It is also important for senior executives to protect people who exhibit unnatural behaviors. In some organizational cultures, leaders who act unnaturally are castigated. "This isn't the way we do things around here," they are told. These risk takers may need some organized protection: a senior executive who shelters them from questions about their effectiveness or other subtle sanctions for example.

But the more important thing top executives can do is model unnatural leadership behaviors themselves. Marcia is the CEO of a large organization who shared the results of a feedback survey with her five hundred top executives. The survey results were not all favorable, and a number of weaknesses were identified. Nonetheless, she was willing to reveal her vulnerabilities, a dramatic gesture that made a huge impact on the leadership cadre of the company. It has had a ripple effect, in that many of these top executives began acknowledging their vulnerabilities to their direct reports.

Another COO we worked with began stopping every meeting he chaired with five minutes remaining and asked people how they thought it went, what could have been improved, and what might have been done differently to make the meeting more productive. This had a much more profound impact than if this COO had issued a memo about making meetings more productive and suggesting that an assessment process be instituted. By encouraging reflection and dialogue, this COO opened up the conversation to real learning. Actions do speak louder than words, and other executives imitated this COO's action. The unnatural action of democratizing the decision-making process was picked up by many other leaders because the COO had clearly modeled how it could be done and had given his seal of approval by his action.

If you were to ask us what reduces resistance to unnatural leadership behaviors fastest, we would say, "A COO who models these behaviors."

Assessing Your Resistance to Unnatural Leadership

Everyone has some difficulty using unnatural leadership behaviors. What resistance do you have to overcome to be an unnatural leader? Rate the difficulty of each type of resistance for you.

Resistance Point	Your Susceptibility
Allowing yourself to do something counterintuitive to your leadership instincts	1 2 3 4 5 Not Difficult Very Difficult
Forming your own singular, personal point of view on leadership	1 2 3 4 5 Not Difficult Very Difficult
Refusing to blame your organization ("They won't let me be an unnatural leader.")	1 2 3 4 5 Not Difficult Very Difficult
Challenging your current leadership pattern	1 2 3 4 5 Not Difficult Very Difficult
Giving up some of your power and control	1 2 3 4 5 Not Difficult Very Difficult
Trusting your direct reports to handle the truth	1 2 3 4 5 Not Difficult Very Difficult

What Makes You Resist?

Think about the points of resistance that you assigned the highest rating. What do you think makes you resist? What prevents you from taking on new unnatural leadership behaviors?

Overcoming Your Resistance

List three specific actions that you can take to overcome your resistance and adopt unnatural leadership behaviors.

1.

2.

3.

Assessing Your Resistance to Unnatural Leadership (Cont.)

Becoming an unnatural leader often requires focused practice. What project or assignment can you use to experiment with new behaviors?

Creating an Unnatural Leadership Culture

What do you need to do to lower resistance to unnatural leadership behaviors for others? How can you encourage others to become unnatural leaders?

What actions can you take to create an environment that encourages unnatural leadership? How can you coach, recognize, reward, and model the behaviors that will build an unnatural leadership culture?

Part Two

Personal Challenges for the Unnatural Leader

Chapter Four

Refuse to Be a Prisoner of Experience

To a certain extent, we are all prisoners of our experiences, and this is not necessarily a bad thing. We learn from our past successes and failures, and this experience helps us be more effective because we are not entering every situation as a neophyte. The most natural thing in the world when you face a difficult business situation is to think about how you dealt with a similar situation successfully in the past and repeat that action.

We are not suggesting that leaders ignore their experiences. Rather, our suggestion is that they question them. People who are prisoners of experience repeat their actions and decisions with metronomic regularity. They have great difficulty doing something that did not work in the past or trying something new that is foreign to their experiences. In essence, they deprive themselves of options; they lack the ability to see alternative strategies or think about situations in fresh terms the way unnatural leaders can.

In a world of slow change, leaders could use a basic formula to deal with most situations; it was a formula contained in well-known case histories and best practices. Leadership programs taught by business schools encouraged leaders to study abstract cases and second-guess the decisions made. Large corporations fostered a leadership image, subtly shaping their layers of leadership through selection and training to think and act alike. They hired people from very similar backgrounds who were then promoted through the leadership ranks with similar experiences. Potential general managers were shipped to Europe for development, and finance leaders were rotated throughout the function to gain perspective.

As a result, these companies moved with reassuring predictability. Everyone knew what companies like P&G and IBM stood for, and their leaders were reassuringly similar. Their cultural confidence, certainty of purpose, and unspoken shared knowledge about how to be a leader served these organizations well—that is, until the world began to become more unpredictable. Once the business environment became global, volatile, unpredictable, and ambiguous, experience became less a teacher and more a constraint.

Common Experiences, Common Problems

Being a prisoner of experience adversely affects leaders in a wide variety of ways. Let's examine some of the most common problems in different areas.

In just about every organization today, a leader exists who is having trouble adapting to the new casual dress norms decreed by the company. Having been raised in a time when formal dress codes were the rule, they often unconsciously associate a casual wardrobe with being unprofessional and indicative of sloppy work habits. They have some difficulty, never vocalized, not only selecting their own dress on casual days, but accepting that this new dress style reflects different values and has nothing to do with an individual's ability or willingness to work hard. In fact, personal preference regarding dress is remarkably variable across generations and work styles.

We have a client, the head of an operating unit of a very large, traditional, global Fortune 100 company, who related the story of visiting the CEO of a Fortune 100 technology company that was created less than a generation years ago. Our client and his team flew in their company plane in business suits, arrived at the technology company, and were escorted to a conference room. While they were waiting for the other CEO, a young ponytailed man in a Grateful Dead T-shirt and blue jeans entered the room and began setting up the audiovisual equipment. Our client asked the technician where they could get some coffee, and the technician responded pleasantly and got them some coffee himself. Later, when the technology company's CEO arrived, our client was stunned to see the technician sit down at the conference table for the meeting and even more surprised when he learned that this technician was actually the company's CFO. As our client apologized for not recognizing him earlier, he became aware of how easy it was to make assumptions based on experience.

These assumptions can be costly. For instance, leaders who are locked into traditional work values struggle to attract, retain, and develop talent. Jay Conger, in a 1998 *Harvard Business Review* article, noted that employees are no longer content with the answer to the question, "What do you want me to do?" They now are asking, "Why should I do what you want me to do?" They are also questioning how a particular assignment will contribute to their career development and evaluating a job based on whether the work is "meaningful." Because of various trends—including the fact that most people will make a number of job moves during the course of their career—they do not just ask "what" questions. And a leader who is unprepared to answer the "why" queries will quickly alienate direct reports.

Consider the case of Andrew, a senior executive with a larger corporation, who was supervising Nancy, a talented young manager who had spent the past several years in a staff position designed to help her obtain technical skills and an understanding of the company and industry. She had reached the point where she was becoming a significant contributor but was frustrated because her learning had come to a standstill due to the nature of her job. Andrew was well aware that Nancy would leave the company if he did not find a way to help her develop herself in new functions and skill areas. Yet he felt it was the wrong thing to do. Andrew had been stuck in a number of positions where he had been bored, but his patience had ultimately been rewarded by the organization. He assumed that Nancy's good work would ultimately be noticed and lead to a better position, and the move would happen when it was right for the organization.

Andrew, however, was able to challenge his assumptions. He knew that some of his leadership peers had complained bitterly about losing talented people because the company was so wedded to the ways things had been done in the past. For this reason, he moved Nancy into a position where she could learn more about business operations and achieve greater visibility within the company. Nancy was delighted with the move and stayed, becoming an even more productive and valuable contributor.

On a larger scale, many senior leaders grew up in companies and became confined by their organizations' traditions and business models. Business schools are still teaching the notorious example of John Akers, the former CEO of IBM who faced the uncomfortable choice of destroying his current business success to ride the PC curve upward. Leadership of PC manufacturing and sales has shifted constantly over the past few years. Companies such as Dell, Apple, Compaq, and Microsoft introduced personal computers and other innovations first that left IBM, NEC, Wang, Nixdorf, and other traditional marketplace leaders trailing in the areas of product and software development. Akers and other senior leaders were unable or unwilling to move IBM away from mainframe market dominance and toward software sales because their experience told them software innovations were insignificant. Fortunately, IBM has found a new niche in services that has remade it as a dominant player.

We are working with Pacific Gas & Electric in California, the utility involved in the well-publicized controversy involving energy price caps in California. Its predicament (bankruptcy and restructuring) is not a result of its leaders being prisoners of experience—it's much more a result of a confluence of events, such as huge demands for power, the inability to raise rates, and semideregulation of the industry—but the company has worked hard to redefine its experience given new opportunities. For many years, the utility was run in a traditional manner with a command-and-control management style. In the past few years, it has revised that style and invested heavily in process management, quality improvement, and cost control. Even more recently, in the midst of a highly volatile political and economic situation, it ran a series of Action Learning programs to challenge senior leaders' assumptions, look at the situation, and question their own thinking. The company will undoubtedly emerge stronger and reconfigured as a result of these investments in learning.

Another organization we know well, Levi Strauss & Co., missed the initial window of opportunity when teenagers turned to the street style of very wide jeans. The company assumed this was a passing fad, like many other passing fads of the past, and believed that the market would soon return to the basic Levi's 501 product, a leader in the industry for years. For many years, Levi's executives focused on improving operations but missed the substantial shifts in their core business, and were reluctant to acknowledge that this passing fad had become a significant trend. In the late 1990s, revenue declined by almost $2 billion as young people turned to trendier brands and fabrics. Since then the company has restructured itself, reduced manufacturing costs, and brought in new leadership and has begun the slow climb back to market dominance. The problem was that Levi's leaders, by their own admission, were locked in their own very successful experience. They defined value based on their position in the marketplace and their products and services. To them, the traditional look of the 501 product, its quality, and its price provided customers with great value—and for years this was true. What they failed to factor into the equation was that customers were redefining what they valued.

How the Experience Trap Works

You would think that smart, savvy leaders are alert to the dangers of relying too heavily on experience. After all, the business press is filled with stories of companies that win one day and lose the next. Who hasn't heard repeatedly that companies and individuals must adapt in order to survive? In practice, however, we frequently fail to integrate this question into our leadership behaviors. Let's look at four well-known shifts in the environment and how leaders are responding to them:

• *An increasingly diverse workforce.* With all that has been written about this subject and all the training programs in this area, you would think that all leaders would recognize the need to adapt their leadership style. Many of today's leaders, however, began in companies where the majority (often the vast majority) of managerial employees were white males. Today, the workforce of most companies includes women, minorities, foreign nationals, and all generations—all of them with very different value systems. Motivating someone who intends to stay with the company for no more than five years (for example, because he or she is planning to retire or return home to another country) is much different from motivating an up-and-coming twenty-five year old who thinks he is ready to become CEO. Nonetheless, many leaders motivate as they were motivated. Certain leadership lessons that did not take diversity into account were drummed into their heads, and they reflexively fall back on what they were taught. "I treat everyone the same" is often a badge of honor for traditional leaders, but this approach often disregards the importance of individual differences.

- *The accelerating pace of change.* This is something that everyone knows, yet we still see leaders refusing to move unless everyone is on board. In other words, they prioritize agreement when the real priority is quick response. You have probably met business unit or functional leaders who required reams of data before making a decision, even when there was not enough time for the analysis. Digital Equipment Corporation (DEC) was a wonderful, consensus, people-oriented company that dominated the market in the 1980s. Why it missed the technology shift from minicomputers to PCs is still debated in business schools, but its culture and leadership relied on slow, methodical, and consensus management even though changes in the industry were occurring at mind-boggling speed. Fast unilateral decisions were crucial, but they were not made. Because DEC's egalitarian, consensus-driven culture had helped the company become successful, everyone assumed it would help keep it successful. There's an old saying to the effect of "dancing with the one who brung you to the dance." Sometimes, however, you need to move past your gratitude for being brung to the dance twenty years ago and consider other partners.

- *Technological shifts.* How many top executives do you know who still eschew e-mail, do not communicate on-line with employees, and rarely explore the Internet for information? They like to communicate and obtain information the old-fashioned way, and there are still many assistants who do the translating from e-mail into the executive suite. Some of these leaders insist that there is no substitute for a face-to-face encounter, and they are right in some cases. In others, however, they are absolutely wrong. Their preferred mode of communication limits them because they will not invest themselves in adapting to reality and can cause them to be less well informed than their competitors who surf the Net. Leaders who are prisoners of their experience may fail to use technology to obtain and convey information efficiently. Even more important, they may not have the foundational experience to understand technology investment alternatives for their own company because they do not live with it themselves.

- *Globalization.* The worst prisoners of experience here are still thinking in unilateral rather than global terms. American leaders especially do not learn and use foreign languages compared to leaders in European countries. Traditional leaders who want to develop a new market in another country may transfer a talented leader with a strong track record of success and ignore the importance of cross-cultural skills and sensitivity. Even enlightened leaders, however, are still stuck in the old global-versus-local paradigm. Our colleague Stephen Rhinesmith argues that globalization is more about mind-set and behavioral change than structure and strategy. What he means is that the best global leaders learn how to manage the paradox of global-versus-local rather than attempting to solve it. While companies want to take advantage of the local ability to produce goods at the lowest possible costs, they also want to capitalize on best practices created by the home office and rolled out globally. It's very difficult to do both (since local executives know that local practices are necessary to produce goods at the lowest possible cost). Prisoners of experience will try to achieve both global and local goals consistently, and they will be consistently frustrated. If you're willing to try an unnatural act, you will forget what you have been taught and recognize that some problems cannot be solved (but they can be managed).

Why can't leaders break with their experience in these four areas and learn to lead unnaturally at times? First, their reliance on experience is precisely why they became leaders. By practicing natural leadership behaviors, they were successful and were promoted. We have observed in many industries (pharmaceutical, banking, consumer goods, medical devices, retail, oil and gas, telephone, entertainment) a similar pattern. People who have been promoted to top jobs exhibited competitiveness, personally delivering outstanding results, besting others to shine and obtain credit, and exerting control in order to deliver predictable, steady results. Now, however, these industries have become interdependent, and the leadership qualities that must be integrated into the mix include coordinated interplay, achieving shared objectives, and looking beyond one's own silo. As much as everyone knows these qualities are important, they are not the ones that helped senior leaders become senior leaders. Consciously or not, most executives are reluctant to adopt these new qualities.

Second, many executives have a relatively narrow range of personal and professional experiences to draw on. If you interview enough corporate executives, you often find a remarkable sameness in terms of the colleges they went to, the places they have lived, and the steady success they have experienced. Many live in the suburbs, earn a comfortable salary, and have not experienced personal hardship. As smart and talented as they are, they often have never experienced the ambiguity of living and working in another country for a sustained period of time or having friends from significantly different backgrounds. Broader experiences tend to make people less likely to be prisoners of one particular type of experience; they are more willing to be flexible in their leadership behaviors because they have been in a variety of situations.

Third, people tend to habituate in order to reduce life's complexities. Faced with environments and problems that challenge them, most people reflexively turn to a familiar approach in order to restore equilibrium. We recently ran a senior-level Action Learning program for a group of senior executives employed by a company well known for its change management focus. Each day during the program, these executives invariably sat in the same chairs surround by the same people. These executives demonstrated the same habitual behaviors of insecure high school students who cluster at the same lunch tables. When we confronted them about their seating habits, they responded by saying that it was "easier" and they could "collapse time" during the assigned exercises by working with the same people each day. Although they might have saved some time in this way, they also were nervous about the exercises (which called for them to discuss their views frankly), and they gravitated to familiar faces and familiar tribal groupings. In a similar manner, leaders seek habitual approaches when an assignment is unfamiliar or anxiety producing. They gravitate to familiar rather than new approaches.

Moving into the "I Don't Know" Zone

It's natural for successful leaders to reach the point where they think fast and act faster than they did in the past. In fact, many people become unconscious leaders, making decisions intuitively and reflexively rather than reflectively. They have accumulated sufficient experience to tell them what they should and should not do in most situations.

When you refuse to be a prisoner of experience, you make a vow to view situations with fresh eyes. Instead of rushing into meetings, interviews, customer conversations, and programs with a subtle but clear "I know everything" confidence, you take a step back and admit, "I don't know." This is a very difficult step for some natural leaders to take because saying "I don't know" feels weak and indecisive. We rarely work with an executive committee whose members openly reveal their honest confusion or genuine concerns. The confidence required to ascend the organizational hierarchy becomes almost impenetrable at the top. That is why we recommend they take an interim step: questioning their assumptions. Once people realize that their assumptions (drawn from their experiences) are invalid, they are much more willing to refuse to be a prisoner of experience.

How do you get people to question their assumptions? One way is to encourage them to face reality: the world has changed. Presenting or teaching leaders facts and statistics documenting social, economic, and industry changes is insufficient for them to challenge their assumptions. In many executive leadership programs, we have witnessed leaders who simply say, "Yes, that's true, but our company is different." For this reason, Action Learning programs are designed to create new experiences for leaders. A temporary system is set up that thrusts executives into unfamiliar environments. They may spend a week or two working in another country or may become part of a team that is equally foreign to their experiences; they may also be required to volunteer next to social workers in a nonbusiness environment, such as a homeless shelter or inner-city AIDS clinic that allows them to connect closely with people who are different from them and challenges their assumptions about the world in a different way. Whatever the new experience, however, these leaders usually respond by being less certain about what they know and more willing to look at new situations with an open mind.

Another way to help people question their assumptions is to demonstrate the stranglehold their experiences can have on their decision making. For instance, managers often ignore facts that do not jibe with their personal experiences. In one tradition-rich

organization, the CEO recognizes that a number of veteran executives are basing their decisions on similar past decisions. As one
of these executives said, "Our plan of action didn't work the first
time we tried it, and I see nothing to convince me that it's going
to be any more effective this time." This may be true. The problem, of course, is when experiences take precedence over
irrefutable facts and result in poor decisions. In this organization,
a number of leaders were demeaning the credibility of the information they received because of what various events and situations
from their past told them was true.

The company was about to launch a new product, and the
executives behind the launch had great confidence that it would
do well because a similar product they had introduced five years
ago had been a big success and the customer base was still intact.
A pilot test, however, indicated that customers' requirements had
changed, the product was not designed in a way to meet their new
requirements, and they could find similar features at a lower cost
with a competitor's product. These executives dismissed the pilot
test, arguing that the test was flawed and not a good barometer of
the market. The product was launched and failed miserably.

This sort of cautionary tale can prompt people to question
their experience-based assumptions. In many instances, however,
more direct intervention is needed. Experience is a powerful and
useful teacher, and it's difficult for some people to let go of what
are clearly valuable experiences and see things fresh. Consequently,
it's useful to have a variety of techniques at your disposal.

Techniques for Escaping from Experience-Based Prisons

Some people need a bit of a nudge to commit this unnatural act.
Others need more of a push. As you'll see, the following
approaches, ranging from simple exercises to more involved coaching methods, can achieve both goals:

• *Take a personal retreat.* This can be a nature excursion, a sab-
batical, or checking into a spa. The idea is to put some distance
between you and your experiences by "getting on the balcony," a
term Harvard University professor Ron Heifetz has used to
describe the act of gaining perspective and detachment. Most

senior executives, enmeshed in their work and their work environment, are too close to the action. It's difficult to gain perspective on these experiences without a physical and emotional remove. A retreat is a time to reflect and start to see other possibilities. This technique is not a panacea and may need to be combined with other approaches. But it is something we recommend for hard-working executives who cannot remember the last time they were in a place (physically and emotionally) where they could reflect.

• *Act against type.* One way to refuse to be a prisoner of experience is to seek out new experiences. We have found that when people are given specific assignments that run counter to their personality type, they often respond positively and unnaturally. For instance, we asked a highly autonomous leader who is concerned about his effectiveness but does not notice his isolation to pick up the telephone and call people to arrange meetings in order to practice inclusion. Or we might suggest to a conflict-avoidant executive that he pick a fight by engaging in an argument with someone he legitimately disagrees with. When leaders participate in these new experiences and discover that nothing terrible happens as a result, they are more likely to deviate from their pattern of leadership behaviors.

• *Seek consciousness-producing feedback.* Leaders who are prisoners of experience are unconscious prisoners; they are unaware of how their policies and decisions are limited by their past. To counter leading reflexively, leaders should seek continuous feedback. Asking, "How am I doing?" and "What can I do better?" will make them much more conscious of their options. When they learn that there are ways they might improve as leaders, they will start thinking before acting as their past dictates.

We have gathered a leader's team in a room, had him ask, "What can I do better?" and then had him leave the room. The team, armed with a flip chart and marker, then answers that question in detail and shares their answers with this executive. The force of this collective feedback often prompts even the most imprisoned individual to think and act in unnatural ways.

• *Intervene during teachable moments.* At certain times, leaders are in no mood to be told that they are too reliant on their experiences or unwilling to consider changing their leadership behaviors. In many cases, this unwillingness is related to their current situation. For instance, their organizations or teams are performing well, and they have no impetus to change. Conversely, certain moments occur when they are more open to change. These teachable moments often take place during a period of transition. In their book *The Leadership Pipeline*, Ram Charan, Steve Drotter, and James Noel identify specific leadership passages—from first-time manager to manager of managers, for instance—that are frame-breaking events. Teachable moments arise when leaders realize that they cannot draw on their previous experiences as extensively as they once did; they learn that their new roles demand new ways of leading. At this point, they are more open than they have ever been for coaching and other interventions.

• *Reward and recognize people who refuse to be prisoners.* Admittedly, this can be a more difficult technique to implement than some of the others. As much as you may want your sales manager to move away from her obsessive focus on results and become more of a team person, your company may continue to offer the rewards for sales performance but not for teamwork. We see this regularly with companies that emphasize the importance of people development and coaching but do not reward anyone for doing so. At the same time, you can offer people praise and other recognition when they demonstrate they are not hamstrung by the way they have always done things. In some cases, leaders know that they need to break with the past but need encouragement and approbation from someone they respect to make that break.

• *Reduce the risk of breaking with the past.* Good coaches challenge people, especially when they are holding on to ideas or methods that are no longer as viable as they once were. They ask questions designed to force a reexamination of current performance and encourage breakthroughs. By encouraging leaders to assess these approaches and articulate their feelings about them, coaches make it less risky for leaders to try something different. What feels tremendously risky when you do not think or talk about it becomes easier to do after it has been expressed. Here are some questions designed to trigger reflection about experience prisons:

What are the advantages and disadvantages of doing things differently?

What impact could you have on the organization if you tried a new approach?

How will others in the company benefit if you do things differently?

What is the worst thing that could happen if you refuse to be a prisoner of your experience? What specific negative events might take place? Would you categorize these events as catastrophic or moderately annoying?

What would it mean for you personally to change the way you operate?

What are your sacred beliefs about how you operate that might be challenged by committing this unnatural act, and how do you feel about them?

Finally, one "technique" does not actually need to be implemented by anyone. We have found that circumstance can sometimes jar people sufficiently that they resolve not to be prisoners of their experience. An industry shakeout, a corporate downsizing, a merger or acquisition, an economic downturn, or any number of other highly charged events can cause leaders to become aware of their unconscious reliance on experience and be more open to nonexperiential alternatives. In the past few years, many dot-com executives have learned that their experiences were insufficient for them to navigate tough times successfully.

When people move to new organizations, for instance, they often develop an awareness of their limitations. Don has recently been hired as a division president by a Fortune 500 company. In his former organization, he could move quickly without worrying about the politics of the organization. His new employer, however, has a more politicized culture, and who you know is as important as what you know. Out of necessity, Don has had to commit the unnatural act of building and maintaining relationships and assessing the political implications of his decisions. Although he has achieved impressive business results in his new position, he has been frustrated by how he has had to achieve them. Still, with the help of coaching, Don has made the transition to a more unnatural leadership style. Although he has not dismissed his experiences and still uses what he has learned over the years, he is now willing to slow down his decision making a bit and consider who might be offended by a given move.

Personal and Cultural Attitudes Toward Experience

Some companies seek out leaders who refuse to be experience prisoners. Game manufacturers such as Radica, Electronic Arts, and Sony have created cultures that reward people who challenge sacred cows; they pay extra for leaders who push back and at times are willing to move away from rather than toward the comfortable and familiar. In these types of organizations, it's much easier to commit this unnatural act.

Unfortunately, many companies lack this type of culture. A few years ago, a pharmaceutical company asked us to coach Jenny, a highly talented (and heavily recruited) executive from a marketing organization who had been hired a few months before. She had been hired to shake things up and get the company more focused on marketing and the customer and less focused on dosages, product, and clinical trials. Despite this ostensible purpose, we were asked to coach her because she was abrasive and, they said, "didn't quite fit in." In reality, what she was doing was injecting new experiences into the culture, and a lot of people were becoming anxious as a result. Jenny was challenging the organization's collective experience, and this caused resistance to her style and ideas. In fact, Jenny was a bit abrasive. Just because you reject certain experiences does not mean you have to throw them in the organization's face. Over time, she learned to be more of a team player, which facilitated introducing new experiences into the culture.

It's not only the culture that influences whether a leader is predisposed to refuse to commit this unnatural act. Sometimes people seek refuge in tried-and-true ways because they attempted to break out of their experience prison and were discouraged. Dan, for instance, was brought up in an organization where standard practice was to follow the boss's orders with few questions, and he became used to executing commands without asking questions. When he joined a new organization, he felt that he had found a company that encouraged openness, dialogue, and confronting disagreements head on. After a month on the job, Dan's boss came out in favor of fully funding a new initiative. Dan disagreed with this decision and voiced his disagreement diplomatically and thoughtfully. Dan's boss responded with a steely glare that made Dan feel as if he had committed a terrible sin. Even worse, Dan's boss gave him the cold shoulder for the next few weeks. For a while, Dan was reluctant to deviate from his experiences. Unconsciously, he assumed that all bosses hated to be challenged in any way. Consciously, he did not want to receive another steely glare or worse. It took months of coaching (and the use of some of the techniques we have discussed) before Dan could commit this unnatural act again.

The point is that cultures and negative episodes can militate against this act. It is more difficult for some people in some organizations to refuse to be a prisoner of experience than for others. From a coaching perspective, leaders in these situations present particular challenges, but they are not insurmountable challenges. Just about everyone can overcome these individual and cultural obstacles if they learn to be highly conscious about their behaviors as leaders. Once they stop relying on unconscious, reflexive decision making and start opening themselves up to previously unconsidered options, they will see the benefits of breaking away from experience in certain circumstances. No matter if they tried and failed to commit this unnatural act in the past or if their culture favors natural leaders, they can change their way of thinking about common leadership issues without any negative impact. From there, committing this particular unnatural act is a much easier step to take.

Refusing to Be a Prisoner of Experience

Most leaders experience their worlds as more and more unpredictable. From the following list, identify the top three factors that are making your world more unpredictable (there is room to add your own factors):

____ Unrelenting need to be customer focused

____ Dynamics of the Internet economy

____ Constant reinvention of my organization

____ Working across boundaries

____ Operating in a matrix structure

____ Constantly shifting priorities

____ Complexities of globalization

How often do you practice leadership behaviors that prevent you from being a prisoner of experience?

Behaviors	Your Rating
Challenging what creates value in the eyes of customers	1 2 3 4 5 Never Always
Learning quickly and adapting to chaos	1 2 3 4 5 Never Always
Taking action even in the face of uncertainty	1 2 3 4 5 Never Always
Giving up control and trusting others	1 2 3 4 5 Never Always
Reflecting and thinking through what is happening in order to put it in perspective	1 2 3 4 5 Never Always
Challenging yourself to do things differently rather than doing the same things just because they worked in the past	1 2 3 4 5 Never Always
Looking at problems and opportunities with a fresh eye	1 2 3 4 5 Never Always
Encouraging responsible risk taking	1 2 3 4 5 Never Always
Trusting others with backgrounds different from your own	1 2 3 4 5 Never Always

Refusing to Be a Prisoner of Experience (Cont.)

List three new behaviors from the preceding list that you can practice immediately.

1.

2.

3.

Steps for Developing Yourself as an Unnatural Leader

Use teams of individuals with different types of skills and experience to encourage creativity and breakthrough thinking.

Conduct or participate in brainstorming sessions.

Set goals and objectives that encourage creativity and innovation.

Recognize and reward suggestions for continuous improvement.

Prevent fear of failure from blocking opportunities for breakthrough thinking.

Learn how to overcome your own fears of "doing the wrong thing" and taking prudent risks. Practice asking yourself, "What's the worst that can happen?"

Chapter Five

Expose Your Vulnerabilities

The illusion of invulnerability has long been an aspect of natural leadership. Many top leaders have cultivated this illusion, assuming that the worst thing for both themselves and their organizations would be for them to be perceived as weak or indecisive. We have come to expect leaders who are confident, assertive, and knowledgeable and know that failure is not an option. As a result, many leaders refuse to say, "I don't know," or admit they have never encountered the situation now facing them, or lack the experience or information necessary to make a good decision. In the past, it was easier for people to pretend to be omniscient because there was a lot less to know; it was easier to bluff their way through a situation. Just as significant, the stakes have been raised. The strong, confident but not completely competent leader is likely to get his organization in more difficulty today than he would have in the past. As we will see, leaders who refuse to admit they do not know can create tremendous problems.

Executives can avoid these problems by committing the unnatural act of exposing their vulnerabilities in appropriate circumstances. Such exposure can take many forms; here are three of the most common:

- Saying, "I don't know"
- Communicating continuously, honestly, and openly, including emotionally
- Taking the risk of being a learner rather than a teacher

Being vulnerable in this way provides leaders with greater access to knowledge, a valuable currency in today's environment.

Denying There Is a Problem

It's difficult to be open about your lack of knowledge if you are in denial about it. Whether it's self-denial or hiding your vulnerabilities from others, you are preserving your own perfection at your team or company's expense. For instance, many leaders are seeking to establish learning organizations where people are committed to improving, exploring new ways of doing things, listening to customers, and sharing knowledge from associates and other stakeholders. The great irony is that many of these leaders refuse to model the very learning behaviors they espouse. Although they may invest millions in training programs, they unconsciously adopt an attitude that communicates that learning is for others. They lead surrounded by an aura of invincibility that minimizes other people and their ideas. Although they may sincerely believe in establishing a learning organization, they delude themselves into believing they personally do not have time. Thus, no matter how much they might talk about creating learning organizations, their behavior symbolically limits the concept and makes it difficult for others to take it seriously.

We recently consulted with a major corporation that wanted to increase accountability. After much discussion, the top executives decided that the best way to increase accountability was to rank every employee's performance relative to that of their peers. We suggested that accountability began at the top and raised the possibility of ranking all the people who were gathered in the room. An uncomfortable silence followed, and then we were told that the accountability problem was "in the ranks." It may well have been, but these leaders were unwilling to allow themselves to be measured—perhaps because it would expose their own vulnerabilities.

Denial of reality, especially external reality, can be equally detrimental. Denial of customer feedback or reinterpreting it through a positive lens, for example, can make companies oblivious to small changes on the horizon that arrive months later as tsunami waves. Having spent ten years in the mainframe computer industry in the 1980s, I (David) can tell you there was plenty of evidence that the PC would change the industry. But because of the investments companies had made in mainframe manufacturing, research, development, and installed customer systems, leaders believed they could defend their niche until the tide somehow turned. They were psychologically unable to accept the ramifications of PCs. A majority of industry leaders were slow to learn about and acknowledge the importance of software and PCs because of the sea changes it would impose on their current reality and favorable position.

This denial often is not conscious, as Dr. Seuss's tale of Yertle the Turtle demonstrates. Yertle builds an empire on the backs of other turtles, ordering them to keep climbing on each other's backs so that Yertle, who is on top of the tower, can see farther, be more important, and rule more wisely. Although the turtles underneath Yertle try to warn him that they are having problems, he ignores them until the tower becomes too high, one turtle at the bottom sneezes, the tower tumbles down, and Yertle is returned to his place in the swamp.

Like Yertle, natural leaders can become so caught up in their own importance and the importance of their own goals that they unconsciously deny new information that may deter them from achieving those goals. In coaching senior executives, we must often help them sort out the difference between determined focus and absurd denial.

We have worked with several executive committees of large pharmaceutical companies. These teams have to make an extraordinary effort, with great intellectual rigor, to understand the data produced by clinical trials of new drugs. It's enormously tempting to filter out ambiguous results or possibly disturbing data and focus on the marketing promise of a new drug. Given a huge potential market and a breakthrough formulation, it can be challenging for senior pharmaceutical leaders to get their minds around potentially negative data, but lives literally hang in the balance. Even at this level, it can be tempting to reinterpret the data and deny that a problem might exist if the data are not conclusive. Fortunately, the skilled executives we work with avoid this pitfall. The natural leader focuses on the positive, refusing to be deterred by distractions.

Another variation on denial is to avoid responsibility for a negative outcome (or only taking superficial responsibility). Being vulnerable means admitting that you made an error, and leaders who can make this admission foster a culture of accountability.

Unfortunately, many executives find scapegoats and shift the blame to other shoulders—regulators, upper management, peers in another function, and even their own team. The *New York Times* recently reported the story of a Colorado software company CEO who wrote an e-mail to his top five hundred employees accusing them of leading a lazy organization in which the parking lot filled in too late in the morning and emptied out too early in the afternoon and stating they were responsible for the company's poor performance. This e-mail eventually made its way into the hands of investors and analysts, and the company's share price plummeted. Rather than scapegoating others, this leader should have begun his fault-finding mission with himself. If his data were accurate (and hopefully he would have had more information than observing the parking lot), how had his management practices created a climate in which people did not feel committed to work hard? If he had been slower to blame others and quicker to admit that he was part of the problem, he would have engaged others in the company with his own vulnerability.

Natural leaders can also translate denial into diversionary tactics. To avoid confronting a difficult situation or admitting blame, they may divert attention away from difficult issues. Rather than address the core reasons for poor quarterly performance, some public leaders direct attention toward tangential causes of those results. Instead of addressing how their vision and strategy or execution may need improvement, they cite the weather, fluctuating currency, unpredictable customers, or a competitor's surprisingly successful foray into a new market. While some of this communication has become almost ritualistic, it works to undermine integrity and authenticity. Similarly, leaders embarking on significant change programs may divert attention from the role they have played in creating current circumstances or the role they will need to play in order to make lasting change happen and instead focus attention on "middle management resistance" or "enrolling the troops."

An Environment That Requires Open, Vulnerable Leaders

Leaders could still succeed with these various types of denial when technical change was all that was called for. When change was incremental—that is, the biggest change that people were asked to make was learning to use a new software system or conforming to a new work process—natural leaders were effective. Relatively little ambiguity or complexity exists in many technical changes, and leaders directed when, what, and how something had to be done and expected others to follow.

Today, however, most companies are confronting what Harvard University professor Ron Heifetz characterizes as "adaptive challenges." The old ways of doing things no longer work, change is needed, and no easy solutions exist. As a result, organizations and people must discover how to adapt to messy situations or paradoxical and conflicting forces. When the Internet creates new distribution and delivery systems and scores of new competitors appear, or when a strong competitor leverages off its current brand to enter new and competitive markets, a Darwinian adaptation is necessary. How to adapt a new business model, or redesign work processes to get the same amount of work done with fewer resources, or how to become a global company while preserving local autonomy, are questions that require significant changes in both thought and action. They require continuous adaptation rather than implementation of a precise solution.

All-knowing, all-seeing leaders must facilitate adaptive change. Executives who present a flawless front to the world will not generate the ideas necessary to cope with adaptive challenges. People will be reluctant to confront leaders who never seem to be wrong, or they will reinforce this flawless role playing by looking to the leader to fix everything and solve all problems. They will shy away from presenting ideas that they assume run contrary to a leader's philosophy or positions or turn to the leader with endless dilemmas to be fixed. People expect invulnerable leaders to tell them what to do, and to adapt to a perplexing, ambiguous, and complex world, a variety of voices must be heard.

As we will see, inviting these voices to speak up communicates vulnerability. The adaptive leader must be able to say, "I don't know," but retain the respect of the troops. Leaders who sincerely request other people's ideas and opinions are admitting that they do not have all the answers.

Real Conversation

The act that leaders find unnatural is creating an ongoing, open conversation with others when the goal is not to persuade or command but to connect. Real conversation is a two-way street; both parties are changed or affected. To create such a dialogue, leaders need to drop their pose of being in charge and in control and be willing to express their own concerns. They have to communicate to the other person that the conversation does not have rules and they are willing to explore feelings and not just throw information back and forth. They have to connect with others.

Many managers, however, have been indoctrinated in a different form of corporate communication. Manipulation and coercion are often the goals of the motivational methods used in organizations. Leaders use upbeat messages ("We can do it"), techniques, and other tools to convince people to think or behave differently. They believe they demonstrate emotional edge by exhorting others to perform. They have clear agendas and are not interested in the back-and-forth dialogue that is the hallmark of real conversation.

Similarly, some leaders use conversation as a battering ram to break down resistance to a given point of view. In many conversations between managers and direct reports, the manager hurls arguments, reasons, and evidence until his direct report has yielded, and this constitutes a conversation. Meetings too may be nothing more than the team leader's throwing his verbal weapons at others in the room. Direct reports may fire back, but the leader's weapons are more powerful, and he prevails.

Many senior executives remember the oft-heard industrial era reprimand: "Stop talking and get back to work." A natural leader instinctively distrusts meandering conversations or ones where people talk about their reactions, their concerns, and their fears. It seems too social and unfocused to qualify as real work. In reality, these conversations are where the real work begins. When people connect with each other emotionally and intellectually, they are much more likely to uncover useful information and risky ideas. When direct reports do not feel constrained by a leader's controlled image or positive expectations, they are much more likely to challenge his traditional thinking.

As unnatural as it might seem, leaders need to keep conversations going around the following topics:

- Why are we doing what we are doing?
- Are we doing the best we can?

- Are we committed to what we are doing?
- What else should we be doing (or, What should we be doing differently)?

David Whyte, author of *The Heart Aroused,* who has led many of our Action Learning programs, notes that leaders should have five types of conversations. We have adapted these types into six unnatural conversational acts a leader can commit:

- *Explore the unknown future.* Too often, leaders act as if they know what the future will bring; they lecture about where the company is going based on previously decided strategy and vision. These known future conversations invite head nodding. When leaders are willing to say that the future is unpredictable and they need help exploring different scenarios, discovery takes place. People are eager to speculate and share their personal visions, and through these exchanges better strategies can be created.
- *Find out what is running smoothly and what is broken* (from the people who know). In other words, talk to direct reports, customers, and others about the reality—not just the intent of various business processes and measurement systems. Focus on what is happening and what is not happening now. Be open to both good and bad news.
- *Encourage conversations between disparate people and parts of the organization.* The $400 million Mars probe was lost because one research group measured the probe's path in centimeters and another group measured it in inches. We paid a high price because they did not communicate. Leaders with a sense of invulnerability often do not see the need to talk to people from different parts of the organization, or they do not see the need to engage in continuous, meaningful dialogue with other employees who are not part of their group. This creates silo behavior in which marketing talks but does not connect with sales and real conversation does not occur across boundaries. One function attempts to control another. Vulnerable leaders, however, are willing to go against tradition and openly share and receive best practices with other functions and adopt a learning mentality rather than controlling posture when it comes to other business units. The marketing manager is willing to admit that he does not know anything about

the priorities and objectives in sales and believes it's important for him and his staff to start learning. We live in a time when hybrid solutions are increasingly important; the joining of dissimilar minds creates answers to questions that cannot be addressed in traditional ways. Disparate conversations help generate these hybrid solutions.

• *Hold regular team verbal practices.* Just as sports teams improve through physical practice, work teams improve through verbal practice. We have seen teams that meet and work on projects together but rarely engage in the type of real conversation we have described. Natural leaders may avoid these conversations because they can get messy and prefer conversations that are orderly and purposeful. This unnatural act, however, means leaders should stimulate conversations and have teams practice listening, open themselves up so they are affected by what others say, adjust course based on what is said, and sometimes change their mind and position. Sometimes blue-sky sessions, brainstorming, and expanding the universe of topics can achieve this outcome.

• *Talk to yourself.* What is unnatural for many leaders is not just engaging in real conversations with others but also with themselves. Our point is that it is not enough just to encourage and participate in dialogues with others The natural tendency is to shut out disturbing or complex ideas. These ideas are not always easy to come to terms with and may require some intense and time-consuming thought. Conversations with yourself about who you are at work and what you want to be is crucial. It might be uncomfortable to think about how your role might change in a changing organization—you might believe it's a waste of time because there is nothing you can do about it—but it can help you redefine your leadership in a highly productive way. Asking yourself tough, far-reaching questions and giving yourself the time and space to get your mind around them is a truly unnatural act.

• *Identify the conversations you are not having.* What topic is your team avoiding? What issue is no one willing to raise? What subjects do you talk about superficially but never address with complete honesty and openness? Leaders need to be the ones to bring taboo issues out in the open through discussion. This can be a painful conversation; talking about the possible need for reorganization is difficult. As much as an executive might worry about how people will react to a potentially threatening or explosive subject, however, sometimes it's critical to make this worry known and diminish it through discussion of options and possibilities. This is true even if airing it means that the leader opens himself or herself to criticism (for example, that her or his mismanagement contributed to the need for downsizing).

Techniques to Increase Capacity for Vulnerability

Making yourself vulnerable is not about being weak. You can be a very strong, influential leader and still be open and honest about yourself. Similarly, being vulnerable does not mean foolishly exposing your Achilles' heel to your competitors or those you are negotiating with. If you are convinced someone is angling for some of your role or responsibility, you do not tell him about the recent blunders that have cost the company. In the same way, you should not disclose information to competitors that would give them a competitive advantage.

As with all other unnatural acts, leaders need to use this one with discretion. The goal is not to be vulnerable but to develop your capacity for vulnerability so that you can use it when needed. With that in mind, we'd like to share with you some techniques that increase a leader's capacity for vulnerability:

• *Focus on the parts of yourself that do not belong to the organization.* Business leaders typically experience moments of creativity or insight on the golf course, relaxing with a drink on the deck, or even in the shower. Free from the stress and detail of work, leaders can get in touch with ideas that do not surface in business settings. Some of these ideas might seem risky or odd, and natural leaders might reject them out of hand (perhaps because of the setting in which they emerged). In many Japanese companies, it is accepted practice for executives to go to bed with pencil and paper on their nightstands so they can write down whatever inspiration comes to them before falling asleep or in their dreams. The next day, these leaders bring their ideas to work, and the source is acknowledged as legitimate input. You may want to adopt this practice or use your Palm or hand-held computer when you are lounging by the pool or walking in the woods. In other words, take your work ideas seriously even though they might emerge in unlikely environments.

• *Put yourself at risk in some way every day.* We once witnessed a fifty-five-year-old CEO take lessons from a twenty-three-year-old techie on how to navigate a new software installation. The CEO made mistakes and struggled to master a program that was second nature to the techie. Rather than avoiding this public lesson because he would appear foolish, the CEO relished it and appreciated the humor and kindness that his young teacher displayed. His willingness to risk appearing ignorant not only encouraged the technician to share information, open up, and take a few risks in joking with the senior leader but modeled vulnerability as an acceptable leadership behavior. Although there are all sorts of ways of taking organizational risks, one of the best is for leaders to communicate clearly and loudly that they do not know or understand something.

• *Allow yourself to display passion for your work.* Steely stoicism is a hallmark of military leaders and sports heroes, as well as traditional business leaders, and to appear in public without this armor is to appear vulnerable. For many years, business executives acted as if it were wrong to display their love for their job, much less their family. Leaders were expected to take their jobs seriously, and somehow displays of pure enjoyment for the tasks at hand were considered unserious. Even today, executive suites are modeled to evoke decorum, control, and reverence. No one runs up and down the halls celebrating the latest sales order or complaining about the competition. Executives who want their staff to approach their jobs with energy and inspiration, however, need to exhibit the same traits. We frequently coach executives who need to figure out what specifically they love about what they do or need to rediscover the joy of work. They are not passionate as leaders because they have lost sight of what drives and excites them. Once they get in touch with what makes them joyous about coming to the office each day, they find it easier to express these feelings to their people.

When and How to Express, "I Don't Know"

You would not think the three brief words "I don't know" would be so difficult for leaders to utter, but they are. To a certain extent, they carry more psychological baggage with them than other vulnerability-creating acts. That is because we expect leaders to know what to do, and we reinforce them for acting accordingly. We look to the president of the country to know how to fix the economy; we expect generals to know how to win wars; we assume that investment gurus will know the direction the stock market is heading and the head of the Federal Reserve to fix the economy. Most leaders reinforce these expectations through their words and deeds, and as a result it is very difficult for anyone to admit a lack of knowledge.

Most of the time, of course, a leader should know the answer or have a strong position. Specifically, when a problem is technical in nature, leaders need to be sufficiently informed to make a decision. For instance, they should know enough to make a good choice among competing information systems. They should know when a given action is against the law. They should know how to make investment and budget decisions that are in the best interest of the company. It's fair for employees to trust that their leaders know enough about these technical matters to make wise choices.

On the other hand, an equal number of situations today cannot be decided effectively by one person. There are too many complexities, too much information, and too many alternatives for any leader—no matter how smart or skilled—to know what to do. If she gives the impression that she does know what to do, however, she will remove any disincentives from her staff for learning, discovering, or contributing their ideas. When she wants to reduce a group's dependency on the leader for answers and motivate the group to create their own ideas, the vulnerable "I don't know" is quite effective.

Actually, leaders do not have to make this specific statement in words as much as in deeds. For instance, astute CEOs meet with their executive committees and create disequilibrium when they fail to take a position on an important matter. We have witnessed many executive committees engage in debate while subtly eyeing the body language of the CEO for cues as to her position. Otherwise confident executives hesitate because their leader has essentially communicated that she does not know the answer or will not take a position. Or the CEO may lay out her case for making major changes in the organization without offering a prescription. Again, this action creates discomfort and tension in the room. She's saying, "Here are all the reasons we need to change, but I don't know what we should do."

This disequilibrium will affect people differently. It can create arguments and resistance as well as great ideas. In most instances, however, people respond to the leader's vulnerability with more energy and out-of-the-box thinking than they usually exhibit. If they are talented, committed leaders, they respond positively to the CEO's open invitation for help. They are much more likely to be energized by the absence of an answer than the presence of one.

In Action Learning programs, creating an "I don't know" environment is a basic foundation for success. Leaders are placed in situations and teams and asked to solve a real and serious business issue. They cannot rely on a leader with position power and a clear answer or past experience to solve the problem. Senior leaders in Action Learning programs are often discombobulated and resistant, and express a desire for "clear direction from the top about what we are supposed to be doing." They often want prescriptions, to learn the playbook and have the final answer delivered clearly by someone in charge. Eventually, initial tension and chaos segue into people becoming enmeshed in the problem, diagnosing the situation, weighing alternatives, choosing a path they passionately believe in, and defending it to senior leaders. In the process, they discover a lot about themselves and the company they work for.

Therefore, try replicating the disequilibrium that Action Learning participants encounter by communicating that you do not know the answer to a problem you outline in vivid detail, and creating a context for debate and dialogue to occur. You will discover that after an initial period of confusion and resistance, they will engage with a degree of emotion and creativity you do not usually see from them.

We want to leave you with the story of a truly effective leader, Norbert Becker, a partner in Andersen, who has taken over management of Andersen's worldwide Information Systems division, with over twenty thousand employees. A deal maker and grower of new businesses and markets in Europe, Norbert is not a technology expert. He was named head of this division, however, because he has been asked to orchestrate significant changes: centralizing the function, rationalizing costs, investing in new knowledge software, and so on. No doubt, Norbert has many ideas about how to make these changes, but rather than post them, he has adopted an "I'm not sure" learner's stance. He is asking many questions, such as whether the partners are willing to change their systems and centralize their technology staffs. He has taken his team off-site and engaged them in the type of real conversation we described earlier. Norbert has listened and taken his cues from what he has learned from them about how to implement change within the division. As of this writing, he is beginning to experience real success as his team takes hold and appreciates his firm but open and learning stance.

Exposing Your Vulnerabilities

Exposing your vulnerabilities is not easy for many leaders. On a scale of 1 to 5, indicate how frequently the following natural leadership behaviors apply to you and may inhibit your ability to expose vulnerabilities.

Behaviors	Your Rating				
I refuse to admit that I lack the experience or information necessary to make a good decision.	1 Rarely	2	3	4	5 Always
I have trouble saying, "I don't know."	1 Rarely	2	3	4	5 Always
I bluff my way through many situations.	1 Rarely	2	3	4	5 Always
I pretend to be omniscient.	1 Rarely	2	3	4	5 Always
I hide my vulnerabilities from others.	1 Rarely	2	3	4	5 Always
I shut out other people and their ideas.	1 Rarely	2	3	4	5 Always
I have an attitude that communicates I don't need to learn anything more than I already know.	1 Rarely	2	3	4	5 Always
I resist thinking about external realities, new information, and existing problems.	1 Rarely	2	3	4	5 Always
I avoid taking responsibility for negative outcomes.	1 Rarely	2	3	4	5 Always
I divert attention away from touchy issues.	1 Rarely	2	3	4	5 Always
I don't see the need to talk to people from different parts of the organization.	1 Rarely	2	3	4	5 Always
I tell people, "Here's what we are going to do," rather than seek their ideas and input.	1 Rarely	2	3	4	5 Always

Exposing Your Vulnerabilities (Cont.)

Focus on the behaviors that you assigned the highest rating. What can you do to overcome these behaviors and start exposing your vulnerabilities?

Practicing Real Conversations

Plan to meet with your team to have a dialogue related to the following questions:

Why are we doing what we are doing?

Are we doing the best we can?

Are we committed to what we are doing?

What else should we be doing?

What could we be doing differently?

What is your point of view on each of these questions? What do you want to share with your team?

1.

2.

3.

4.

5.

Exposing Your Vulnerabilities (Cont.)

Using David Whyte's six categories of unnatural conversation, evaluate how well you are using each of these six approaches.

Type of Unnatural Leadership Conversation	How Well Do I Use This Approach?
Exploring the unknown future Are you willing to say the future is unpredictable and that you need help exploring different scenarios? Do you encourage people to speculate and share their personal visions in order to create better strategies?	___ I am very good at this type of conversation and have it frequently. ___ I am good at this but don't do it enough. ___ I rarely have this type of conversation with my staff.
Finding out what's running smoothly and what's broken Do you talk to direct reports, customers, and others about the mechanics of various processes and systems? Do you focus on what's happening and not happening? Are you open to both good and bad news?	___ I am very good at this type of conversation and have it frequently. ___ I am good at this but don't do it enough. ___ I rarely have this type of conversation.
Encouraging conversations between disparate people and parts of the organization Do you talk to people from different parts of the organization? Do you take ownership of issues and seek resolution across organizational boundaries?	___ I am very good at this type of conversation and have it frequently. ___ I am good at this but don't do it enough. ___ I rarely have this type of conversation.
Holding regular team verbal practices Do you stimulate conversations with your team to practice listening, open up to what others say, and adjust course and position based on what was said?	___ I am very good at this type of conversation and have it frequently. ___ I am good at this but don't do it enough. ___ I rarely have this type of conversation.

Exposing Your Vulnerabilities (Cont.)

Type of Unnatural Leadership Conversation	How Well Do I Use This Approach?
Talking to yourself How much time do you spend on reflection and self-discovery? Do you shut out disturbing ideas that aren't easy to come to terms with? Are you clear about who you are at work and what you want? Do you ask yourself tough, far-reaching questions and give yourself the time and space to get your mind around them?	____ I am very good at this and do it frequently. ____ I am good at this but don't do it enough. ____ I rarely take the time to reflect.
Identifying the conversations you are not having Is your team willing to raise issues and not avoid topics? Do you talk about subjects superficially and not with complete honestly and openness? Do you bring taboo issues out in the open through discussion?	____ I am very good at this and do it frequently. ____ I am good at this but don't do it enough. ____ I rarely take the time to do this.

What can you do to engage your organization in real conversations, listen, and seek their ideas and input more often?

Steps for Developing Yourself as an Unnatural Leader

Admit your mistakes.

Encourage people to talk about how work is affecting them.

Be willing to express your fears.

Create conversations with back-and-forth dialogue.

Engage in meaningful dialogue with people who aren't part of your group.

Adopt and encourage a learning mentality for parts of the organization that you and your team don't know much about.

Make time for reflection and self-discovery for yourself and your team.

Chapter Six

Acknowledge Your Shadow Side

All leaders have shadow sides, although not all leaders acknowledge them. In the 1970s, comedian Flip Wilson had a catch-phrase—"The devil made me do it"—that describes actions we cannot fully explain. The shadow side may be anything from perfectionistic tendencies to destructive inclinations to demean direct reports. Natural leaders frequently deny they even have a shadow side; it does not fit their ideal of the flawless, heroic leader. Direct reports, of course, may be well aware of this dark aspect of their boss and have learned to work around it. Some natural leaders may admit to themselves that they have certain dark traits, but they may also rationalize these traits ("It's really not affecting my work") and refuse to discuss them.

Despite its ominous name, the shadow side is not all bad. In fact, a leader's strengths are often inextricably linked to this shadow side. The micromanaging leader who drives everyone nuts with his mania for control may also be brilliant at identifying flaws early and saving the organization millions through his attention to detail. If this person were to acknowledge his shadow side, he would still maintain his strength but would not have such an adverse effect on the people he works with. By reflecting on this dark tendency and discussing it openly with others, the unnatural leader defuses the shadow's potentially destructive power.

Every leader has a shadow side. In fact, some of the most creative, powerful leaders in the world have had it in spades. National debates raged over the shadows cast by Presidents Richard Nixon, Jimmy Carter, and Bill Clinton. At the time, it seemed inexplicable why such a brilliant, compassionate man as Jimmy Carter would get bogged down in detail. Similarly, Richard Nixon's Machiavellian schemes at the height of his power turned out to be political suicide. Bill Clinton's moral turpitude undermined his authority and prevented him from realizing important goals. Their actions were obviously irrational; their shadow side caused them to act in ways that were not in their own best interest (or the best interest of others, for that matter).

This concept of the shadow side has its origins in Carl Jung's work in 1912, which built on Freud's notion of the repressed side of the personality. Although there is a good deal of debate about how and why this shadow side develops, what is agreed on is that people often deny it exists or try to keep it a secret from others. Our goal is to help you see the benefits of acknowledging this shadow side and learn how to use it to become a more effective leader.

Shadow Side Traits and Types

Psychologist Robert Hogan has conducted extensive research about different shadow personalities and developed the CDR International Derailment survey based on this research. We have found it to be very useful in helping executives in our Action Learning and Action Coaching programs break their denial about and understand their shadow sides. It consists of eleven scales that identify the probability of engaging in counterproductive behaviors under stress, with each scale corresponding to eleven shadow side types we frequently encounter among leaders:

- Volatile—moody and unpredictable with a tendency to be enthusiastic one moment and doubtful the next
- Distrustful—suspicious and dubious about others' motives and intentions, with a likelihood to see the glass as half empty versus half full
- Overly cautious—unassertive, fearful of making mistakes, and appearing indecisive or resistant to taking action when necessary
- Aloof—withdrawn and seeming to lack empathy and concern

for others, with a tendency to avoid conflict and fail to communicate when necessary

- Passive-resistant—seeming to cooperate and agree but maintaining private reservations that lead to pursuit of a personal agenda
- Arrogance—overly confident with feelings of entitlement and inflated views of self-worth, frequently resulting in diminishing other people's contributions
- Mischievous—socially skilled but likely to push the boundaries of possibilities and go over the line in terms of what is acceptable in a culture or an organization
- Melodramatic—likes to be the center of attraction, tends to dominate, and often misses social cues
- Eccentric—acts and thinks in sometimes odd and unusual ways
- Perfectionistic—attends to details and may be compulsively conscientious, often micromanaging and failing to delegate
- Pleaser—eager to meet other people's expectations and reluctant to take independent action that goes against the opinions of others, particularly those in authority

Typically, we work with an executive who has completed the CDR International Leadership Derailment Report. We might begin by helping him see the positive aspects of the shadow side type that applies to him. By helping him understand that arrogance can be self-confidence pushed over the top by stress, for instance, he may recognize that his positive belief in his own abilities is transformed into the negative unwillingness to consider other ideas besides his own. A book, of course, precludes this type of intensive, one-on-one discussion. Still, you may examine these scales and find that your shadow side is one of the eleven listed.

It is also possible that you have a different type of shadow side or that you do not recognize the shadow that fits you like a cloak. The following discussion is designed to illuminate the subtleties of shadow side detection. We share some examples of leaders struggling with these dark behaviors, as well as the three most common negative leadership repercussions. In this way, we hope to spotlight the destructive nature of an unacknowledged, destructive behavior as well as help you become more practiced at spotting a particular shadow side type.

Subtleties of Shadow Side Detection

The first common shadow side tendency involves *avoiding or delaying decisions*. This type of leader is often prized by his organization for his thoughtful, steady approach to issues; he is viewed as the calm in the center of the storm, and others view him as wise. These may well be strengths, but the shadow side repercussion is that this person becomes overly cautious when faced with competing alternatives. In an era when most leaders are faced with more options than they know what do with—and it's quite difficult to discern which option is the best one with any certainty—this shadow side can create serious problems. Typically, this leader sits back in meetings and says very little; others do not know where he stands on issues. He always needs more data before making a decision but never has enough data. The result is that his reticence and indecision frustrate others. The group never seems to get anything done, and they are reluctant to voice their own opinions because their boss is so hard to read. In most instances, this type of leader is terrified of being challenged and appearing foolish, and this fear is especially counterproductive for companies grappling with complex issues that require bold decisions.

A second shadow side repercussion is *arrogance*. Highly confident leaders can easily slip into arrogance during times of high stress. Confidence, certainly a good trait for leaders to possess, can turn malign under certain conditions, and people can start ignoring their direct reports' ideas and exhibit excessive faith in their own opinions. Intimidation of others and unwillingness to listen to negative feedback are additional consequences.

Highly confident, successful leaders frequently are unwilling to acknowledge this arrogant shadow side. Sally, for instance, was a brilliant technician and had helped her large organization solve critical business problems. As a result, she was promoted to a top managerial position. Although Sally always displayed some arrogance, it did not hurt her early in her career because her work was focused on technical issues and she managed relatively few people. In fact, she was so talented at solving technical problems that her bosses, peers, and direct reports gave her a wide berth, knowing how valuable she was to the company. Because she had never received much negative feedback, she was shocked to learn that she was not considered a viable candidate for the company's soon-to-be-open CEO position. When we were called in to coach her and provide feedback on the impact of her arrogance, Sally was surprised. She said she knew she could be forceful and certain in her opinions, but she had no idea that others considered her patronizing and condescending. Her shadow side was virtually invisible to her.

The third repercussion is an *inability to execute.* In a *Fortune Magazine* article "Why CEOs Fail," consultant and CDR International colleague Ram Charan cited many examples of CEOs who got their companies into trouble because they failed to execute sound strategies. This jibes with other experience of working with highly creative, intelligent leaders whose shadow side revolved around putting ideas into practice. Many of them felt that coming up with a great idea should suffice; other people should figure out how to make their great ideas work. Typically, they became bored with the details of implementation. It was almost as if they were too good to get their hands dirty with the details. Astonishingly, they did not see how this shadow side negated the impact of coming up with great ideas.

As you reflect on your own shadow side and that of others, keep in mind that it's much easier to identify the shadow aspect of others. We do not realize that we are execution phobic, arrogant, or indecisive. Or if we do realize we have these tendencies, we tend to discount them. Perfectionistic leaders honestly believe they are merely being detail oriented now to avoid rework later. Pleasers cannot see that in their effort to empathize and help their employees grow, they are failing to hold anyone accountable. Like Sally, they are honestly shocked to discover that people have problems with this part of their personality and that it's hurting their work performance.

Consider Will, who was recently brought in to a well-known corporation in a top executive position. As one of his first tasks, Will met with a large group of organizational leaders in a two-day session. His goal was to communicate the importance he placed on openness, taking risks, and assuming responsibility for results. It was a great meeting, and Will was terrific, by turns supportive, charming, and funny. By the end of the meeting, most of the leaders had warmed up to Will and were looking forward to working with him. In the closing hour of the meeting, a question-and-answer session, one executive asked another executive in the meeting about whether she and others in the room were supportive of a key proposal facing the company. Will leaped out of his seat, grabbed the microphone, and proceeded to berate the questioner for being naive, bullying the executive into admitting that he had erred in asking the question. In that moment, Will's shadow side took over, and he undid everything positive he had accomplished over the previous two days. Will did not acknowledge that he had this dark side or that it had ruined the meeting. The odds are he rationalized his outburst as "teaching people an important lesson" or perhaps that the meeting attendees did not even give it a second thought. The point is, he was oblivious to his shadow side.

Considering the Consequences

For years, leaders have been successful despite their shadow side; however, the negative consequences for ignoring it today are much greater than in the past. Traditionally, companies learned how to manage around a CEO's or other top leader's dark nature. They accepted that Jack had an explosive temper and tiptoed around him when he was in a foul mood; they knew this decreased productivity and stalled decision making but figured it was the price they had to pay for an otherwise excellent leader.

In our politically correct times, Jack's temper is likely to result in lawsuits filed by individuals who are offended by what Jack says in a moment of pique. His outbursts will also probably drive good people out of the company and cause the organization to suffer significant losses in the war for talent. Fear of his temper may cause his direct reports to withhold ideas that they feel might trigger Jack's temper—ideas that are crucial for teams to work at maximum capacity. For the good of the organization as well as his own career, Jack needs to acknowledge this shadow side, as unnatural as it might feel to reveal this unflattering secret to the world.

Unlike our hypothetical Jack, Pedro is real; a high-potential finance director for a Fortune 50 company, he was named the head of the company's sales organization with an eye toward his next promotion: leading a major Latin America subsidiary. Pedro inherited a sales group whose key members were at odds with each other, and these interpersonal problems had largely been ignored for years. As bright and talented as Pedro was, he had a low tolerance for interpersonal problems. He simply could not understand why two people would not work together for the good of the company, and when he encountered these situations, he tried to use his positional authority to straighten things out. If this did not work—and it rarely did—Pedro would explode and try to bully people into patching up their disagreements. Pedro's shadow side—a lack of empathy combined with an explosive temper—lowered the sales organization's morale and failed to boost sales revenues as a prelude to awarding Pedro stewardship of the Latin American subsidiary. Pedro simply did not see that motivating people required more than use of positional authority, that he needed to empathize and understand what was at the root of interpersonal conflicts if he hoped to resolve them, and that his fury made a bad situation worse.

Pedro, like most other leaders, was unaware of the consequences. As a natural leader, he operated on instinct and experience. He did not realize that his shadow side was compelling him to act irrationally or in ways that were at odds with the situation. The shadow side obscures our normally acute perceptions. Leaders who might otherwise foresee negative consequences develop a cloudy vision when their shadow side takes over.

What makes this issue of consequences tricky is that there may not be any negative repercussions for years. The shadow side is situation sensitive. Leaders can spend years before it emerges and wreaks havoc. If an executive occupies a cozy corner of an organization and does not have many people reporting to him, his aloof nature may not cause problems. It is only when he is transferred or promoted to a group where he must interact with others more frequently that negative consequences emerge. Years ago, people used to be better able to establish themselves in isolated corners of companies, and their shadow sides would cause little or no damage. In an era of volatile job movement, team structures, and diverse relationship-driven environments, it is much more likely that leaders will encounter situations that catalyze shadow side activity and negative consequences.

Acknowledging One's Shadow Side

Acknowledgment must be to both oneself and others. In terms of oneself, this is difficult when leaders have failed infrequently or faced relatively little adversity. As a result, they are not motivated to engage in introspection and discover their shadow side. In fact, successful businesspeople frequently convince themselves they are without fault (or at least without major ones); they believe that leaders should be justifiably confident.

This mind-set makes it difficult for some leaders to commit this unnatural act. We human beings are clever about avoiding taking close looks at our personal characteristics; psychologists term this avoidance tendency *defense mechanisms*. Certain leaders use the defense mechanism of minimizing the full impact of their shadow side. Others rationalize the problems they cause by maintaining that any problems lie with others or with circumstances beyond their control. No doubt you have encountered executives who intellectualize their shadow-produced problems and offer their own off-the-mark theories about why things went wrong. And of course there are leaders who respond with hostility when they are confronted with problems they have actually created, and their anger at others effectively keeps them from looking inward.

To break down these defense mechanisms and help leaders acknowledge their shadow sides, we usually provide them with direct feedback from someone they trust. Although they may not accept 360-degree feedback that detects the presence of their shadow side, they find it hard to ignore this information when it comes from a person they trust. It may be that their closest aide never had the courage to confront the boss about this hidden aspect of his personality. It may be that this person's boss was afraid of alienating or losing him with talk about this delicate subject. Whatever the reason, when they talk straight, their message usually is powerful enough to get through.

Certainly it is better to get through to leaders before their shadow side throws them into crisis mode. Unfortunately, some people are not willing to listen until a crisis looms. As coaches, we have found that people are willing to look at themselves in different ways when their actions have resulted in a major failure or caused significant, undeniable problems in their group.

Public acknowledgment of the shadow side brings up other issues. It's one thing to admit your shadow side to yourself; it's something else entirely to broadcast this dark, dangerous aspect of yourself to friends and enemies alike. Here are the most common concerns that prevent leaders from making this public admission:

- Fear that their credibility as a leader will somehow be diminished.
- Concern that other people will take advantage of their admission of this flaw.
- Lack of self-confidence to admit that they, like all other human beings, have flaws.
- Confusion about what to do next. After acknowledging their shadow side to others, they are uncertain about what they should do or say; they do not know what they should be doing differently, and it's unsettling to think about.

People are ready to acknowledge the shadow parts of themselves only when they see that doing so is a positive though difficult act that has these benefits:

- It communicates that admitting weakness is acceptable and can foster honesty and openness from direct reports.
- It helps other people recognize their own shadow sides and be open about these issues (rather than hiding them and allowing them to do damage).
- It brings difficult issues out in the open, making it easier to develop approaches for managing them.

Finally, companies whose cultures place a premium on openness and self-awareness facilitate both private and public acknowledgment of the shadow side. One organization we work with had virtually institutionalized discussions of leaders' shadow sides. At open forums, people can talk about how shadow side tendencies affect the quality of leadership, and the organizational culture encourages self-awareness and being aware of how personal style affects relationships.

Tips and Techniques

The CDR International Leadership Derailment Report, which provides development suggestions to manage shadow side issues, as well as other tools such as the Myers-Briggs Type Indicator are useful in helping people discover and talk about these issues. By pointing out the link between a negative trait such as arrogance and a positive one such as self-confidence, you can help people accept the bad with the good.

When you talk about shadow side issues with leaders, the discussion invariably comes to rest on the gap between intentions and actual impact. At this point, people typically express dismay at the gap between how they would like to be seen and how they are seen, and you can ask them what accounts for this gap. Leaders are usually eager to explore this issue; sometimes the problem is that they do not know what they are expected to do or lack the skills or training to build a strategy or develop others. In many cases, however, the gap is a reflection of shadow side tendencies that are deeply rooted in their personalities. In these instances, steer the discussion toward situations that people found particularly challenging or problematic. Reflection on adversity related to these situations and analysis of previous failures (and what went wrong) may lead to shadow side epiphanies. To help leaders experience these epiphanies, ask the following questions:

- In a situation where you were under significant stress, how did you handle it?
- In what ways could the situation have been handled more effectively?
- What behaviors undermined your ability to achieve maximum effectiveness?

Look for recurring themes when examining their behaviors under stress by exploring the following questions:

- Do the same problematic behaviors occur repeatedly when you find yourself in these high-pressure situations?

- What emotions kick in during these difficult experiences, and do they create problems?

Then ask some questions that allow them to think about whether they have observed negative impacts of other leaders' behaviors:

- Have you ever observed another leader in your organization behave in ways that caused problems?
- Can you identify with any of these behaviors?
- Why do you think leaders engage in behaviors that they know are counterproductive? Why would they do things they know are wrong?

The point of all these questions is to push them gently (and sometimes not so gently) toward the acknowledgment that they too have a shadow side that can get them in trouble at times.

Whether you are coaching someone to acknowledge her shadow side or you yourself are attempting to come to terms with it, the following suggestions may help:

- *Label the tendencies.* Give words to shadow side behaviors that cause problems rather than talk about them in vague terms (or not at all). Use the CDR International Leadership Derailment Report traits or the other terms we've used to categorize shadow sides.
- *Avoid defensiveness.* Everyone has a shadow side, and while some shadow sides are more troublesome than others, they are something all leaders need to deal with.
- *Anticipate situations that create problems for you.* The shadow side will not emerge in all circumstances, so be alert to the specific factors that cause it to emerge in you. By being aware of your tendencies, you can reduce the likelihood that they will cause you or others problems.
- *Recognize the flip side of the shadow side.* It's easier to deal with your hidden destructiveness as a leader when you see that it has a positive flip side. Most of us want to deny something that is completely malignant. When we see that a trait is a mix of good and bad, it's easier to accept and deal with it.

Benefits of Acknowledgment

People who acknowledge their shadow side do not become better leaders overnight. They do, however, eventually become better leaders because they have this unnatural act in their arsenal. Let's look at some of the leadership benefits of having access to this unnatural act:

- *More choices when compelled to behave a certain way.* Ed was the CEO of a well-known global corporation when we began working with him. Highly organized, precise, and systematic, Ed presided over his team's meetings like a silent wise man. As members of his team engaged in passionate debate, Ed would take notes and at the end of the meeting summarize the conclusions in a dry and detailed brief. His summations were always brilliant, but they left everyone cold. Unable to inspire or motivate his team, Ed welcomed us when we were called in to coach him. But despite his efforts in the direction of acknowledging his shadow perfectionism, Ed never really accepted that it was *his* problem. After completing the CDR International Leadership Derailment Report, he would dutifully add "acknowledge shadow side" to his to-do list. He was stuck in his natural leadership mode of never acknowledging an imperfection in a meaningful way. As a result, when he was compelled to act like a perfectionist, he did not have another option. If he were highly conscious of his shadow side tendencies, Ed could have chosen a more productive behavioral path on occasion, telling himself, "I'm being anal-compulsive again. The 80 percent solution might work here. I need to try another approach so people realize I'm a fully engaged human being."
- *Becoming aware of being part of someone else's reality.* Natural leaders often are wrapped up in their own worlds and do not realize the tremendous impact their behaviors have on others, especially their direct reports. When people become aware of their shadow sides, they possess a greater ability to measure their actions against their impact; they realize that these actions have a profound effect on whether people are excited, motivated, inspired, creative, and so on. Being able to view a situation through someone else's eyes is a great unnatural talent, and shadow side awareness helps develop it.

- *Improving organizational productivity.* So much effort goes into managing the boss or anticipating the leader that it drains people of energy that could more profitably be expended elsewhere. We worked with one global energy company with a widespread ritual of almost daily 11:00 A.M. check-up calls, generated by the direct reports to a top executive who denied his by-the-numbers shadow. They put in much effort in preparing for these telephone queries, and the whole situation was viewed largely as a joke in the ranks. Nonetheless, the bosses who made the calls had lunch with the top executive at noon each day, and they wanted to be prepared should he ask them an unexpected question about their business. Acknowledging the shadow side eliminates the need for these ritualistic games.

- *Managing under stress.* Stress often causes the shadow side to emerge. When we are under great pressure, we often allow our shadow side free rein; the dark qualities we might manifest only some of the time now become omnipresent. We have been coaching a senior executive whose company is experiencing severe problems, and since they arose, he has been constantly complaining to anyone who will listen to him about his personal situation and how his stock options and pension benefits are in danger. His shadow side of victimization and self-pity has emerged with great intensity, and scores of people who work for him are demoralized by his complaining and lack of sensitivity to the impact on them. If he could acknowledge his shadow side, he would be able to moderate this effect, use his many talents to help his people through this difficult period, and retain the best of them for the reorganized company without personalizing his difficulties. Just as stress brings out the shadow side, acknowledging it makes us aware of this tendency and allows us to control it.

- *Creating powerful emotional connections with others.* Acknowledging our shadow side also means acknowledging our humanity. Natural leaders who deny this side of themselves come across as being perfect. Of course, they are not and everyone knows it, but their air of invincibility keeps others at a distance. When people admit they are perfectionists or confess to being a pleaser or a whiner, they humanize themselves and open the possibility of a real emotional connection with others. Relationship management has become critical, and leaders who are unable to form the strong relationships that involve an emotional component are short-changing their companies and themselves.

Even Nearsighted People Can See Their Shadow

We conclude this chapter with the story of Kate, a leader we coached who initially seemed incapable of committing this unnatural act of acknowledging her shadow side. Bright, articulate, and highly motivated, Kate received feedback that she was alienating others with her inaccessible and overcontrolling manner. Even worse, Kate's discussions with us demonstrated that a huge gap existed between her intentions and her impact. Kate viewed herself as a "people person" who cared about her direct reports and advocated their interests to senior management. When she received feedback that called her brusque and accused her of running over others, Kate was shocked and denied the validity of what she was hearing. Then she attacked the feedback methodology and proceeded to blame her boss, claiming that she was surprised the feedback was not worse given how difficult it had been to deal with his demands. Finally, she took on the organization, saying that it was not a particularly caring culture and that people there laugh at anyone who shows much empathy or kindness.

Although there was some truth in Kate's description of the culture, she had exaggerated; in fact, many leaders in her company were emotionally intelligent. Kate, however, looked everywhere but at herself to explain what we and the feedback were communicating. It took a great deal of coaxing and questioning before Kate's resistance began to diminish. Kate began by admitting that she was somewhat insecure—she had been at the company only for a year—and she was struggling to fit into its culture, saying she had felt at home in her previous company, which she had left because it was experiencing a downturn. She had been struggling to build a network of support at her new employer and was under a lot of pressure for results. In addition, relocation was a hassle, and she was experiencing personal difficulties.

Clearly, the accumulated stress of all these things caused her shadow side to erupt. Her controlling nature prompted her to be overly critical and nitpick. At times, Kate would become obsessed with details and lose sight of the big picture. Every assignment had to be completed perfectly, and even a small glitch might catalyze her to take over a project from a direct report.

Kate did not want to be viewed as an overbearing nitpicker and did not believe she was viewed that way. It was only when we began coaching her that she could take a step back and view the past year with hindsight and reflection. Gradually, she could see the theme of her micromanaging and how it was causing direct reports sleepless nights and much angst. This was not Kate's intention, but it was her effect. Through the shared feedback, the use of the CDR International Leadership Derailment Report (Kate was a perfectionist), and ongoing discussion about the difficulty of transitions, Kate saw how she was trapped in a self-defeating cycle: she took on more and more work in the new job, experienced a greater desire to do the work perfectly, and felt tremendous pressure as the challenges became overwhelming. Gradually, we helped Kate move to the point that she could begin to she how she contributed to problems with her direct reports and could acknowledge her shadow side. First to herself and then to others, she acknowledged that she was not perfect but was trying to be. These admissions, done hesitantly and with some embarrassment at first, helped Kate become a much more self-aware and self-controlled leader.

Acknowledging Your Shadow Side

Reflect on what happens to you when you are under stress. Read each of the descriptions that follows, and rate how susceptible you are to each of these vulnerabilities.

Vulnerability Description	Your Susceptibility				

Volatile: Energizing and active but moody and irritable; easily annoyed; tends to give up on projects; critical of others' work; may seem self-doubting and tense

1	2	3	4	5
Low				High

Distrustful: Insightful about others' motives but skeptical and critical; takes criticism personally; can be argumentative; builds few long-term relationships

1	2	3	4	5
Low				High

Overly cautious: Tense, quiet, careful, and indecisive; fearful of making mistakes; tends not to state opinions; is uncomfortable around strangers

1	2	3	4	5
Low				High

Aloof: Tends to be unconcerned about the feelings of others; seems stiff around strangers; seems not to read social cues; unintentionally bruises feelings

1	2	3	4	5
Low				High

Passive-resistant: Overly cooperative but privately irritable, resentful, stubborn, and uncooperative; dislikes interruptions; puts off unpleasant tasks

1	2	3	4	5
Low				High

Arrogant: Challenges, confronts, and intimidates others; tests the limits; unusually self-confident with inflated views of competency and worth

1	2	3	4	5
Low				High

Mischievous: Clever, charming, impulsive, and adventurous; unafraid of risk, easily bored; needs variety and excitement, very quick to act

1	2	3	4	5
Low				High

Melodramatic: Enjoys being the center of attention; makes a strong first impression; easily irritated; often overcommits; may become angry when challenged

1	2	3	4	5
Low				High

Eccentric: Acts and thinks in creative and sometimes odd or unusual ways; makes unusual decisions; attracts attention to self

1	2	3	4	5
Low				High

Perfectionistic: Meticulous, precise, compulsive, and conscientious; supervises others closely; maintains high standards; tries to do everything rather than delegate

1	2	3	4	5
Low				High

Pleaser: Eager to please and reluctant to take independent action or go against popular opinion; polite; rarely challenges policy

1	2	3	4	5
Low				High

Acknowledging Your Shadow Side (Cont.)

Focus on the vulnerabilities that you assigned the highest ratings. How do your vulnerabilities undermine your performance?

How do your vulnerabilities affect your working relationships?

Think about a specific situation when you were under significant stress and did not handle it as well as you should have. In what ways could you have handled the situation more effectively?

In what situations is your shadow side most likely to emerge?

List three actions that you can take to manage your vulnerabilities and adopt unnatural leadership behaviors.

A.

B.

C.

Steps for Developing Yourself as an Unnatural Leader

Adopt a learning attitude toward your vulnerabilities. Anticipate situations that may give you problems, and mentally rehearse for them. Talk with others who have faced what you are facing to get advice and coaching. Watch people you believe handle these situations well.

Learn to look at negative feedback and criticism as potentially useful information that you need to understand more fully.

Think about how you handle high-pressure situations, and identify ways you can handle them more effectively.

Solicit feedback from others regarding how you handle stressful situations.

Make a point to observe how other leaders deal with stressful situations.

Encourage your direct reports to acknowledge their shadow side, and provide coaching and feedback that can help them learn how to manage negative consequences.

Chapter Seven

Develop a Right-Versus-Right Decision-Making Mentality

In the old days, leaders had problems and solutions. Today we have paradoxes and continuous choices. Previous generations of leaders routinely relied on a tried-and-true, either-or analytical methodology to solve problems. Using conventional analysis, they made business decisions based on the facts. In the vast majority of cases, they could look at a problem and decide the right course of action and the wrong one. Although they made mistakes, their alternatives were clear, and the results of their decisions generally were unambiguous. A strategy either worked or it didn't.

Leaders now must make decisions in a volatile business environment rife with ambiguity, paradox, and complexity. Natural leaders often try to force the problem-solution methodology on problems that defy traditional analysis. Many times, leaders are faced with decisions with no obvious answer that will emerge, no matter how detailed or astute the analysis. The decision is often between two or more alternatives that are right. Global or local? Centralized or decentralized? Equity or individual difference?

The unnatural act is learning how to manage and make many continuous choices rather than make one big choice and defend it to the death. As we will see, it takes a confident leader to make a decision knowing that it's not "right" and that circumstances may force him to modify that decision in the near future. Natural leaders have been acculturated to act as if they know the right thing to do in all situations. As a result, they find it unnatural to admit that they are confused and uncertain by the equally attractive alternatives before them.

Let's look at the source for much of this uncertainty and confusion.

Unsolvable Paradoxes

What distinguishes a paradox from a problem is that the paradox has no real long-term solution. Instead, leaders must manage two opposing forces, both of which have merit. For instance, leaders are faced with the paradox of making decisions quickly but accurately. They need to decide whether to buy a company that has suddenly become available for purchase but do not have the time to gather all the facts to make an informed decision. The paradox in this situation is that the need for speed compromises the need for accuracy (and vice versa). Similarly, leaders are faced with the paradox of trying to make their companies more diverse and inclusive, yet at the same time creating a meritocracy in which people are rewarded based on results. How do you decide between two people up for promotion when one will add to workforce diversity but is not quite ready for the position and the other is ready now but fits the current mold perfectly?

The following paradoxes that we have encountered in coaching senior leaders present particularly vexing right-versus-right decisions.

Short-Term Versus Long-Term

The classic example of this paradox is long-term investment in research and development (R&D) versus quarterly earnings objectives. Do you reduce the R&D budget in order to achieve quarter-by-quarter short-term earnings? Or do you increase the budget for future growth even though it might have a negative impact on quarterly figures? Although this paradox has been with organizations for years, industry analysts and portfolio managers and the business media have put more pressure on companies recently to deliver shareholder value consistently. At the same time, business critics have been chiding organizations that are overly focused on short-term goals, and there is widespread acceptance that organizations have to retool and reshape themselves, even cannibalizing profitable products, in order to catch the next wave of innovation.

Avon Products, for instance, is attempting to transform its business by improving its global business processes and moving into new areas such as retail. As it makes this transformation, however, it cannot neglect its core direct-sale business. There is no right answer or magical solution about how to address both the existing requirements and future opportunity. Instead, the unnatural act is to accommodate the apparent contradictions of focusing on both the present and the future, constantly adjusting strategy so that both short- and long-term goals are met.

Global Versus Local

Our colleague Stephen Rhinesmith has written an excellent article, "The Five Steps of Global Paradox," in which he examines the corporate impulse to globalize in order to achieve economies of scale, share best practices, create global brands, and meet the needs of global customers. If companies globalize too much, though, they lose touch with customer needs in local markets, reduce opportunities for customization, and appear out of touch with local management. Although localization also has benefits—empowering local leadership, being sensitive to local customer needs, and so on—too much localization can result in increased costs, duplication, and problems with cross-organizational communication.

The natural impulse is to search for a magical solution. More than one leader has chosen global over local and paid the price when country organizations floundered. More than one leader has opted for local over global and paid the price when she could not control escalating costs. This paradox, like the others discussed here, comes down to optimization versus maximization. Managing a paradox effectively means finding the optimal balance between two competing forces rather than maximizing the benefits of each. This means accepting that there will be a downside to balancing local versus global interests but managing in such a way that the downside is minimized.

Professional Versus Personal

The drive for bottom- and top-line performance has led to remarkable gains in U.S. productivity, but as the standard is being raised, demands on individual workers have increased. Workforce reductions and head count freezes have made it necessary for fewer people to do more, and global companies require more travel. To advance in one's career, working long hours in the global tournament is now inevitable. At the same time, a cultural emphasis on family, being a good parent, and self-actualization has caused leaders to want to spend more time at home as well as pursue activities they love outside work.

Achieving the right balance is tricky, especially when a natural leader believes that the professional is more important than the personal. Become a workaholic and you may advance your career, but your personal life will suffer (and eventually your productivity may decrease because of burn-out). Refuse to work more than forty hours a week to focus on family, and you may doom your career.

The unnatural act is to accept that there is no perfect balance between professional and personal. *Work-life balance* is a misnomer; it is impossible to achieve. As soon as you think you have achieved this balance, you may encounter unexpected business reversals and need to work harder and longer. Or you may find that your relationship is in trouble, and you must shift the balance more toward the personal. Unnatural leaders recognize that what works today might not work tomorrow. They are vigilant for shifts in one direction or another and willing to make course corrections when they occur. Being alert for feedback from a boss that they are letting important projects slip or from a spouse that their priorities need realignment can enable them to adjust the balance continuously and achieve work-life flexibility.

Individual Versus Team

This too is a difficult balancing act. With the development of matrix organizations, broad spans of control, and the need for more cross-cultural decision making, teams have become increasingly vital. As a result, leaders have been faced with a series of difficult choices between meeting individual needs and satisfying team requirements. It's very difficult to get these choices right. Leaders want to emphasize individual objectives and needs to provide a straightforward focus on performance and clear accountabilities. But if they put too much focus on the individual, they do not benefit from the collective efforts of teams. Leaders also want to emphasize teamwork because it fosters shared learning, creates synergies useful in executing tough business challenges, and facilitates interorganizational networking and best-practice sharing. An overemphasis on teams, however, can result in a drag on decision making, informal competition among team members, and lower morale among people who feel that although their individual contributions exceed those of others, they are not recognized or rewarded for these contributions.

Just about every day, leaders confront team-versus-individual decisions. If they increase rewards for teams, will such an action demotivate individual efforts? If they allow certain talented individuals to function outside team structures, will teams be resentful? Should the organization's culture focus on hiring and rewarding the talented few or a culture that motivates everyone?

Direction Versus Delegation

As companies have flattened and leaders have delegated downward, right-versus-right choices have proliferated. Leaders recognize that people still need direction, but how much is too much, and when does it impinge on their autonomy? A certain amount of direction helps people focus on addressing clear priorities, but too much can make people feel as if they are being told what to do, and as a result they do not feel empowered or motivated to create. Delegating is empowering for direct reports and frees leaders to concentrate on high-priority responsibilities, but it can also confuse people about what they are supposed to do and disconnect them from the organization.

Leaders need to weigh the pros and cons of direction versus delegation regularly. Two factors are useful in this assessment: the criticality of the task and the capacity of the person responsible for the task. If, for instance, the task is of immediate and high importance, the leader may find it necessary to provide more direction than she usually does. If the person assigned the task is highly competent, the leader may want to delegate more responsibility than usual with less direction. In coaching senior leaders, we ask them to weigh these two factors and make constant adjustments as the only feasible way to deal effectively with this paradox.

Jay, a senior executive leading his business through a major change in business value creation, encountered this paradox as he dismantled silos, put together cross-functional teams, and did what many change agents do. He found, however, that despite the urgency he felt, his direct reports were resisting these changes. They were subtly protesting the amount of work involved in making the changes a reality and complaining that there were too many priorities, that it was impossible to get everything done, and that Jay's time frame was unrealistic. They began asking Jay to be more specific about what he wanted and to clarify his priorities. Jay struggled with how to respond to their complaints. He did not want to provide too much direction and rob his team of what he perceived to be a valuable struggle to come up with viable ideas. He also wanted to create an organization of empowered leaders who could operate effectively on their own. At the same time, if their grumbling and inaction continued, he risked negative business results in delivering new services to customers. If he erred on the side of delegation, he might hurt his team's morale as they floundered; it was possible that he might lose some very talented people who wanted to work for a leader who could provide clear direction.

There is no happy ending to this story. Jay continues to struggle with these issues as he moves forward with the organization's transformation. In fact, most executive teams we work with are wrestling with the question of how to provide a clear strategy and respond to employees' expectations for precise direction, while also requiring them to take responsibility, set direction, and lead. Jay has learned that there is no magical solution and that he must experiment with delegation and direction decisions and adjust them depending on the situation. For executive teams, this requires constant conversation and adaptation about direction and delegation.

The Impulse to Find the Correct Answer

Imagine taking a multiple-choice test and the teacher instructs you that some questions may not have a correct answer. When you are used to circling A, B, C, or D, such an instruction can confound you. You may believe that she is not being serious or is trying to confuse you. In either case, you do not want to believe there is no correct answer, because then you have no logical way to deal with the question.

This correct-answer impulse runs deep and strong in many executives. Although they may have learned to accept one or two types of paradoxes, they insist on finding the correct answers to others. The centralization-versus-decentralization paradox, for instance, is one that leaders often believe they can solve. And perhaps they can solve it—at first. But the decision that appears correct initially may prove incorrect six months later.

Elizabeth, for instance, the new CEO of a company, determined that because of spiraling costs, the organization should centralize and move away from its traditional practice of granting spending decisions to those in the field. In the interest of reducing costs and gaining control, Elizabeth began to review spending decisions, require approvals, and oversee appointments to various positions, efforts that were met with predictable resistance in local offices. Still, as costs decreased and some sharing of best practices began, the directives seemed to be working. Over time, however, sales began to decline in key markets because global franchise leaders were immune to country input, and product development lagged significantly behind market demand. As Elizabeth steered the company into greater emphasis on globalization and as some countries began to lag, she needed to act fast to modify her initial decision. But she was convinced she had made the right decision initially and began to make the classic leadership error of interpreting the data to support her own theory. She was unable to commit the unnatural act of second-guessing herself, monitoring the situation, and comprehending that she had to shift back in the direction of decentralization. Because she was unable to adjust this balance, she ultimately was fired.

Another trait of natural leaders is an intolerance for ambiguity, and this intolerance mitigates against making right-versus-right decisions. Many leaders like to think of themselves as decisive and in control. They favor structure, order, and closure. They hold to rigid schedules, run tight meetings, and avoid messy situations. To admit that a challenge has no solution strikes them as heresy. They may have difficulty admitting this fact to themselves. It's also possible that although they can acknowledge it to themselves, they cannot acknowledge it to others. They assume that others want and need answers and that it's their responsibility to provide them.

We want to emphasize that in certain instances, these natural traits are necessary. Certain problems, especially those requiring adaptive rather than technical solutions, need leaders who can come up with the right answers. The most effective leaders, though, can differentiate a solvable problem from a paradox. At times, they risk being viewed as indecisive in order to monitor a changing situation and adjust their earlier decision accordingly.

How to Adopt a Right-Versus-Right Perspective

Both right-versus-right and right-versus-wrong decisions require facts. At every choice point, data must be analyzed and decisions made. The natural approach to decision making, unfortunately, is to focus only on the facts, and many leaders pride themselves on fact-based decision making. It is as if a leader places all the facts of the argument on a scale, and whichever way the scale tips determines the decision. In right-versus-right decisions, though, the scale is perfectly balanced. Many leaders who move up in the company hierarchy discover what Stephen Rhinesmith has called "the ascendancy level of decision making": the higher you go, the more that alternatives and choices become equally attractive because the easier decisions have already been made lower in the organization. At the top, the choices must often be based on values, vision, and strategic purpose rather than clear facts. Here are some suggestions for viewing and making decisions from a right-versus-right perspective:

• *Factor your values into the decision-making equation.* Janet, the head of a global business for a Fortune 100 company, struggled with how much to centralize operations and install shared services in Europe to achieve economies of scale without losing touch with local markets. She weighed the facts—cost savings of centralization against the risks of losing customer focus and responsiveness—and was stuck. Her team lobbied for greater centralization, but Janet believed that general managers of subsidiaries needed to be able to run their own businesses and have the resources to do so. Perhaps because Janet had been a general manager herself, she personally valued a certain amount of local autonomy. As a result, she resisted her team's sentiment and struck a balance between centralization and local autonomy that satisfied her values and achieved her purpose.

Charles, a new CEO, was in the process of forming his executive committee and was trying to decide whether to place all his direct reports or just some of them on the committee. Because he had a large number of people reporting to him, including everyone would create a somewhat unwieldy team and make it more difficult for them to hold open discussions and move quickly. On the other hand, he thought highly of his direct reports and believed their diverse viewpoints would result in a richer mix of ideas. Charles valued inclusiveness over speed. He recognized that one was not necessarily more important than the other in an absolute sense, but throughout his career, he had seen that inclusiveness produced high morale, fostered great ideas, and yielded a more holistic approach to issues. As a result, he decided to include all his direct reports on the team.

Janet and Charles could not have made these decisions as effectively without knowing what they valued. Leaders need to be attuned to their own beliefs and not just adopt the beliefs of mentors, bosses, or what is in vogue at the time of a decision. Values do not make one choice better than another, but they do instill greater integrity into the process and enable the leader to execute with commitment. Janet and Charles made decisions that they truly believed in, and their beliefs served as a guide between two otherwise equal alternatives. Both moved forward with confidence, convinced that their principles had helped steer them in the right direction.

- *Tolerate uncertainty, and become comfortable with ambiguity.* Some executives become anxious when faced with equally compelling alternatives or when the facts point them in multiple directions. Uncomfortable with uncertainty or ambiguity, they decline to keep themselves open long enough to explore all options and facets of a situation before making a decision. They make hasty decisions to resolve a situation and put uncertainty behind them.

Unnatural leaders condition themselves to become comfortable with choices that are complex and unpredictable and to tolerate the expectations of others that they be more clear and precise. Rather than plunging forward, they force themselves to be flexible, open, and vigilant. When a situation becomes volatile and many courses of action present themselves, they consciously take a step back and reflect rather than taking a step forward and decide. This does not mean that they are indecisive but that they are willing to adjust to an uncertain environment and operate thoughtfully and comfortably within it.

Jamal is a great example of someone who has learned to adapt to uncertainty and ambiguity. A senior business unit leader who is in the middle of transforming his organization, he reached significant milestones in his first six months on the job, combining information technology and marketing services to create cross-organizational opportunities for on-line services that the company could not envision in the past. After those first six months, however, Jamal's team began to push back. They began complaining that they were uncertain how to implement the next phase of service innovation, that they had a number of options for moving forward that involved major costs that they needed Jamal to decide, and that they were worried that they were moving the company in the wrong direction. This type of team and organizational pushback is not uncommon after the initial enthusiasm of a change initiative wears off.

Jamal did not dismiss their expressions of uncertainty. He was concerned that they were struggling and might not be able to implement the next phase of their strategy effectively. But he had led change in other companies and had learned to deal with these expressions of uncertainty and the ambiguous nature of the transformation that was unfolding. Because of his experience, Jamal was convinced that his team had to discover for themselves how best to implement the new direction; it was the only way they would completely buy in to the strategy, and he believed that buy-in was important. He listened to their complaints but did not fix them. A natural leader might have stepped up to the challenge of their uncertainty and attempted to resolve all issues for the team. Jamal, with support from us as coaches, insisted that the team members work things out on their own. Eventually, they came up with a plan to make the strategy work and successfully executed it.

• *Empathize with people in other positions within the organization.* Most traditional leaders acknowledge the importance of empathy, but they themselves do not empathize. Why should they labor to view a situation from other people's frame of references when their job is to create a singular vision and drive it into the organization? How does listening to the naysayers and critics, these leaders argue, add value? Managing a paradoxical situation, however, is difficult if you do not empathize with other people involved in the paradox. By this, we mean that it is difficult to manage a right-versus-right decision when there's no sensitivity to the people involved on both sides of the decision. Let's go back to our centralization-versus-decentralization example to illustrate this point.

A New York–based global company decides that all product development for Asia will take place in one location. The New York executive who favors this decision sees it as a way to improve the company's overall profitability. The manager of the Malaysian office, on the other hand, views it as a reduction in his authority and argues that it will impair his ability to meet customer needs. Without understanding these and other perspectives, a leader will be tempted to move forward with the centralization decision, believing that local managers will get over their objections. Without understanding how they are feeling about centralization, he will decide with the arrogance of being right. But this attitude will alienate local managers and prevent him from revisiting and possibly revising his decision as events unfold.

Making an effort to understand what another person is truly thinking requires pushing one's own ego aside and listening deeply to the other individual. Listening deeply is not just the act of hearing another person's words but sensing the emotional struggle going on in his head. For instance, the real issue for a local manager concerned about centralization has little to do with economies of scale; it has to do with power. The manager of the Malaysian office is angry that his power and influence in the field are being transferred to headquarters and that he must deal with real consequences. Given that, a leader should ask himself the following questions:

How does it feel to have your power reduced?

What would I be concerned about if I were in this person's position?

How might I react if I were told about this centralization plan?

What would I need to hear or what actions would headquarters have to take to accept this decision?

• *Develop cognitive complexity.* F. Scott Fitzgerald wrote in *The Crack-Up* that "the test of a first-rate intelligence is the ability to hold two opposed ideas in the mind at the same time, and still retain the ability to function." Developing cognitive complexity is what Fitzgerald was describing. Too often, leaders respond to paradox—two opposing ideas—by becoming dysfunctional. They either become paralyzed and unable to make a decision, or in a quest for clarity they ignore the reality of a paradox and make a decision as if one of the alternatives is the perfect solution.

You do not need to be a genius to develop cognitive complexity, but you do need to stop trying to simplify issues. "Keep it simple, stupid" (KISS) is a cynical statement that has been embraced by more than one leader. The temptation to reduce complex and contradictory issues down to their essence is difficult to resist. Trying to figure out how to sell through e-commerce and traditional distribution networks without competing against oneself produces headaches; sending mixed messages to customers because of the competing selling models turns headaches into migraines. It is much easier to simplify the situation and decide, "No one in our industry can make e-commerce work; dot-com companies are imploding. Let's put all our effort into our traditional selling channels!"

We have found, however, that leaders can be coached to accept a world of seeming contradictions and mind-bending complexities. They develop a Zen-like acceptance of things as they are, not as they should be. Rather than fighting against waves of paradox, the unnatural act is to learn to work around them and recognize that it's possible to function effectively despite these paradoxes.

A Tool for Developing an Unnatural Decision-Making Mentality

We've developed a tool that we've used successfully at Avon Products to help executives become right-versus-right decision makers. It's based on the work of Barry Johnson and his book *Polarity Management*. The following five-step tool helps leaders learn to make decisions when vexing paradoxes are involved:

1. *Define the paradox.* A decision can be defined as a paradox when two or more opposing forces exist, each force has an upside and a downside, no long-term solution exists, and the upside of each force must be increased while the downside must be decreased. What is the paradox that you're facing (for example, global standardization versus local customization, recognizing teamwork as well as individual contributions, or pressing for business results while still maintaining a people-friendly environment)? List the competing forces:

   Force 1

   Force 2

2. *Test the paradox to be sure it is a paradox.* The following two questions will separate old-fashioned problems from paradoxes:
   - Can the situation be solved once and for all with a specific solution? If so, it's a problem to be solved.
   - Are there two or more solutions, both of which are right in the short run but could have negative consequences in the long run? If so, it's a paradox to be managed.
3. *Place the names of the forces on either side of the matrix* (for example, team versus individual, centralization versus decentralization, people versus performance).

Positive Aspects	Positive Aspects
Force 1	Force 2
Negative Aspects	Negative Aspects

A Tool for Developing an Unnatural Decision-Making Mentality (Cont.)

4. After identifying the two forces, write down the positive and negative consequences of each in the appropriate boxes. For example, what are the concerns and consequences if you focus only on business results and not people? Possibilities are burn-out, attrition, and lower morale. After you think about the negative consequences, write them in the lower quadrants for each force. Then identify the positive benefits of each force. Using the same example of business results, some ideas may be financial success and increased shareholder value. After you think about the positive benefits of each force, write them in the upper quadrant for each force.

5. Now list the ways in which you would manage the situation to ensure that you don't go too far below the line distinguishing between the positive and negative aspects of each issue. In other words, how would you "live in the positive" and "manage the negative" of each of the four quadrants? What specific action would you take to keep the forces in balance?

Steps for Developing Yourself as an Unnatural Leader

Use the paradox management tool for decisions that have no real long-term solution.

Avoid trying to answer questions when there is no solution just because you believe people can't handle uncertainty.

Pay attention to changes in the external environment that could have an impact on a significant paradox you are trying to manage.

Work on clarifying what is important to you (for example, your values and beliefs), so that it can be applied in situations where the data available do not provide a clear direction.

Be open about the existence of paradoxes, and teach how to manage them.

Challenge yourself to understand the upside and downside (the competing forces) for each key decision you need to make.

Part Three

Leading Teams as an Unnatural Leader

Chapter Eight

Create Teams
That Create Discomfort

Among the paradoxes in business today that underlie the need for unnatural leadership acts is that leaders must create teams that work well together yet also embrace conflict and openness. As important as it is for people to offer each other mutual support and to drive toward consensus, it's equally important for them individually to adopt a strong point of view and challenge the boss's and their peers' positions.

Because of this paradox, creating teams that create discomfort is difficult for some leaders but increasingly common in high-performing companies. Many companies today have adopted matrix structures that are designed to create conflict, and yet their company culture discourages conflict.

By *discomfort,* we mean feelings that range from anger to unease, produced by team members who disagree with and dispute other people's (including the leader's) point of view. We are not suggesting that discomfort should be the goal but that it should become a crucial ingredient to effective decision making rather than something to be avoided. Obviously, no leader is going to assemble a team whose members constantly confront each other or are constantly checkmating the leader. Anarchy is not the answer, even in a world that rewards unnatural leadership behaviors.

Discomfort, however, signals that different viewpoints are being aired and that established viewpoints are being challenged. In highly volatile and complex environments that are driving for performance, this discomfort signals that teams are grappling with difficult problems in the most open ways possible. Rather than playing political games or letting one powerful voice dominate, they are listening to and debating a range of ideas. In a very real way, discomforted teams are capitalizing on conflict, using it as a springboard to innovative solutions and real, rather than superficial, commitment.

Often, leaders pick as team members people they have worked with before, known to be loyal or with viewpoints similar to their own, in an effort to capitalize on an opportunity or shorten the time for getting up to speed. Or they choose a diverse team but create an atmosphere in which people are reluctant (or even afraid) to be open and honest. Many leaders unconsciously equate being on the team with keeping your opinions to yourself. As natural as these leadership behaviors are, they are no longer as effective as they once were. A little discomfort can go a long way to increasing team performance.

The Benefits of Criticism and Conflict

When we are coaching leaders to improve their performance, we frequently collect information about an individual's behavior and style from people he works with. We then summarize that information and share it with the person we are coaching. Invariably, the leader responds with surprise or even shock at the feedback. The problem is that leaders hold power over the careers (not to mention the salaries, bonuses, and other rewards) of the people who are providing the feedback, thereby restricting the flow of information. The anonymity of 360-degree feedback or the involvement of a neutral third party opens up information.

Typically, the higher the leader is in the organization, the more restricted the flow of information is. This is especially true for natural leaders who rely on power, authority, expertise, and experience, creating the perception that they want to hear only certain things (good news, not bad news, or positive ideas, not negative remarks). In these situations, leaders can find themselves in difficulty. Because they have not received all the information they could use, they are less effective; they do not realize that their policies or leadership style are the cause of high turnover or poor morale in the group, for instance. This basic truth is at the heart of Action Coaching for senior leaders.

Some of these leaders may well have included people on their teams who hold different perspectives from their own, but these teams fail to create discomfort because individual members do not feel free to do so. Their leaders have not communicated effectively or created an environment that conveys that they are open to all sorts of ideas and feedback, and thus they receive only reinforcing responses. They assume that team members will be willing to open up, failing to realize that their personality or position keeps them closed up.

The other common experience we have as coaches involves leaders complaining, "There's conflict on my team," often using this complaint as a way of explaining why they are having problems implementing a strategy across organizational boundaries. In many instances, our clients communicate to us that conflict makes them and members of their team uncomfortable. Although they may not state this problem explicitly, their responses to our questions indicate that they are extremely wary of the emotions that conflict engenders. Consciously or not, they work toward reducing or eliminating conflict, or they signal that conflict is not acceptable, and this often makes for an uninspired team and uninspired ideas.

Leaders who avoid team conflict and create environments in which team members are loathe to voice contrary or untraditional opinions find it very difficult to achieve productive outputs in matrix structures In many companies we work with, such as Johnson & Johnson, companies rely on contention, which they have turned into an energizing, creative force. For instance, the global franchise leader is going to make budgeting decisions about marketing that irritate certain country marketing directors. Achieving global launches, rationalizing products globally, and deploying worldwide advertising budgets can bring country managers and global franchise leaders into contention because local and global requirements can differ. Their conflict, however, is not destructive; it's not the type that translates into winners and losers, with the latter losing their self-respect. Instead, their conflict is constructive, because team members at Johnson & Johnson understand that conflict is inevitable and embrace it, and also because they have a corporate value system, the Johnson & Johnson credo, to help guide their behavior. Typically, great solutions emerge from the friction.

Committing this unnatural act is tremendously beneficial. When teams create discomfort, they are creating a rich stew of ideas, as well as bringing weak approaches and potential pitfalls into the open. Why, then, do leaders shy away from this unnatural act?

Harmony: A Natural Goal

Let's start with the fear of emotions associated with conflict. *Discomfort,* as we use the term, is an emotional state that many leaders find difficult to accept. Their reflex is to appease unhappy individuals, find compromises that do not make anyone too upset, and pretend that the team is one big, happy family. Most companies today aggregate their appraisal systems results to discover their company consists of only high performers. This may be true, but it is more likely that their leaders have trouble delivering negative feedback, facing strong emotions, and dealing with conflict. The leader who is afraid of feeling uncomfortable may select team members who think as she does. Or she may communicate that everyone in the company should keep certain ideas and opinions to themselves and focus on the positive.

Many companies eschew expressions of strong emotion except at sales conferences, when a motivational speaker exhorts the troops. Instead, feelings are repressed or funneled into griping, graffiti, opinion surveys, and anonymous feedback instruments. The genuine expression of feeling is messy and complicated, which is why many leaders find it off-putting. But expressions of passion and feeling signal commitment, an increasingly elusive and desirable commodity in the workplace. Energy and edge drive performance. Teams that operate with few, if any, arguments quickly achieve consensus and enjoy a cool, calm operating environment that may be easy to lead, but they are not easy to push to breakthrough levels of performance.

Sometimes even the most brilliant leaders work overtime to ensure that discomfort does not "infect" their teams. We are working with two senior leaders at a well-known high-tech company; both are brilliant scientists in charge of major research and development projects that require them and their teams to work together. We were brought in to work with them because their personal conflict is sapping the energy from their teams. It's not that they bicker in front of their teams. Just the opposite is the case. They believe that they keep their conflict, competition, and personal animosity hidden and are proud that they do. When we interviewed people who worked with these two leaders, however, they told us that they were well aware of the hostility between the two men and that whenever they were in the same room, the atmosphere was polite, controlled, and emotionless. Although the scientists never said anything to each other that conveyed this animosity, their body language spoke volumes. It was difficult for anyone to be relaxed and open when they were around. Both, however, were convinced that the right thing to do as leaders was to prevent their groups from witnessing the conflict. By their avoidance of open debate, they sent mixed signals about how to view and work with the other team.

When leaders encourage open communication and pick at least a few team members who are willing to voice discomforting opinions, good things often happen. We ran an Action Learning program for the top leadership of Quantum, a large California-based disk drive manufacturer. In an industry that has been called structurally flawed, five or six key players are continuously engaged in cutthroat price competition to obtain one of the big computer manufacturers as a customer. Leadership in disk drive innovation passes back and forth among the key players, and the few customers play the disk drive manufacturers off each other. This causes each competitor to go through bust-and-boom cycles. Quantum had suffered through these cycles for years as it worked to develop a viable strategy. As part of this process, we were asked to develop its top leaders through an intensive Action Learning program.

During the program, we challenged the senior leadership group to find out what Quantum should do to increase shareholder value, and to help them answer that question through Action Learning, they participated in a "temporary system" designed to create openness, facilitate reflection, energize conflicts, and stimulate new ways of thinking and a willingness to deviate from standard thinking. Through the use of a number of team challenges, we helped the CEO, Michael Brown, and his team build an Action Learning environment that was significantly different from the typical Quantum meeting. Typically, the press of time, the pressure for short-term performance, and other factors made it difficult for leaders to challenge corporate strategy or offer fresh perspectives.

The Action Learning teams worked hard on the team challenge: to determine the best course of action for Quantum to increase shareholder value. After some time, the teams reported to Brown on their analysis of the industry, competition, customers, and prospects for growth. What most of the teams said was: "Find a partner and merge, or sell the company." The teams believed that the industry dynamics were not going to change and it would be impossible to sustain shareholder value growth over time. The best scenario would be for industry consolidation to occur and for Quantum to lead it. These teams demonstrated enormous courage and risk, and the Action Learning environment created the opportunity for them to debate their circumstances openly. As a result of this process and other inputs, Quantum sold its disk drive business to Maxtor, one of its biggest competitors.

Whether this was the right strategy, only time will tell; there may not be a "right" strategy, as every unnatural leader recognizes. The point here is that these teams contained a diverse membership and had the freedom to reach a highly discomforting conclusion. Under a purely natural leader or in most corporate settings, selling the company would never have been considered an option to be discussed.

Discomfort is a difficult unnatural act for another reason. Consider the chaotic times in which we live and work. Leaders are under pressure to achieve unrealistic growth targets, rationalize costs, install ever improving business processes, and accelerate the pace of decision making. In the face of all this pressure, complexity, and uncertainty, leaders tend to close ranks and seek a chaos-free decision-making process. They feel more comfortable knowing that at least their team will perform in a predictable, efficient manner.

The problem is that the environment makes discomfort even more important than in the past. For instance, with the complexity of product design, global delivery, and meeting customer requirements has come the need to work more effectively across internal departments and units. *Boundarylessness* often means unclear reporting lines and authority because the focus is on results. Leaders need and must cultivate the input of a diverse group of people to make effective decisions.

Leaders need to be comfortable with the inevitable discomfort these teams produce and learn to manage it. If instead they attempt to reduce or eliminate debate and conflict, these teams will not produce superior results. Globalization increases the likelihood that teams will be created with different cultural backgrounds, priorities, and points of view. As we have noted, the global-versus-local paradox is the reality in most companies today, and the conflicts need to be thrashed out in open debate, which accounts for cultural differences but achieves individual commitment. A leader must orchestrate and encourage debate and find a way to manage them in order to deal effectively with the issues and move forward. Leaders who attempt to stifle debate and force their own solutions on a team will inhibit performance.

We do not want to underestimate the natural leadership drive toward harmony. Many leaders believe that to be culturally sensitive, they must be agreeable. Many leaders have spent years in systems advocating a dispassionate approach to decision making. Many, especially in science- and research-based organizations, have arrived at decisions based on their ability to command data and sort through alternatives logically. Trusting your own judgment above all others has been the norm of leaders. A highly unnatural act, on the other hand, is being comfortable with your own judgment yet also willing to encourage and entertain opposing viewpoints authentically.

One senior leader we know encouraged his team to challenge him and offer ideas that deviated from his chosen direction. During meetings, he would verbally encourage challenges and untraditional ideas. His body language, however, was not encouraging. When someone ventured a contradictory opinion, he would shoot that person an icy stare that would communicate his displeasure, or he would begin reading his mail while others debated with each other. Soon his team learned to follow his lead and keep their out-of-the-box ideas to themselves.

To create teams that create discomfort, leaders need to be highly conscious about incorporating this unnatural act into how they select and lead teams.

Guiding Principles for Creating Discomfort

The following guidelines will make it easier for leaders to create teams that are willing to challenge leadership and offer ideas and solutions that vary from traditional ways of doing things. These guidelines are not designed to create a team of anarchists and rebels but one that has the ability and green light to challenge the status quo. If you are a veteran manager, expect these guidelines to contradict what you have learned about team selection and management. To commit an unnatural act, you need to unlearn some of the things you have been taught about teams. The first three principles are focused on team composition and the second three on the environment in which the team operates.

- *Pick some disagreers for your team.* In other words, find at least a few individuals who do not share your views on strategy, operations, or execution. For instance, find people who have different views on the competition, the stage in market evolution, customer requirements, or even what leaders in the company should do to succeed and what the key organizational levers for change are. This does not mean you should look for people with untenable perspectives or who are disruptive and disagreeable. Nor does it mean you should staff your entire team with disagreers. Working a few into the mix, however, guarantees that you will consider options and ideas that might not otherwise surface.
- *Make diversity a priority in team selection.* We are talking about diversity from the broadest possible vantage point. You are not just looking for differences in race, gender, and age, but also differences in experience and thinking. For instance, a leader of a U.S. global company might create a team of U.S.-centric individuals because of the challenge of communicating across languages, time zones, and cultures. Such a team might miss subtle non-American market issues, and the makeup of this team might send a message to the rest of the organization that non-U.S. issues are not signifi-

cant. We have seen this as employees in a global corporation look at a top team made up only of country nationals.

Natural leaders might be tempted to ignore this precept because they want a team that can reach agreement quickly and because they think it's going to be too much trouble to factor global issues into decisions consistently while remaining responsive to local needs. Or they might believe there are no non-U.S. leaders who are ready to join the team and provide their input. This unnatural act may well be a bit of a hassle at first, but it will result in a team that is more proficient at reconciling the global-versus-local paradox, a reconciliation that all global organizations are increasingly confronted with.

• *Consider including "enemies."* We are using *enemies* as a synonym for what the British refer to as "the loyal opposition." These are not people who have a personal vendetta against leaders but who work in other business units or research teams, have staked out strong positions, and hold opposing views on business direction. Including them on a team not only alerts leaders to where implementation obstacles might reside—they will be vocal about the politics and policies that might block effective implementation—but can co-opt the opposition. Rather than forming an underground movement that is difficult for leaders to deal with, enemies are allowed to function as part of the establishment. The danger of this unnatural act is that enemies will be intransigent and cause teams to become bogged down in endless disagreements. To avoid this possibility, leaders must establish ground rules for decision making, communicating that although all team members have the right to express their point of view, at the end of the day they must buy into the decision that is made (whether or not they agree with it). We have found that when this buy-in takes place and opposing viewpoints are debated, this process actually accelerates decision making.

• *Model status quo–challenging behaviors.* Sometimes it's insufficient to include contentious people on your team because they believe that stating an opposing or unpopular viewpoint will not advance their careers. Leaders therefore should model the discomfort-creating behaviors they want their team to emulate. Demonstrating intellectual curiosity and honesty, rigor in considering alternatives, taking on sacred cows, bringing up uncomfortable topics, and breaking with traditions will give your team permission to do likewise. Keeping the debate open long enough before making a decision on a course of action for the team also invites challenge and disagreement.

• *Accept the challenges of others with a nondefensive, learning demeanor.* One of the most difficult things for leaders to do is to avoid the defensive posture that comes naturally to many leaders when faced with criticism or conflict. Natural leaders grew up equating disrespect with challenge; they expected their positional authority to produce verbal agreement when they shared their ideas with direct reports. Strong leaders naturally have strong viewpoints, and it is paradoxical to be both strong and not overwhelm all others. Unnatural leaders recognize that respect comes from the integrity of their ideas rather than their position. They are able to keep their ego in check and suffer some challenge or even embarrassment in order to encourage others to speak their mind. When faced with challenges, they are able to say, "I don't know," or, "I made a mistake," if they feel this is the case. Admitting you do not know the answer or made a mistake is tough to admit, especially when team leaders are strongly associated with a position or decision. But what a leader suffers in short-term ego deflation is more than made up by the long-term gains in free-flowing, problem-solving ideas.

• *Share information.* Natural leaders are sometimes reluctant to share new positions, strategies, plans, reorganizations, and other information, though not necessarily for obvious reasons. Some natural leaders might refuse to share because they want to maintain control, but most keep things to themselves because sharing information creates additional time-consuming work for them. They realize that informed people tend to be more likely to express opinions, ask questions, and issue challenges, actions that slow the decision-making and implementation processes. In the name of speed, therefore, they withhold more than they should or choose to send critical decisions or information through e-mail or memos.

Many leaders in large organizations complain about the "plague" of Web site chatrooms and bulletin boards where their strengths, weaknesses, and decisions are openly discussed and tough questions are asked. In response to this employee drive for more information, some top teams sometimes drive to control information and eliminate leaks as a sign of discipline and team loyalty. Just as problematic are situations where the CEO, COO, or top leaders try to create more challenge through listening sessions, brown bag lunches, and open-door policies but are thwarted by managers who are threatened by such actions. We have witnessed a few company meetings in which a young challenger was dressed down after the meeting for asking an inappropriate question. Having information, however, is a tremendous stimulus for teams to offer fresh ideas and challenge existing programs. It provides a base for people to launch initiatives and confront strategies from a position of knowledge.

Facilitating This Unnatural Behavior

With the previous six principles in mind, here are more specific actions designed to create teams that create discomfort. We have found that these actions encourage team members to challenge the accepted wisdom as well as their leaders.

- *Rate team meetings.* At the end of every meeting, ask people to rate the meeting on a scale of 1 to 10. Some teams use the GRPI model of team effectiveness for team members to rate the meeting in four categories:

Goals	Are they clear, understood, and accepted?
Roles	Does everyone know what is expected of him or her?
Processes	Are there clear ways to decide?
Interpersonal	How do people feel about each other and express their feelings? How do they deal with conflict?

Rating each of these four areas and talking about them gives the team a forum for honest, open discussion. Leaders who implement this rating system clearly communicate that they want feedback that addresses urgent issues and provide a structure for encouraging debate and focusing attention on key aspects of team effectiveness.

- *Ask for personal improvement feedback.* Go to direct reports after a meeting, program, or coaching session, and tell them one or two things you learned about yourself from the meeting. This does not have to be a long-winded lecture or emotional confession. Make it short and sweet: "I realize I was starting to dominate the discussion, something I tend to do, which is why I shut up for the last half of the meeting." Then ask your team if they have one or two ideas how you can perform better or improve at something. Leave the room for thirty minutes (and tell the team you'll be back in a half-hour), and ask them to brainstorm and come up with a mini-report about what you might do to improve.

- *Institutionalize the question, "How have we screwed up?"* Johnson & Johnson holds Credo Challenge sessions: small-group meetings that take place around the world in which teams and business units ask themselves, "How in the last year have we not fully upheld the Johnson & Johnson Credo?" a statement of beliefs and values that has guided the company for over sixty years. Credo Challenge sessions provide structured opportunities for people to discuss where they are falling short and how the company or team can improve around their key values.

In many organizations, these types of discussions are infrequent. People feel they need special permission to broach what they consider to be taboo subjects. If you can institutionalize the question of falling short, however, you will make it far easier for people to talk about issues they perceive to be off-limits.

We believe that Action Learning creates an ideal atmosphere for productive challenge and conflict. It sets up a temporary organizational environment in which people are encouraged to investigate and then challenge a company's culture, the competition, business strategy, and management practices. Participants are encouraged to engage in dialogue with and confront senior leaders based on their research and facts and suggest ideas that they might be reluctant to offer in typical meetings.

We recently ran an Action Learning program for high-potential development in which a company's executive committee held a "fishbowl" meeting. They were surrounded by a number of young "high potentials" who observed the executive committee wrestling with decisions about a key product launch, which the observers were working on. Although these high potentials learned a lot from the discussion, the true value of their participation was their feedback to the company's leaders. They expressed concern that the executive committee seemed to be taking a very cautious, passionless approach to a new-product opportunity. They stated that a product launch required risk taking, emotional investment, and strong commitment on the part of the executive team. They suggested to the committee how their decisions and actions might play out when filtered throughout the company, how they and their peers might interpret the decisions of the executive committee, and how they may not be able to execute the launch in the same way the executive committee intended. This session created a catalytic learning moment in which both groups understood the viewpoints of the other, as well as their own limitations.

Like the other tools discussed, this Action Learning program gave people permission to express opinions that might otherwise not have been expressed.

A Word of Warning: Creating Discomfort Entails Risks

Any leader who attempts to use the principles and methods described here needs to have a strong sense of self. It takes a certain amount of self-confidence to preside over a team where conflict is common and people are challenging your decisions. Daniel Goleman's *Emotional Intelligence* provides a good framework for the types of traits a discomfort-creating leader must possess.

First, leaders must be extremely self-aware. To make the right selections for their teams, leaders must have a good grasp of their skills, values, personal style, and beliefs. This awareness not only helps leaders choose people who will complement them from a value and skills standpoint, but also allows them to gauge their impact on other members of the team. Bosses who are not self-aware often do not realize how intimidating they are. As much as they might want to create a team environment of positive discomfort, they create negative discomfort instead, causing people to keep their opinions to themselves for fear of chastisement. Leaders who are self-aware know how to modulate their impact on other people, no matter how powerful or aggressive their personalities might be. In *Action Coaching*, we describe self-awareness as the foundation for individual performance improvement and breakthroughs.

The second element of emotional intelligence, according to Goleman, is self-regulation. When we are faced with conflict under stress or are overworked or tired, many of us undermine our effectiveness. Some people become overly cautious and fearful of making the wrong decision; others attempt to dominate a discussion and do not listen to differing points of view. Creating discomfort also creates conflict and stress, and leaders must know their behavioral tendencies under these conditions. If they do not, they can easily come down too hard on direct reports and stifle great discussions and debate or withdraw and allow the discomfort to get out of hand. Self-regulation—the ability to monitor one's moods and behaviors and adjust them accordingly—is critical.

Optimism is another quality that leaders who exhibit this unnatural behavior should possess. Debates within teams can become heated and in some cases foster a sense of despair: the more people argue, the more distant a solution or dismal a situation seems. Optimistic leaders communicate that debate is healthy and that the team will be better off because of it. By being optimistic, leaders convey that conflict has a purpose and that no matter how mired the team gets in its discussions, they will ultimately get through and benefit from them. As a leader, it is important to keep reminding the team that conflict is natural and can be managed.

Empathy is a fourth emotional intelligence trait valuable for unnatural leaders. If you intend to invite ideas and opinions, you should be prepared to see things from others' frame of reference. This means understanding not only the logic of the argument but why the argument is important to an individual. Leaders with empathy are neither quick to dismiss ideas they disagree with nor to dismiss them in ways that antagonize team members.

Finally, Goleman refers to social skills as an emotional intelligence component. From a leadership perspective, this translates into an ability to influence others and find common ground that can produce a good outcome. Socially skilled leaders get to know their team members, and especially their needs. They are able to persuade others not just based on what they themselves think but what a given individual requires. In short, they possess the skills necessary to navigate the sometimes turbulent whirlpool of a discomfort-producing team. Although they may have purposefully created this turbulence, they can still move the team forward through it using their capacity to influence people.

A Second Word of Warning: Discomfort Is Not Enough

We are not going to get into a long discussion of what it takes to create an effective team; plenty of books have been written on the subject. We would be remiss, however, if we were to give the impression that if you select a diverse team and create an environment where productive conflict can flourish, the team automatically will become high performing. Many other factors are involved in performance, including direction, alignment, execution, understanding the objectives, and selecting members who possess the skills to achieve those objectives.

Our point, however, is that leaders need to select people who have the capacity to function effectively in discomfort-producing situations. It is much easier for a team to disagree or even verbally fight it out if they are good listeners, flexible, and respectful. Without these and other qualities, debate can turn acrimonious, and arguments can turn personal, destroying team chemistry. For this reason, unnatural leaders ask the following questions of potential team members:

- Can they solve problems and make decisions?
- Can they show flexibility, and are they open to other points of view?
- Are they willing to voice their opinions even if they are unpopular?
- Are they aware of their impact on others?
- Can they sacrifice personal interest in the best interests of the team?
- Can they show empathy with other team members?
- Are they able to regulate their emotions in discussions with others?
- Do they have a high level of self-awareness?
- Can they openly recognize the contributions of others?
- Can they be counted on to meet their responsibilities?
- Do they listen well?

- Do they have high performance standards?
- Do they understand the organization and what it is trying to achieve?
- Can they establish trust in relationships?
- Do they show respect for other people?

In other words, can team members exhibit the same traits of emotional intelligence required of a leader plus a number of other crucial qualities? The more people who possess these qualities, the easier it will be for the team's leader to commit this unnatural act and achieve positive results.

An Example of a Discomfort Creator in Action

Jeff was brilliant at building and running teams that produced positive discomfort. A senior research executive in a renowned global corporation, Jeff expertly assembled project teams that were guaranteed to challenge him and each other. He went beyond technical or functional expertise when making his selections, looking at potential members' capacity to develop strong positions and deliver them openly. He chose not only scientists he did not know well or had never worked with before but ones with reputations for being fearless in discussions no matter who else was in the room. Some of the people he tapped were difficult to manage, and other senior research leaders had refused to work with them.

Although Jeff may have appeared misguided to some of his functional leaders, there was a method to his madness. Once he had his team in place, he launched the team by helping members define their personal styles and identify their vulnerabilities. He wanted them to be aware if they were likely to ignore other people's input and stubbornly insist on working in isolation, for instance. Jeff orchestrated an initial discussion among team members about their strengths but also their weaknesses, and they identified a few potential problems that could derail the team's efforts. One of his teams decided they needed to monitor whether they communicated as much as necessary and made the effort to share successes that could help other team members. Jeff and his team set up ground rules, processes, and standards to deal with these issues.

Although Jeff often had teams containing people who were known as troublemakers, iconoclasts, and loners, his teams invariably developed research breakthroughs, conducted trials, and delivered results faster than other teams in the organization. They were more innovative, more flexible, and better able to push established boundaries in order to come up with effective ideas. Jeff admitted it wasn't easy, but it was worth it.

Creating Teams That Create Discomfort

How often do you use behaviors that create teams that create discomfort? Rate yourself on the following behaviors.

Behaviors	Your Rating				
I use different methods for motivating others, not just my power and authority.	1 Rarely	2	3	4	5 Always
I create an environment of openness and challenge that is constructive.	1 Rarely	2	3	4	5 Always
I openly acknowledge the value of different points of view.	1 Rarely	2	3	4	5 Always
I choose team members who are willing to disagree with me.	1 Rarely	2	3	4	5 Always
I encourage team members to challenge my thinking.	1 Rarely	2	3	4	5 Always
I select team members who are willing to encourage debate within the team.	1 Rarely	2	3	4	5 Always
I accept the emotional side of conflict.	1 Rarely	2	3	4	5 Always
I create the type of climate that encourages breakthrough ideas.	1 Rarely	2	3	4	5 Always
I show courage by challenging the status quo.	1 Rarely	2	3	4	5 Always
I accept the challenge of others with a nondefensive and learning mind-set.	1 Rarely	2	3	4	5 Always
I share useful and relevant information.	1 Rarely	2	3	4	5 Always
I take on our organization's sacred cows.	1 Rarely	2	3	4	5 Always
I ensure that all sides of an issue get examined.	1 Rarely	2	3	4	5 Always

Creating Teams That Create Discomfort (Cont.)

Attitude Toward Conflict

Choose a recent situation involving conflict. How did you handle it? How comfortable were you dealing with conflict? What does this situation tell you about your attitude toward conflict?

Set the Tone for Challenging Status Quo

List three examples of behaviors you use that encourage others to challenge ideas and decisions constructively.

1.

2.

3.

What sacred cows in your organization do you need to challenge?

Creating Teams That Successfully Manage Conflict

Think about the behaviors necessary to manage conflict successfully. How much does your team practice each of these behaviors?

Team Behaviors	Your Team Rating
Debating with facts rather than just opinions	1 2 3 4 5 Rarely Always
Developing multiple alternatives to enrich the level of debate	1 2 3 4 5 Rarely Always
Sharing commonly agreed-on goals	1 2 3 4 5 Rarely Always
Injecting humor into discussion and debate	1 2 3 4 5 Rarely Always
Maintaining a balanced power structure	1 2 3 4 5 Rarely Always
Resolving issues without forcing consensus	1 2 3 4 5 Rarely Always

Creating Teams That Create Discomfort (Cont.)

What actions can you take to create a team that successfully manages conflict? List three specific actions.

1.

2.

3.

Action Planning

What are the most significant actions you can take to create teams that create discomfort? List three specific actions.

1.

2.

3.

Steps for Developing Yourself as an Unnatural Leader

Encourage people to say what's really on their minds.

Don't withhold your ideas and opinions, even if you don't agree with others.

Hold open monthly meetings with no agenda. Encourage people to ask questions and communicate barriers interfering with their effectiveness.

Spend time with your team to analyze barriers to timely, honest, and clear communications.

Create task forces and project teams comprising people with different experiences, skills, and abilities.

Avoid shooting the messengers with bad news.

Make sure that all sides of an important issue get examined. Assign someone to be the devil's advocate.

Design meetings that encourage group discussion and debate.

Survey the team at the end of the meeting to assess how effective it was (for example, was everyone's voice heard?).

Chapter Nine

Trust Others Before They Earn It

One principle of natural leadership is that people receive trust when they demonstrate they are worthy of it. This means that every new employee is considered to be on probation and are not given real responsibility, assigned to lead the most critical projects, or allowed access to classified information until they have proved themselves.

If you think this sounds like a military definition of trust, you're absolutely right. The military model is one where the generals feel absolutely no reason to trust the privates (or any other officer except their long-time aides, for that matter). This approach is based on the belief that people will unquestioningly follow orders, and trust is irrelevant. Furthermore, it's rooted in the view that people are prone to misdeeds and must be managed.

We would like to suggest a definition of trust that is aligned with unnatural leadership. It involves extending trust to people you believe will meet your positive expectations. This means giving most people the benefit of the doubt right from the start. Certainly, there are situations when trust may be withheld, but generally, trust is given before it is earned. At the same time, leaders recognize that they must earn the trust of others. This, of course, is highly unnatural: leaders are reversing the military equation of trusting no one but demanding that others earn their trust.

It is true that leaders can get burned when they trust others before they earn it. The alternative, however, is far worse. As we will see, withholding trust today has more devastating consequences.

Seven Reasons to Trust First, Ask Questions Later

Leaders who have been schooled in traditional leadership methods often find it unconsciously difficult to trust people they do not know well or who have not proved themselves. They become much more willing to commit this unnatural act when they are aware of the powerful forces making trust so crucial in today's workplace.

The Need for Speed

In most high-performing companies, leaders often lack the luxury of a linear, orderly decision-making process. Customers have gained so much power and choice and are constantly expecting better products or services at a faster pace, and this need often eliminates the possibility of slow, methodical planning and decision making. Numerous other competitive factors—the need for blockbuster products, regulations, financial trade-offs, bundling of products and services, and increased merger and acquisitions, among many others—prevent the type of painstaking analysis that characterized decision making in the past.

Today, in order to act fast, leaders must make many decisions intuitively without a lot of information. They place much greater reliance on "trusting their gut," as well as trusting other people's guts. If a leader's direct report tells him he thinks the product launch should move ahead, that leader often does not have the time to do research and verify his direct report's statement. Leaders need to trust their direct reports' logic as well as their hunches because they often lack the time to gather all the facts.

Empowerment

In most complex global organizations, leaders are empowering those who are closest to the customer, have the best information, and are on the front line. To give up control over people and outcomes to this degree is unprecedented. Natural leaders often balk at these actions, if only because it feels as if they are giving up a significant amount of power. Empowerment in complex organizations, however, is absolutely essential; it's impossible to compete and grow if the people who are furthest from customers are making the decisions. Leaders need to trust that those on the front line are in the best position to make decisions. If they believe this is so, the power trade-off is worth it.

Interdependencies

To get things done in today's companies, complex, interdependent, boundaryless networks across departments and functions have arisen designed to serve customers. New matrix structures demand cooperation between diverse parts of an organization, and the boundaryless company is highly interdependent. This is especially true in global companies such as Johnson & Johnson, Merck, Colgate, Honeywell, and others where different country or geographical units must make decisions in tandem with product or service units, corporate centers of excellence, staff departments, and others.

If leaders in one discrete part of the organization distrust those in another part and think of them as outsiders, the impact of the whole is reduced. There is no room for suspicion of others who come from different functions or work in different countries or divisions. Because of the need for speed, there can be no "get-to-know-you" period where everyone is on probation. There cannot be the luxury of intramural squabbles or petty differences. This is especially true in fluid, organic organizations of shifting assignments and temporary project teams. When you have a task that requires quick-cycle performance, you need to develop quick-cycle trust. If leaders hold back information or do not fully commit to people because of a insufficient trust, collaborative efforts will deliver average results. People sense when leaders do not fully trust them, and their behavior becomes a self-fulfilling prophecy. Why should they fully commit for someone who clearly views them with concern? In addition, leaders who distrust others from lateral departments or teams fail to get close enough to be plugged into their universe. In other words, they unintentionally keep them at a distance and are unable to learn from them, share best practices, and uncover synergistic opportunities.

Alliances

Joint ventures and partnerships have become the preferred way to spread risk, share expertise, amortize future costs, and divide capital expenditures among competitors. In every industry, especially capital-intensive ones, market leaders have established global joint ventures. These new alliances often demand that people from very different cultures and with different philosophies trust each other. In some instances, these new allies were formerly bitter competitors and have to overcome years of distrust. Leaders need to get past their tendency to divide the world into us-versus-them and start extending trust to partners who look, act, and lead differently.

The Technological Remove

In an increasingly virtual world, we are missing the nonverbal cues that we relied on as precursors to extending trust. Leaders would unconsciously absorb the voice tone, facial expression, appearance, and other cues to determine if someone really could be trusted. Leaders would express their judgment in simple terms: "He's a good guy," or "She's all right."

Today, how can you trust someone without the reassurance offered by face-to-face interaction? The real question, however, is how can you *not* trust someone when so much work gets done virtually? Leaders must work to develop a comfort level with people they never see and communicate with primarily on-line. Without this trust, the free-flowing, rapid exchange of information and ideas will not occur on-line.

Talent Scarcity, Diversity Abundance

In a policy- and procedure-driven world, leaders were able to replace one talented person with another. If they did not feel quite right about a direct report, they could move him and find an equally talented replacement. In the new paradigm, talent is golden, and there are not enough nuggets to go around. Therefore, leaders must trust talent implicitly and wherever they find it. In many cases, they find talent in unusual people and places. Given a diverse workforce, leaders need to trust individuals who are not at all like them. They must trust people who are different in age, with different lifestyles and preferences, who may dress differently, and sport nose rings and tattoos; they must trust people who do not speak their language (literally and figuratively); they must trust individuals who have never before worked in traditional organizational structures. These people represent fresh ideas and provocative points of view. As much work as it takes, the best solutions derive from these diverse viewpoints. In a diverse organization, leaders must intentionally extend trust to those who are different and not just those who are the same.

Distrust of Leadership

Perhaps the most compelling reason for leaders to extend trust is that their direct reports typically do not trust them. Or rather, people are more cynical and skeptical of institutional leadership today than ever before, and leaders need to earn back their trust by being open and honest. Leaders who demonstrate that they have faith in their direct reports and are willing to risk failure by extending trust are more likely than purely natural leaders to repair the damage done in large companies during the past two decades. If you doubt that this damage is significant, consider the conventional wisdom today about how companies should be managed and how leaders should act:

- People are employed at will, and periodic downsizings should be expected.
- Don't hire too many people because of costs. Keep things lean and stretched.
- Outsource whenever possible, and don't worry about building loyalty within.
- Rank individuals, rely on individual incentives, and reward the highest performers; pay for performance.
- Buy people and talent rather than make a commitment to develop and coach them.
- Move people when they are no longer needed.
- Focus on the shareholder and the bottom line first, last, and always.

Unnatural leaders recognize the limitations of this conventional wisdom and know that people hunger for leaders and institutions they can believe in. There is a great opportunity for leaders who are strong enough psychologically and emotionally to take the risk of extending trust. Ironically, the so-called tough leaders focus on results at all costs but often are not tough (soft) enough to treat people with respect, dignity, and honesty.

Obstacles to Extending Trust First

Given the previous seven factors, you would assume that most leaders would feel compelled to trust others. Some leaders are aware of these factors and do recognize that the health of their organizations (not to mention the health of their own careers) depends on extending trust, but the majority are either not aware or choose to follow their instincts and do otherwise. Many senior executives have grown up in companies where it was considered unwise to trust anyone outside their own function, department, or corporate tribe. If you are in manufacturing and you openly trust your peer in marketing with the real product schedule or hidden budget resources, he might use it against you when the year-end shortfall arrives. Trust your direct reports too openly, and they will try to take your job. Trust your boss, and she will consider you weak or ineffective. Mentors sometimes schooled their protégés in distrust by offering advice about how to survive and "play the game around here." Everything from Hollywood dramas about big business to cynical locker-room talk about nice guys finishing last conspired to make real trust an unnatural attitude.

Other obstacles exist besides this general sentiment against trust. We look at three major ones.

Our Sense of Vulnerability

When you feel vulnerable—a not uncommon feeling in the current business environment—extending trust seems counterintuitive. Why make yourself any more vulnerable than you already are? In fact, many senior leaders seek us out as coaches in order to become more defended, tough, and armored. Many cite the problems they experience in hiding their sense of vulnerability in an internally and externally competitive business tournament and wonder how to toughen up.

In the past, even ten years ago, when companies dominated markets, leaders had more control, and the environment was more predictable, vulnerability was not a big issue. Today, however, we are dependent on people delivering for us who are thousands of miles away, whom we may rarely see, and who come from very different backgrounds. Vulnerability creates anxiety and fear, and these emotions feed distrust. You would think that the higher you go in an organization, the less vulnerable you would feel, but it's just the opposite. Ask any CEO whose organization did not deliver the results promised to Wall Street last quarter if he feels vulnerable.

Historical Precedent for Distrust

When executives have been burned by others in their organizations, not only do they have difficulty trusting the guilty party, but they fear trusting anyone else for fear that history will repeat itself. Many senior leaders try to distinguish among allies, friends, and enemies. Allies receive only limited professional trust; friends, who are usually few in number, receive more but still limited trust; and enemies are not to be trusted at all.

Jack, one of our clients, was the CEO of a global corporation, and Andrew was his COO. Jack and Andrew endured a relationship of limited trust because of an incident that had occurred a few years earlier. Through a variety of circumstances, Jack discovered that during the CEO selection process, Andrew had lobbied for another CEO candidate and against Jack. It was not clear if Andrew had actually betrayed Jack's trust or whether his lobbying for the other candidate represented his sincere belief about who was the better candidate. The point, however, is that Jack felt betrayed. From that point on, although these two worked together and treated each other with professional respect, in his heart Jack viewed Andrew, as well as Andrew's close associates, with some suspicion and was very guarded when talking to them about sensitive issues. We worked hard to help Jack and Andrew improve their relationship, and only when the root cause was finally uncovered did the trust-building process begin.

Many times, leaders make assumptions about an individual's trustworthiness based on second-hand information. In succession planning meetings we have observed, discussions often circle around the issue of trust. Succession planning participants sometimes relate one anecdote about an individual under consideration that conveys volumes of information and limits a career—for example, "I wonder what was really going on at that sales meeting two years ago when Martha didn't disclose the shortfall in her revenue forecasts?" The implication is that Martha should not be trusted, although the basis for this lack of trust may be limited at best.

Personality

Some people are naturally distrustful, and this "Nixonian" personality type presents a formidable obstacle for coaches who are attempting to help someone learn to trust. Certain leaders arrive at organizations with a suspicious or even paranoid worldview firmly in place, and it's tough for these leaders to become open and honest with other people, especially under stress. Others, though, are simply cautious and skeptical, and these leaders are much more likely to commit the unnatural act of trusting.

We have also found that leaders are willing to trust certain types of personalities and not others, attributing this to chemistry or simply instinct. For many reasons, a particular type of person rubs a leader the wrong way. While he may be perfectly willing to trust some direct reports before they earn it, he is unwilling to trust others. Sometimes the disliked personality represents negative past history.

Janice, a client who is a senior executive with a major company, is effusive, outgoing, and emotional. She finds it easy to trust most other people: direct reports, peers, suppliers, and others. But when she encounters someone who is introverted, analytical, soft spoken, and hesitant, she immediately becomes suspicious. She is convinced this person has hidden agendas, wonders what is really going on, and reflexively keeps him or her out of the information loop. Although Janice has been told she has a problem in this area and her boss and coach have encouraged her to overcome it, she still falls into the trap of distrusting this personality type.

Techniques and Tools

As coaches, we are frequently asked to coach someone who is a natural leader and in the past has produced great results through position power, charisma, and iron will. Although his company has evolved—it is working much more closely and frequently with outside partners—he still treats these outside partners as if they were outside the circle. He does not level with them, politely but firmly orders them to deliver results rather than asks them, and makes them feel as if they lack the track record and expertise to be a true partner at the competence level of his own company in any project. Naturally, these partners have complained, and his boss is worried about his attitude.

To help him make an unnatural adjustment to his attitude, we may try a number of approaches. Here are the ones that we have found to be most effective:

• *Encourage belief in people.* Some leaders operate under the unconscious assumption that some of their direct reports are inadequate, mediocre, and unimaginative. It's difficult to trust anyone whom you hold in such low regard. These beliefs may have formed because of a bad experience in the past (the history obstacle we referred to earlier) or they may be the result of prejudice against certain groups (from a given country, for example). Whatever the reason, we attempt to help our clients work to view people through a different lens, a technique that often dissipates negative attitudes about people's capabilities.

Chris, for instance, is an engineering leader in a technology company that has traditionally placed more confidence in numbers than people. She comes from a "quantify everything" school and does a good job measuring everything from product performance to customer satisfaction. In leading her team, she makes key decisions by polling team members and even charting their discussions, arriving at decisions through statistical consensus. Although Chris has great personal integrity, her rational, analytical approach unconsciously sends a message to her team that she does not fully trust them. By providing Chris with our reactions and feedback from her team about her overly rational style, Chris is beginning to change. She never realized that she did not believe in other people; it was a nonissue to her. To Chris, numbers were facts. She never realized or intended that her team would wonder if she trusted them because she relied so heavily on the numbers (she was an engineer, after all). By hearing that they wanted her to have more confidence in their abilities and evidence of her trust, Chris eventually learned to moderate her approach and work toward the unnatural act of trusting people before they earned her trust.

- *Hold positive expectations.* Ideally, leaders go beyond belief in others to the point that they hold great expectations for those others. This attitude is based not on evidence—for example, that they produced great results in the past—but on a highly optimistic view of human capacity for superior work. Sometimes this is hard to do and requires "choosing your attitude."

A truly unnatural act is to have great expectations of people you have never met in person or who reside in a country you have never visited. Time and again, we have seen this unnatural act turn into a self-fulfilling prophecy, and much research has confirmed this observation. If you hold high expectations of someone, that person will sense it and work zealously to meet these expectations. Many leaders do not realize the impact they have on their direct reports and teams and how much this impact differs from their intentions. People are so sensitized to leaders' moods and words that if the leader is positive and energetic, other people with whom she works will be positive and energetic too. It is not unusual for team members to share information with each other about the boss's mood, and for good reason. Her mood is a big factor in their universe. If a leader believes her staff are capable of clearing a high-performance bar and they sense she trusts their talent and that they can reach ambitious goals, they will respond accordingly.

An interesting example of high expectations is the story of Kerry Killinger, CEO and chairman of Washington Mutual, one of the fastest-growing banks in the United States, now seventh largest, and one of our clients. What started out as a small Seattle thrift with $6 billion in deposits has grown to $300 billion in deposits in three years. Although there were a number of reasons for Washington Mutual's growth, a major catalyst was Killinger's continuous and fervent conviction that the bank's employees could surpass everyone's expectations. In one-on-one meetings, group presentations, and leadership development training, he continuously communicated his certainty that they would become a major player in consumer and mortgage banking, despite skeptical industry analysts. As a result, Washington Mutual staffers felt that he trusted their capabilities as people rather than as performers and that his faith in them was a personal belief rather than a logical deduction based on past accomplishments. They felt trusted, and this trust has become a cornerstone of the Washington Mutual culture. Today, Washington Mutual is growing into a national franchise, and the enthusiasm, informality, and service orientation of its culture is helping it win in every market it enters.

• *Stop viewing trust as an either-or choice.* People are much better able to commit this unnatural act when they cease to see trust as a black-or-white issue. When the perception is that an individual either can or cannot be trusted, then it's difficult to extend trust before it's earned. Leaders hesitate to trust because they remember when an individual let them down or fell short of expectations. "I can't fully trust him," he thinks. In reality, trust comes in shades of gray. A leader may be willing to trust an assistant to maintain personnel files but not trust her to deliver a formal presentation. This leader may trust another person to deliver the presentation but might be wary of sharing sensitive information with him about others.

Similarly, leaders sometimes feel betrayed when talented people leave an organization and become convinced they can no longer trust their staff. But these departees have not necessarily betrayed the leader's trust. Usually they left the company for a variety of valid reasons that have nothing to do with personal loyalty.

It's much easier to extend trust when leaders are not expecting blind loyalty or never to be let down. Extending trust before it's earned is simply saying to people, "I believe the odds are good that you're going to meet or exceed my expectations, and I'm going to be supportive and open in order to help you do a great job." Working intentionally to maintain an optimistic outlook about people can facilitate trust.

• *Check one's own assumptions about how others should behave.* Perhaps you've heard the saying, "All reality is projection." It suggests that we project our expectations of how people should behave. A manager often feels betrayed not because of questionable behavior on the part of a direct report but because she expected that direct report to behave differently. Although she may sincerely believe that her direct report violated her trust, the reality is that the violation had less to do with the direct report's actual behavior and more to do with the manager's assumption about the way to behave. Although these assumptions are inevitable, they should not prevent leaders from withholding trust. We have found that becoming conscious of assumptions can make it easier to extend trust. When a leader knows she expects direct reports to be discreet about certain subjects—and when a direct report isn't discreet— the leader realizes that the direct report did not do something wrong; rather, she may not have clearly communicated her expectations about the importance of being discreet.

Ideally, leaders will also endeavor to raise their trust thresholds by challenging their own assumptions. Once you know that you expect everyone to be highly discreet with certain types of information, you can examine whether this is a fair assumption. In a business environment where openness and transparency are important, should you expect staff to be highly discreet? Too often, leaders set themselves up to be betrayed by their team because they have low trust thresholds or unreasonable expectations. They harbor assumptions about correct work behaviors that are almost impossible for people to live up to. Challenging these assumptions can make it easier to trust one's staff.

The Results of Trust

What actually happens when leaders commit this unnatural act? Many people can imagine only disaster when trust is extended before it is earned. They think about a direct report who is entrusted with a major project and does not deliver, dooming the project and putting his manager in jeopardy. Or they visualize a partner in another office who quickly drains the project's resources, taking advantage of a leader's willingness to extend him financial trust and ends up blowing the budget. We will not deny that risks are involved when trust is extended, but we have also witnessed great benefits for leaders and organizations.

First, performance levels are increased. When bosses communicate through word, action, and attitude their faith in their team, those team members work harder to come through. Employees are much more likely to fulfill expectations than thwart them. Trust is energizing, causing people to work harder and longer to demonstrate that trust is justified.

Second, trust extended results in trust returned. As we have noted, much of the workforce views leadership in a cynical light. The relationship damage can be repaired (at least to some extent) when leaders take the initiative and demonstrate (not just state) they view people as more than human resources or labor costs. When people feel they are trusted, they are likely to respond in kind; they are more willing to initiate ideas and volunteer useful information that they may have kept from more natural leaders.

Third, it accelerates the delivery of work. When executives do not completely trust their subordinates, they have a great need to be in control. As a result, they micromanage, monitor, and measure continuously. "Inspect what you expect" used to be the first rule of supervision in many companies. This takes a great deal of time from leaders who instead should be investing their time in strategy and vision. With trust comes a willingness to skip these time-wasting interim steps and focus on results.

Trusting Others Before They Earn It

What factors make trusting others important for you in today's work environment?

Speed

Empowerment

Interdependencies

Alliances

Virtual team

Telecommuting

Scarcity of talent

Distrust of leadership

In what situations do you have the most difficulty trusting others?

Working with individuals who look, act, and lead differently than you do

Working with people you don't know well

Working with people who haven't proven themselves

Giving up control and empowering front-line staff to make decisions

Virtual teams

Telecommuting

Working with others who come from different functions, countries, or divisions

Reflect on the obstacles and beliefs that may interfere with your ability to extend trust before others earn it. Rate each of the following obstacles by indicating the extent to which you agree or disagree with the following statements.

Behaviors	Your Rating				
I feel vulnerable relying on people whom I rarely see or who come from different backgrounds.	1 Strongly Disagree	2	3	4 Strongly Agree	5
I am fearful that my history of being betrayed by others will repeat itself.	1 Strongly Disagree	2	3	4 Strongly Agree	5
I have a personality that is naturally distrustful. I am suspicious of others' motives and believe that people have hidden agendas.	1 Strongly Disagree	2	3	4 Strongly Agree	5
I believe that most people are deceptive and unimaginative and don't want to work hard.	1 Strongly Disagree	2	3	4 Strongly Agree	5

Trusting Others Before They Earn It (Cont.)

Behaviors	Your Rating				
I have a personality that is naturally controlling, and I feel vulnerable relying on others to do the job as fast or as well as I can.	1 Strongly Disagree	2	3	4	5 Strongly Agree
I believe that people should unquestioningly follow orders and that trust is irrelevant.	1 Strongly Disagree	2	3	4	5 Strongly Agree

How much do you practice the following unnatural leadership behaviors?

Behaviors	Your Rating				
Giving people the benefit of the doubt right from the start	1 Rarely	2	3	4	5 Always
Recognizing the need to earn people's trust	1 Rarely	2	3	4	5 Always
Empowering those who have the best information and are on the front line	1 Rarely	2	3	4	5 Always
Trusting someone without the reassurance offered by face-to-face contact	1 Rarely	2	3	4	5 Always
Trusting individuals who are not at all like you	1 Rarely	2	3	4	5 Always
Being open and honest	1 Rarely	2	3	4	5 Always
Risking failure by extending trust	1 Rarely	2	3	4	5 Always
Treating people with respect, dignity, and honesty	1 Rarely	2	3	4	5 Always
Letting go of control and depending on people to deliver	1 Rarely	2	3	4	5 Always
Keeping people in the information loop	1 Rarely	2	3	4	5 Always
Getting to know people as individuals	1 Rarely	2	3	4	5 Always
Conveying confidence in the ability of people to deliver results	1 Rarely	2	3	4	5 Always

Trusting Others Before They Earn It (Cont.)

What actions can you take to extend trust before others earn it? List three.

1.

2.

3.

What actions can you take to create an environment where people trust each other and communicate continuously, openly, and honestly? List three.

1.

2.

3.

Steps for Developing Yourself as an Unnatural Leader

Spend time getting to know your direct reports as individuals.

Express your confidence in their ability to deliver results.

Experiment with giving others the benefit of the doubt instead of doubting their ability to deliver.

Pay attention to how frequently you communicate your faith in others through your work, actions, and attitude.

Challenge your assumptions about trust and whether your expectations are impossible for people to meet.

Be sure that your actions match your words.

Chapter Ten

Coach and Teach Rather Than Lead and Inspire

In this chapter, we focus on the unnatural trait that often gives leaders the most trouble. We have already discussed the conventional wisdom that leaders should be heroic figures. Growing up listening to Ronald Reagan or John Kennedy giving visionary, inspirational speeches as well as being aware of the brilliant speeches of Winston Churchill, Martin Luther King Jr., and other world leaders, people have developed their own leadership gestalt. We use the term "lead and inspire" to get at what this gestalt is about, but these words do not do it justice.

The most natural of leaders view themselves as charismatic, important figures whose words have a compelling quality. They literally see themselves as above the fray and survey the business landscape with a calm remove. In many ways, they believe it is best to take a detached approach to leadership, using others in the organization to get things done. They live for what we refer to as leadership moments: crises, big deals, grand opportunities, and other moments of great significance. This is when natural leaders step forward and lead, delivering a brilliant commentary for the media or employees or making a momentous decision.

This gestalt is reinforced in times of adversity when people look for inspirational leaders. They want to believe that their company is being led by those who are wise and know what to do and in uncertain times can ease their doubts and fears. They take great comfort in a leader's ability to come up with the right words at the right time, and they imbue this leader with a special aura, feeling as if she was destined to lead.

Heroic, inspirational leadership is a wonderful concept and certainly has its place. There are times when the troops need to be rallied, and a leader who inspires confidence during difficult times can hold a team or an organization together. Even in good times, a charismatic, dynamic leader can reassure Wall Street, customers, and employees. The problem, quite simply, is that this type of leadership is no longer enough; the unnatural act of coaching and teaching is just as (if not more) important today. Executives must learn to communicate one-on-one, continuously, empathetically, and with a given individual's interests at heart. They must have a point of view and be able to convey it while establishing a meaningful connection in the process. This may not gratify the ego as much as the more inspirational, natural model, but it is an act that's absolutely necessary for any leader who wants to function at maximum effectiveness.

The Decreasing Value of Inspiration

We have made the rather bold statement that the heroic, inspirational leader has become a bit of an anachronism; that although the classic lead-and-inspire style has its place, it is an incomplete leadership approach. This may strike some as a dubious premise, so let's examine why we find the evidence for it conclusive.

First, cynicism has eroded confidence in leadership across the board. On the political front, presidents from Nixon to Clinton to Bush have made us distrustful of speeches, inspirational and otherwise. On the business front, too many CEOs have sold or destroyed companies and walked away with golden parachutes. Employees do not respond to strong, powerful leadership the way they used to. On the other hand, they are much more responsive to leaders they perceive as honest and trustworthy. Mike, for instance, was a dull speaker; although he was pleasant, he was also rather bland and humorless. He became CEO of a company that was going through major changes, including downsizing and displacement of people. In spite of his personal characteristics, Mike had tremendous integrity. When he said something, people learned that he meant it. As a result, the vast majority of people in the company, including the most talented, did not flee during difficult times or complain about the company's direction. They trusted Mike because of his integrity, not because he inspired them.

Another reason for the devaluation of inspiration is the complexity of being both a leader and a direct report. Direct reports look to their bosses not for inspiration as much as for explanation. The tremendous pressure for performance, the avalanche of information, the rapid pace of change, the complexity of diversity, and many other factors have made it more important for leaders to provide guidance to direct reports and less important for them to provide inspiration. People have numerous questions and concerns every day of their working lives, and they look to leaders for help. This does not mean leaders need to answer their questions (as we have seen, there is not always a right answer), but they do need to engage them in conversations where issues are aired and options are explored.

Third, company loyalty is not what it once was. Speeches that ask employees to "win this one for the company" or appeals for greater effort in order to help the organization overcome a major obstacle often fall on deaf and cynical ears. People's attitudes about work have changed, and although they may sincerely believe in a company's mission (many of our clients' employees have this belief), they also are astute enough to know that they, rather than the company, are primarily responsible for their development. Many leaders at least acknowledge this point, if their speeches are any indication. If you analyze communication to employees in companies today, you will find that the majority are not limited to the company's vision, mission, and strategy but clearly communicate what a particular decision will mean to the individual employee and the employees responsible for executing that decision. Leaders comprehend that this is important but do not always see the importance of the next step: how coaching and teaching can do a far better job than a memo or speech in meeting an individual's needs for development.

This brings us to our fourth point: employees are now more diverse than ever before, not only in their age, gender, nationality, and preferences but in their attitudes. Although some people still might be inspired to greater effort by a heroic leader they can identify with, most are not. We have found that people are self-motivated by an ever-broadening range of goals: being with a winning company, satisfying individual achievement needs, obtaining status and power, altruism, a position and company that is compatible with their values, and the freedom to work independently. Although they may be revved up by the powerful words of a leader whom they greatly admire, they have many other more powerful, internal motivations. Coaching and teaching, on the other hand, allow leaders to connect with these various internal motivations and demonstrate how what is good for the company is also good for the individual. In short, a rousing speech cannot be tailored to each individual need the way coaching can.

Despite all these factors, there are still leaders who are convinced that if they deliver a compelling message and act like a leader, people will follow. We have talked to a number of lead-and-inspire executives who were convinced that they had done a great job of motivating others in the company and were surprised to find that their motivation had failed: productivity did not increase, but turnover did. We have watched many leaders go through media training and speech coaching, only to emerge with their real personalities somehow diminished but their surfaces polished. The danger here is that leaders can fool themselves into believing that they can talk groups into delivering great results. Consequently, these leaders fail to develop the unnatural traits that will more effectively help them achieve their objectives.

What Coaching and Teaching Really Mean

Although everyone understands the general definition of coaching and teaching, we focus on what these two words mean from a leadership standpoint. It's not as simple as offering a direct report some advice occasionally or telling her how to do something; these are natural leadership acts. What is unnatural is to coach and teach continuously, empathetically, and with a given individual's interests at heart.

Coaching and teaching are multifaceted, highly adaptable acts. Leaders can coach people to overcome skill deficiencies, provide advice about developing strategies, target specific attitudes and behaviors that (if changed) will strengthen performance, help newly hired employees make the transition into the company and its culture, and develop staff with high potential. Coaching and teaching can also help leaders align the goals of an employee with the organization and result in individual and organizational success. Sometimes a leader's coaching and teaching involve feedback to an employee, designed to assist that person with understanding his impact on others.

Effective coaching in these various ways unleashes enormous potential within a company, moving people from doing to becoming. The lead and inspire approach to leadership is focused on leading, designed to motivate people to achieve organizational outcomes. Natural leaders communicate these messages:

- This is the direction in which we are headed.
- This is why it is important.
- This is what is required for us to succeed.
- This is what is required for you to succeed.
- This is what success looks like.

Although all of these messages can be useful, they fail to answer the question that is increasingly on people's minds: "What's in it for me?" This is not a selfish question but a logical response to a business environment that is highly volatile and a career path that is no longer linear. The days of thinking "the company will take care of me" are long past. Thus, if employees are going to perform at their highest level, they need to be motivated from both individual and organizational perspectives.

This is what a coach-and-teach approach can achieve. Leaders communicate in ways that not only enhance others' current performance but develop potential. Too often, natural leaders are interested only in sharing their own ideas or conveying their position and are less successful at creating two-way dialogues that allow direct reports to develop their own thoughts. This two-way dialogue enables a leader to grasp what his direct report's goals are and use this information to coach accordingly. In this way, a coaching dialogue becomes a forum for a leader to give and receive information. He not only acquires information from a direct report that allows him to facilitate this development but gains valuable insights about what is going on in the group and organization that increases his business planning effectiveness.

Leaders and their organizations benefit in many ways when they depart from the lead-and-inspire model:

- *Putting the right people in the right jobs.* Assigning people to jobs that are a good match for their skills, attitudes, and behaviors is critical to building organizational capability, and coaching provides leaders with the opportunity to assess an individual's capacities as well as develop him with an eye toward the right job. Coaching fosters awareness of a direct report's strengths and weaknesses in a way that natural leaders never approach.
- *Creating a coaching-teaching culture.* When managers coach others, they clearly communicate that this is an appropriate leadership behavior. One reason that coaching and teaching feel so unnatural to leaders is that their bosses never (or rarely) coached them.
- *Communicating organizational values.* Inspirational leaders give powerful talks about values, but they are often unable to translate these talks into practice. In many companies, values become platitudes and rarely become drivers of behavior. Let's say a core value of a company is teamwork. A leader can coach this value by providing advice and guidance about what this value looks like. She can point to one particular behavior and say, "This is the right way to work as a member of a team," and point to another behavior and say, "This is the wrong way." Through coaching, she can answer a direct report's concerns about working effectively within a team framework ("How will my contribution be rewarded?") and generally make this value operational.
- *Clarifying expectations.* What should success look like for a direct report? Coaching people so that they understand current and future responsibilities in very specific terms often avoids arguments and anger. A gap frequently exists between what natural leaders expect of their direct reports and what direct reports think is expected of them. Coaching closes this gap.
- *Improving morale and commitment.* Coaching and teaching direct reports implicitly communicate that people are valued and their leaders care about them. People recognize that their bosses are making an emotional and time investment in helping them learn, and this makes them feel as if they are more than just a company asset or replaceable part.

- *Increasing knowledge sharing.* A two-way coaching dialogue means that leaders receive as well as give valuable information. One company we work with is intent on becoming customer-centric, and it was only when senior leaders made a commitment to coaching that they discovered why many of their customers were so frustrated dealing with them. Coaching had opened up multiple lines of communication that reached to the front lines, and when senior leaders compared their feedback, they saw customer dissatisfaction themes emerge that they were able to respond to.

The Power of the Lead-and-Inspire Model

One of the great ironies we have discovered is that just about every leader talks about the importance of coaching and teaching but relatively few of them do much about it. Somehow, there is a disconnect between approving of this unnatural act and actually making it part of one's leadership routine. It's useful to understand why this act is so difficult for many leaders to commit.

We have touched on one of the reasons already: the hold that the heroic leadership stereotype has on the imagination. In many organizations, leaders are judged according to this false measure. If they look and talk like leaders and everything seems to be running smoothly, they are judged to be effective. Just as significant, leaders are prisoners of their own arrogance. In the January 2001 issue of the *Harvard Business Review,* Jim Collins examined research that attempted to identify leadership factors in companies that moved from good to great. He determined that the most powerfully transformative executives possess a mixture of personal humility and professional will. In fact, they exhibited a number of paradoxical traits: timid and ferocious, shy and fearless. In addition, Collins found that this top group was focused on developing the next generation of leaders.

Too many executives are trapped by their belief that they have to act the part of leaders. Rather than exhibit the paradoxical traits Collins refers to, they exhibit only the fearless, ferocious, and willful parts. Coaching and teaching are humbling; they demand putting oneself on the same level as a direct report and require honesty and openness. When you are a prisoner of your own arrogance, it's difficult to display these qualities.

A less esoteric reason for resistance to coaching and teaching is that they are difficult, time-consuming skills to implement. It takes much less time to give a speech to a team than it does to coach each team member. In fact, the preparation for a one-on-one coaching session with a direct report demands significant work.

Even for leaders who are willing to invest the time necessary to coach, however, coaching is off-putting. Many leaders feel uncomfortable when trying to coach. After all, they have achieved success as leaders because of their business acumen and technical competence. The typical CFO, for example, probably did not have to display much (or any) ability as a teacher or coach to receive promotions. Just as significant, she was not trained in how to coach and teach.

Most leaders are very comfortable with problems to be solved but uncomfortable with interpersonal events like coaching. Analyzing data and coming up with a solution feels more natural than dealing with the ambiguity and emotions involved in one-on-one sessions with a direct report. In addition, some leaders lack confidence in their ability to understand what makes their direct reports tick and fear the confrontation that may take place during a coaching session. Emotional intelligence and empathy are coaching attributes, and many leaders find it difficult to exhibit these qualities at work. More to the point, they often lack the self-awareness that makes empathy possible. How can they coach someone about his impact on others when they lack knowledge of their own impact on people?

Finally, some leaders refer derogatorily to coaching and teaching as the soft side of leadership. They create a false dichotomy between the empathy, trust, and caring needed for successful coaching and the analysis, measurement, and motivation mind-set needed to achieve results. What they do not realize is that one feeds the other and that coaching must be a combination of a results focus and interpersonal skills.

Making the Transition to Coach and Teacher

Overcoming the resistance factors to this unnatural act involves a number of tactics:

- *Building the business case.* We have found that executives are much more eager and willing to coach when they understand the business benefits. By talking to them about how coaching helps build organizational capacity by improving potential and ensuring people are in the right jobs, they are not so quick to dismiss this aspect of leadership. Actually, most leaders do not dismiss coaching as much as they give it a lower priority than other responsibilities. By putting coaching and teaching in traditional business terms—showing how it can stop the talent drain in their division, for example—they become more interested in experimenting with this unnatural leadership behavior.

Building the business case is also important because it prevents leaders from just going through the coaching motions. If leaders do not sincerely believe that coaching and teaching are valuable tools, their direct reports will spot their insincerity in a second. No one can fake coaching. It takes place on an interpersonal level, and a direct report can sense if his boss is fully committed to helping him or if he is just making a token effort. When leaders grasp the business benefits of coaching, however, they go into it with much greater enthusiasm.

- *Develop a plan.* Alan was the prototype of an inspirational leader. Eloquent, silver haired, and the savior of a division (he had supervised development of a new service that customers loved), he was brilliant when presenting or making any type of talk. One-on-one, however, he was somewhat cold and distant. Alan had always believed that coaching was the responsibility of outside consultants or human resource staff. His boss, however, felt that Alan's direct reports had potential that was not being developed and insisted that Alan work with us to become a better coach. Alan struggled mightily at first, but after a number of discussions, he came to accept the business logic of being a good coach. What stumped him, though, was getting started. He told us that he sat down with one of his direct reports with the intention of coaching but found himself fumbling for what to say and do. Alan, a silver-tongued orator, was tongue-tied.

Alan was missing a plan, and we have learned that such a plan greatly facilitates coaching and teaching. It provides the specificity necessary to raise comfort levels and increase the odds of follow-through. Therefore, leaders should ask themselves the following questions and use the answers to develop a coaching plan for direct reports:

What is this person's major challenge (for example, a performance problem, a transition issue, or the realization of potential)?

What are the key messages you need to deliver, including feedback, performance expectations, and organizational issues?

What do you want this person to learn? Why is this important?

What are this person's aspirations and goals? If you don't know, what can you do to find out?

What is this person's reaction to coaching likely to be? Will you encounter resistance? What form will this resistance take? Are there any tough messages you should deliver, and if so, how will this person respond?

What are your ultimate goals for this person?

What is your time frame for coaching? When will you meet with each of the people you intend to coach? Set target dates.

• *Rehearse coaching and teaching interactions.* This simple tactic helps people a lot and can done in two ways. The first and obvious way is simply to say out loud (when you are alone or with someone else playing the direct report) what you want to say during an upcoming coaching interaction. The second way is to role-play with another person, but the other person takes on the "boss" role and you play the direct report. Both methods enable leaders to test different ways of communicating and anticipating reactions. Ideally, leaders will be able to fine-tune their approach and become more comfortable with the feelings coaching engenders.

• *Experiment and reflect.* Despite the previous tactics, many traditional leaders feel awkward when they start coaching and teaching. This is to be expected, and they should not beat themselves up about miscues or convince themselves they are incapable of handling these unnatural tasks. Instead, they should talk about their initial coaching attempts with a boss, peer, or outside coach. During these discussions, the following questions should be answered:

What did and did not work?

What impact did your approach have on the direct report?

What would you do differently the next time?

How would the approach you took work with other people in your group?

To what extent were your goals achieved?

What did you learn about effective coaching and teaching as a result of this experience?

Unnatural leaders know that the time invested in coaching delivers a return in both the short and long runs. They do it whether or not their organization values and rewards it because they have seen the benefits and believe it is the right thing to do.

Coaching and Teaching Rather Than Leading and Inspiring

Use the following questions to determine how much you value coaching and teaching as well as how effectively you are currently using coaching and teaching as part of your leadership.

Do you give coaching a high priority? If not, why not? What obstacles and factors get in the way of making it a higher priority for you personally?

If you have direct reports, what messages do you give them about the importance of coaching? What do your actions say about the priority of coaching and teaching?

Why do you think coaching and teaching are important for you personally, for your direct reports, and for the organization?

What feedback have you received about your integrity? Are you honest and open? Do people think that when you say something, you mean it? Do people trust you?

How comfortable are you in dealing with interpersonal events like coaching? Do you have confidence in your ability to understand other people? Are you comfortable with the feelings that coaching may create?

Coaching and Teaching Rather Than Leading and Inspiring (Cont.)

Action Planning

What actions can you take to make coaching and teaching a higher priority for yourself and your team? What can you do to make coaching and teaching commonplace in your organization? List three specific actions.

1.

2.

3.

Steps for Developing Yourself as an Unnatural Leader

Set a goal to review the performance of each of your direct reports regularly.

Set stretch goals for your team.

Identify someone you respect who excels at coaching and teaching. Ask her to coach you.

After every conversation with your direct reports, ask yourself, "Have I left them stronger and more capable than before?"

Learn about the abilities, aspirations, and ambitions of your staff, and incorporate this knowledge into your work with them.

Develop a plan for assessing each direct report's need for coaching. Have each one prepare a list of areas in which he thinks coaching would be helpful. Meet individually with each person and agree on a coaching contract.

Set a goal to review each direct report's performance once a quarter and provide feedback.

Don't ignore performance problems; act as soon as they arise.

Talk to your direct reports on the level of involvement they want from you in their work.

Learn how to be effective at giving and receiving feedback.

Set a goal for yourself to assess and develop a full understanding of the knowledge, skills, abilities, and career prospects of each of your direct reports.

Foster peer coaching by example; pick a colleague you trust, and coach each other.

Part Four

Leading the Organization as an Unnatural Leader

| **Connect Instead of Create**

The natural leadership impulse is to do it all yourself. Having been trained in cultures where individuals and organizations took tremendous pride in their own accomplishments and working in companies where getting ahead meant getting credit for yourself, managers logically value their own ideas and product and service innovations above those of others. Not only from a business perspective but from an American one, rugged individualism has been the norm. According to research conducted by CDR International partner Stephen Rhinesmith, the United States and Australia are the most individualistic countries in the world. Our culture has always viewed borrowing an invention from others as a sign of weakness. When American hegemony in technology, software, entertainment, or other industries is challenged or questioned, Americans can become defensive. Conversely, we have always taken tremendous pride in our own inventions and discoveries, ranging from the automobile to stem cell research.

Within our organizations, individual achievement and discovery innovation have been traditionally well rewarded. People who create new products, systems, software, processes, and services that generate revenue and solve customer problems have not only been promoted but have been honored for their accomplishments. Many companies have bestowed internal awards on their best scientists, salespeople, and inventors.

Leaders also know that if they want to rise within an organization, their fastest route is to lead a successful organizational project or solve a critical company problem with a result that has their name on it. If they solve problems by bringing in consultants to help or by extending the ideas or previous product lines of others, they might be rewarded but not as significantly as if they had done it on their own.

Thus, it's unnatural to solve problems by connecting rather than creating. Becoming a networker, alliance maker, and relationship manager may seem antithetical to strong leadership, but in an Internet-driven, connected world, it is becoming required, which is why we need to look at the compelling reasons for committing this unnatural act.

The Technology Catalyst

When the mainframe computer was introduced into organizations in the 1960s, it improved efficiencies and changed the way companies do business. The mini-computers and PCs of the 1980s and 1990s had a significant impact on organizational structure since various units could now do their own information processing. This encouraged decentralization of power and indirectly spurred the growth of leadership development programs. Companies needed more leaders in more places as power moved decision making outward and downward.

In the past decade, and especially in the past three years, we have seen the spread of peer-to-peer computing. Although Napster is the most obvious nonbusiness manifestation of this trend, business employees have capitalized on it to obtain and send information to people in their networks around the world. Work now gets done, ideas are surfaced, best practices are generated, and problems are solved through Internet connections, a nonlinear movement that befuddles people accustomed to a more logical work flow.

In the past twenty years or so, we have watched leadership focus shift from hierarchical structures to business units (core competencies, strategy), to teams, and now to networking. Current organizational models are often organic rather than mechanistic. The emphasis today is on knowledge, learning quickly, and adapting to a constantly changing environment. To do these things, leaders must connect people. Peers have tremendous power in this environment, and even small companies have been highly successful in using peer power and input in order to leverage limited resources. In this democratizing, decentralizing setting, connecting is critical.

Software developments are fueling this trend. Tools such as Microsoft Outlook and Lotus Notes enable people to collaborate and consult with each other without ever meeting face to face. It's not just that people in different companies and countries can exchange ideas and solve problems; it's that they can do so quickly, efficiently, and interactively. It is astonishing how quickly people, especially recent college recruits, have adapted to getting work done virtually and have established their own protocols for making work flow smoothly.

Some leaders we have observed, however, resist the technology-fueled change in how work is done. Rather than encourage their teams to connect with others and provide resources for making these connections, they attempt to control the flow of information and work as if they occupied a well-defended fortress. Made nervous by the complexity, ambiguity, and speed of the world around them, they close ranks and attempt to be self-sufficient in their own business unit, function, or country, creating what they need to survive and declining help from corporate, or other departments, or businesses. Although the isolationist impulse is natural, it is no longer normal. The reality is that leaders need to loosen controls over ideas and information and spur people to search around the world for great new partners and concepts. Many companies such as GE have institutionalized the relentless search for best practices, a manifestation of the unnatural impulse to connect instead of create.

At this point, natural leaders often balk. By borrowing best practices from others, admitting that they do not have the solution, and "giving away" ideas and best practices in order to get some in return, these executives feel they will never get credit for what they accomplish. How can they take credit for an idea that was hatched by a supplier? How are they going to measure the success of a direct report whose main skill is finding resources and borrowing the work of others?

There are no easy answers to these questions except that sharing credit and a willingness to develop new measurements are part of the unnatural leadership mind-set. Consider, too, that success today is not just about connecting the dots but connecting the people. As important as analytical and thinking and problem solving are, being able to secure ideas and information in other ways is also important. Leaders with great connections—with contacts that cross all sorts of boundaries and great relationships with these contacts—have access to more and better ideas than purely natural leaders. Let's look at the eight types of connecting that leaders need to adopt.

Connecting to Information Sources

Natural leaders are often above the fray and dependent on others for news. We still encounter leaders in high towers protected by layers of assistants and outer offices. An unnatural act, therefore, is to position oneself on the information pathway. For instance, some leaders place "sensors" throughout the company; they connect with so many different people that they are able to pick up even weak signals about what is going on. This means taking the time to talk to people outside the usual groups; it means establishing good communication with people in other functions, on different leadership levels, and in different offices. These connected individuals have a significant advantage over others in that they obtain more information faster. When faced with tough alternatives, they can plug into the people network of their organization to test out how a decision will play out. These unnatural leaders are usually in a good position because they know more about what is happening in the business. They might not have the solution, but they have an information edge that makes decisions a little less difficult and situations a little less confusing.

A leader's willingness to put himself on information pathways is contingent on his need for inclusion. In the past, successful executives manifested a strong need for control. Today, successful executives have a strong need for inclusion, manifest by a desire to include others in various projects, programs, and teams. We recently ran a large Action Learning program for two merging banks, and as part of the program, we encouraged leaders who were low on expressed inclusion to commit an unnatural act: reach out and invite members from the other bank to join their teams (the expressed inclusion was measured by the Fundamental Interpersonal Relationship Orientation-Behavior, an instrument created by William Schutz to identify interpersonal needs for inclusion, control, and affection). In a merger, inclusion rather than control is pivotal to success. Those leaders who became inclusionary not only formed better teams but were privy to critical pieces of new information, enabling them to move the merged company forward faster; they knew how to work with their unfamiliar partners, while control-focused executives lacked the information that facilitated this forward movement.

Jill, for instance, was a good example of the control-focused type. She was the head of the Asian region for a global Fortune 100 company and was called the "empress of Asia" behind her back because of her imperialistic style. As part of her controlling nature, Jill stood as a buffer between her region and what she felt was unnecessary help from corporate. While Jill had a point—corporate probably did not fully comprehend what was happening in the Asian region and was providing too much direction—she responded in a counterproductive manner: she built walls around her region to diminish corporate influence. Jill's country managers, however, were frustrated by this wall and soon began going around Jill to work with people from headquarters and global marketing. They belittled Jill behind her back and started to withhold information from her while conveying data to their contacts at corporate.

In coaching Jill, we helped her understand that living in a networked corporation today requires particular skills. She was not connecting with others, especially from an information standpoint.

Connecting to Change

Philippe was the office head in a small European country for a major consulting firm. Although this office accounted for a small percentage of the firm's total income, Philippe had established great relationships with other office heads throughout the world. He was constantly seeking out deals, looking for opportunities to work with other offices, sharing what he knew with others, and inquiring about what was happening in their regions. As a result, his office soon received work from other countries, and Philippe became the person everyone turned to when they needed strategic thinking about expanding in Europe. Still, it was somewhat surprising when the firm named Philippe to the newly created global position for the entire organization. It was surprising because this was a big job for someone from a little country (and someone who was not that proficient in his new role), but the company reasoned that it was about to launch a major change initiative and needed someone to lead this initiative who was well connected and able to make additional connections.

Connected leaders have a sixth sense for detecting resistance to change as well as the network necessary to secure buy-in for change and build momentum for it. When we coach senior leaders on instituting changes, we often request that they create a political map that identifies how key stakeholders view the targeted change, sometimes assigning a numerical value to represent an individual's support or resistance to the proposed change. After they complete this exercise, we know very quickly how connected they are as a leader by how confidently they assign a numerical value. Some leaders do not have an understanding about who will and who will not support a projected change program because they are not wired in to the network. Typically, they are the leaders who try to create change themselves or view change as a technical, rather than political and cultural, challenge. They may have the power to create change, but they lack the connections necessary to spot the people who will set up roadblocks to it and the people who need to be influenced to support it.

Connecting to an Ever-Changing, Far-Reaching Universe

Many natural leaders are accustomed to thinking about leadership in terms of American football. The leader is the quarterback who orchestrates a play that has been planned and rehearsed in advance. At times, however, a more appropriate sports analogy is to the constant scrim in rugby or the movement of a soccer ball that is in swift motion among team members. Today's network consists not only of diverse employees who change jobs or acquire new skills at a rapid rate but of people scattered all over the world and who may include vendors, suppliers, customers, and competitors. Leading within this complex network is not like sitting atop a massive, phlegmatic hierarchy. In fact, it's too amorphous and chameleon-like even to find a perch. The best that leaders can do is stay in the middle of it and find where the action is happening; being connected facilitates this positioning.

As unnatural as it might seem, leaders need to tap into their network for ideas even from individuals who are peripheral to the organization or even if the leader has never met that individual in person. Just as challenging is bringing a virtual team together, encouraging them to work synergistically, defining a clear goal and mission for the team, and helping members clarify their roles. Perhaps even more challenging, the leader of a virtual team must make sure that coordination happens, key assignments are made and understood, and the person with the right skills or knowledge is given the right assignment. This can be tough if the leader has not met many of the people on the virtual team or has had few in-person interactions with them and has to trust a team member located around the world to complete the assignment without traditional supervision and face-to-face meetings.

Leaders who are connected with people, whether through personal relationships or on-line ones, have a decided advantage in this environment. To get things done in the past, the people you knew was important. Today, the key is to whom you're connected.

Connecting to New Issues and Trends

In his book *The Innovator's Dilemma,* Clay Christenson writes that once-dominant companies such as RCA, Fairchild Semiconductors, Firestone, and Xerox lost market share among other reasons because they minimized the reality of market information. Often market leaders are not scared enough to stay broadly and deeply connected, and these once-famous companies depended on their biggest and best customers for feedback about new technologies.

Faced with the prospect of a new product or technology from a trusted supplier, these customers might often say, "We don't need it," while simultaneously a new and significant market was developing for this new product. Because they failed to establish a broader network through market research—of smaller customers, potential customers, and customers in different industries—their connections were limited, as was their perception of the market opportunity.

Connected leaders, however, do not necessarily have to create new technologies to take advantages of trends. In many cases, they can gain a strategic advantage simply by being privy to network information about trends and shaping their strategies so they dovetail with them. Many unnatural leaders today spend a significant portion of their time surfing the Web, e-mailing colleagues, and connecting by telephone. The most successful politicians build up a database of contacts and connections who can be mobilized for elections and legislative decisions. Leading in a networked and wired business world requires the same skills. Being among the first through a network to spot a new service need in a given field or to recognize the formation of a new market is often sufficient to confer competitive advantage.

Connecting to Diverse Resources

The natural leadership mentality involves relying on a small, select group of colleagues and advisers to get things done. They have a few preferred vendors, consultants, and so on. Consciously or not, they divide the world into "us" and "them." In their minds, the us group is the only one that counts. They have difficulty seeing the possibility of leveraging resources in the them group, even though that group is a much larger and more diverse one than the us team.

Johnson & Johnson's vice chairman, William Weldon, is terrific at making the boundaries of teams permeable, shuffling their composition as business needs dictate. Sometimes CDR International is included as a consultant to Johnson & Johnson; at other times, it's McKinsey or one of a number of other consultants. As well, Weldon includes retired executives, customers, individual contributors, corporate staff, functional specialists, and many others as tasks require. As a leader, he makes a point of being aware of and in relationships with a wide variety of people, including doctors, researchers, professors, scientists, employees at all levels, and many others, giving him access to the right people for the right situation. He is a proponent of the philosophy, "If it's invented somewhere, let's use it," as opposed to, "If it wasn't invented here, it doesn't exist." He is as smart as his network, which is vast.

Connecting to the Talent Pipeline

Natural leaders are focused on developing their own team members, assuming that if they have a chance to train and develop them, they will create "their type" of people. While it makes perfect sense to develop as much internal talent as possible, employees are much more mobile today; highly marketable executives, especially, often leave right when they are at their peak value. Many companies today debate the relative merits of "making" versus "buying" leadership talent.

For this reason, unnatural leaders are always recruiting, both internally and externally. They do not view this as only a human resource responsibility but make it their business to look for talent everywhere, from trade conferences to social gatherings. We are coaching the head of a technical development department; he finds talent at bookstores, coffeehouses, and other places frequented by technogeeks. He has established contacts in all of these untraditional arenas, and the result is that he often has his pick of the best people in his area.

Connecting to Different Ways of Thinking

Each company has its own way of approaching business issues. The culture, history, and leadership practices of an organization combine to create conventional wisdom and sometimes bureaucracy. As a result, corporate leaders adhere to certain beliefs and practices and have difficulty considering other theories and approaches. Connected leaders work to keep themselves open to alternative ideas and approaches, continuously reading, attending conferences, and surfing on-line to stay ahead. One of the first questions we ask our coaching clients who want to improve is, "How do you learn? What do you read? What is your strategy for staying ahead?" Unnatural leaders instinctively understand that human assets are more important than physical assets, and they place a high value on talent and knowledge. Rather than focusing on generating new approaches and best practices from within, they constantly scan the environment, looking for the best, the newest, the breakthrough, and the potentially dangerous.

Connecting with Unexpected Allies

Being connected means more than establishing relationships with traditional allies—a major customer, for instance. The unnatural leader considers unorthodox possibilities, resulting in unions such as the one between Pfizer and Microsoft. These two companies are looking at the information management possibilities of identifying medical conditions on-line and finding ways to treat them effectively. The Internet will catalyze many of these unusual partnerships, especially in the area of information management. One of our clients, Merck-Medco, started out as a prescription-dispensing business but has evolved into a major medical information management company. Leaders recognized early that they possessed medical condition and related purchasing information on about 30 million customers and that this database could create new types of information services for their customers.

We are working with Hewlett-Packard to help its leaders understand how to get things done even when they lack control. Under CEO Carly Fiorina, Hewlett-Packard has moved from many decentralized business units to a new front-back organizational structure (the front consists of the areas that deal directly with the customers, while the back produces what the customer actually buys). Executives need to learn to work across traditional boundaries because they do not control all the resources to meet customer requirements and needs. In most large companies today, complex, interdependent structures mean that leaders lack formal organizational authority and can accomplish their goals only by influencing others. Without strong connections with people in other functions and offices, this influence will not be felt.

How to Foster Connective Attitudes and Actions

It's not easy for some leaders to focus on even one of the eight types of connections just discussed. Some have been so thoroughly indoctrinated in the rugged individualist philosophy and are so jingoistic about their companies that they experience great difficulty when asked to connect instead of create. Although the following ideas are not panaceas, they will help leaders shift their thinking and behaviors toward an unnatural approach:

- *Borrow Jack Welch's "borrowing" incentive.* Early on at GE, former CEO Jack Welch recognized that GE had to eliminate the "not invented here" syndrome. Although he did many things to eliminate it, one of most innovative was holding managers accountable for both contributing and adopting best practices from elsewhere in the company. In other words, managers were evaluated on their borrowing ability; Welch was known for grilling managers about what ideas they had appropriated lately and how well they had done in proselytizing their peers.

It's one thing to talk about the need for leaders to adopt best practices and something else entirely to evaluate performance based on how well or how often a leader takes an outside idea and makes it his own. This type of incentive is powerful not only because there's a tangible reward for borrowing but because it sends a clear message that taking the best from others is a good thing to do. Through incentives, organizations must convince people that innovation is happening everywhere, and their challenge is to find it. We are frequently dismayed with how much time senior leaders of large corporations spend on generating new leadership practices, when we are convinced that in their large global corporation, those practices already exist somewhere within their boundaries. When leaders recognize that their company is serious about borrowing and using best practices and ideas from elsewhere—when they grasp that it is no longer necessary for them to demonstrate their brilliance through original ideas or by maintaining tight control of the creative process—they are much more willing to connect. Natural leaders look to create from the relatively narrow base of their organization or unit. Unnatural leaders broaden their view to the entire universe of talent, resources, knowledge, and ideas, connecting with people and concepts that extend far beyond their traditional boundaries.

• *Downplay the three big Cs.* A desire for the three big Cs— credit, control, and compensation—has shaped many leaders, even though they publicly disavow it. They took to heart career advice about making sure they got their name attached to programs and policies to which they contributed. They learned early on that keeping things under control would please their boss. As young managers, they invariably heard their boss say, "The one thing I don't want is a surprise!" They have been interrogated in public meetings about what is happening, what is not happening, and why they are not on top of it all. Thus, they have learned to keep an eagle eye on budgets, deadlines, processes, and programs.

Compensation has traditionally been viewed as the way score is kept. To get more money has always been a career goal, and the way to get more money was to maintain control and take credit.

To commit the unnatural act of connecting, a leader must plug into other rewards beyond the three Cs. In coaching senior leaders, we encourage them to reflect on not only what the organization values but what they value as individuals. It's not that control, credit, and compensation are unimportant but that other rewards, such as developing people, team performance, and personal integrity, are increasingly important. When people stop leading unconsciously and start becoming reflective about a company's reward system and their own belief system, they often are more open to connecting with and learning from outside people and ideas. With some coaching, they see that it makes sense to search the world rather than their own backyard for the best ideas. On reflection, they understand that they will feel good sharing credit and giving up some control if they focus on moving the company forward.

Bosses and coaches should have the types of conversations with others that push them to consider what's really important in their work life. By challenging their assumptions about what the company expects and asking them to define what they stand for, it's possible to make them aware that through their efforts to succeed in one system, they have limited their knowledge and opportunities, which will ultimately curtail their success.

• *Encourage people to embrace (rather than resist) the paradox of connecting.* Natural leaders who are willing to try connecting are sometimes thrown by the resulting paradoxes. When leaders establish diverse connections, they are chagrined to discover that they are being pulled in different directions. In the past, loyalties were clear. A manager was loyal to his boss, his team, his customers, and his organization. Allegiance was unambiguous. Today, when you have established alliances with a number of different teams and types of organizations, allegiances can become confusing.

Denise, for instance, is a member of her boss's team, as well as the leader of her own team. As a member of her boss's team, she is frequently asked to make decisions about budgets and resource allocations that have an impact on her direct reports. Recently, she was asked to engage in a cross-organizational ranking of employees. As a result, her peer group was involved in ranking members of Denise's team. Naturally enough, Denise's team expected her to fight for them and make sure they all obtained top-tier appraisals. As much as Denise believed in her own team and could defend their performance, she also wanted to participate fully in her boss's team goal of ranking employees across all functions.

Denise, as an unnatural leader, did not try to shield her team members from the scrutiny of her peers; she attempted to make sure the performance and potential of her direct reports were ranked fairly. At the same time, she encouraged her own team to network up and bypass her if necessary if they wanted to communicate something to her boss or even her boss's boss. In this way, Denise was able to reconcile the paradox of her connectivity.

Denise's boss encouraged this attitude and coached Denise when she was initially confused about her loyalties. Living within conflicting and paradoxical loyalties is a reality in corporations today, and there is no need to be secretive about these realities or to view the choices in either-or terms. With a friendly ear, people can explore the ambiguities and complexities generated in a connected world and receive feedback that may help them clarify their thinking.

Connecting Instead of Creating

Think about how often you connect instead of create. How much do you practice each of these behaviors?

Behaviors	Your Rating				
Exchanging ideas and information	1 Rarely	2	3	4	5 Always
Embracing "not invented here" concepts	1 Rarely	2	3	4	5 Always
Forming alliances and building networks	1 Rarely	2	3	4	5 Always
Taking the time to talk to people outside the usual groups you work with	1 Rarely	2	3	4	5 Always
Establishing good communications with people from other functions, levels, and offices	1 Rarely	2	3	4	5 Always
Looking for talent everywhere	1 Rarely	2	3	4	5 Always
Seeking out and sharing good ideas and best practices	1 Rarely	2	3	4	5 Always
Placing a high value on acquiring knowledge	1 Rarely	2	3	4	5 Always
Adopting best practices	1 Rarely	2	3	4	5 Always
Staying connected to new issues and trends	1 Rarely	2	3	4	5 Always

Focus on the behaviors that you assigned the lowest rating. What keeps you from connecting with others?

Connecting Instead of Creating (Cont.)

What can you do to send a clear message that taking the best from others is a good thing to do?

List three new connecting behaviors that you can try.

A.

B.

C.

Steps for Developing Yourself as an Unnatural Leader

Reward people based on their ability to connect to others.

Stay informed by being out in the marketplace and in touch with customers, competitors, analysts, and academics.

Develop principles that influence everyone in your organization to work toward the same goals.

Identify colleagues whose support is important to your success, and make it a point to have regularly scheduled meetings or at least informal conversations over coffee or lunch.

Think about other departments and organizations that could benefit from knowing what you are doing, and share information with them.

Form a community of practice around a shared purpose. Check out suppliers that have Web-based products and services for connecting people, such as participate.com, communispace.com, or placeware.com.

Set a goal to learn about the priorities of other departments and functions.

Develop a plan for taking a short-term assignment in another functional area.

Arrange visits to other companies to benchmark best practices.

Look for an assignment with exposure to multiple business functions.

Don't stay in your office. Make sure that you are connecting with people and building relationships.

Seek out best practices both internally and externally.

| Give Up Some Control

No one today would call himself a controlling leader. *Control* has acquired a pejorative connotation in most organizations, at least in the sense of looking over people's shoulders, eliminating all risk, and micromanaging other people's work. That said, we should add that natural leaders have a strong need for control. Although they may not be as overt or insistent on it as they were in the past, they are still likely to want to influence decisions and shape policies strongly.

While some people's need to control is rooted in their personalities, others developed this controlling impulse as a result of their organizational experiences. They were exposed to Murphy's law: "What can go wrong, will go wrong." There was some truth to this law many years ago, as evidenced by low quality, poor processes, and strained employer-employee relationships. At that time, the way to avoid having too many things go wrong was to keep a tight rein on people and processes. Micromanaging, a style of management that is out of favor now, was very much in favor years ago. Typically, the managers who exerted the most control were promoted to leadership roles.

Today, natural leaders attempt to be controlling for other reasons. Some of them are responding to intense pressure for results, believing that the best way to get results is making sure everyone does what he is supposed to do. Others are attempting to establish some predictability in a highly volatile environment; they are trying to control and slow things down because everything around them is moving at such a breakneck speed.

It's unnatural to let go. Many leaders resist giving up even a modicum of control of those things they consider important for fear of what might happen: work will not get done on time; mistakes will be made; others may take advantage; work will become disorganized and chaotic. In coaching executives, we have found that control issues are almost always an issue in how a leader relates to direct reports.

We are not suggesting that leaders give up all control. The operative word is *some,* and the real trick is finding the sweet spot between control and autonomy. Before discussing why it's necessary for leaders to give up some control, let's define our terms.

Control Means Different Things to Different People

There are two basic types of control in business organizations: tangible and intangible assets. Tangible assets cover everything from money to inventory to technology with corresponding systems (financial controls, reporting systems, and so forth) designed to measure and keep track of things. In terms of the intangible assets, there are people and knowledge. In many companies, tangible assets are tightly controlled, while interpersonal processes have relatively few formal controls. For instance, expense reports are highly detailed and closely monitored, ensuring that no one cheats the company of even a few dollars. At the same time, there is no control in place to ensure that a manager who demeans or demoralizes others does not cheat the company of those employees' contributions and potential.

When we talk about unnatural leaders giving up some control, we are primarily referring to control over people. Controls that focus on behaviors and aspects of human relationships (such as checking and reporting) are the ones that today yield fewer results. On the other hand, controls that relate to performance outcomes are often increased by unnatural leaders. Instead of concentrating on restricting employee behaviors, they establish an environment of performance accountability where everyone is aware and committed to meeting certain standards. These standards are not arbitrary or absurdly ambitious but realistic and necessary; they must be met for the business unit to grow, thrive, or survive. To a certain extent, these standards control the pace and quality of work.

As we noted earlier, control may also be a function of personality. It is a need we all have to a lesser or greater extent, and although we cannot change this need, we can control it through awareness of how this need affects others. This need manifests itself in all sorts of ways. Some of us have a strong need to make decisions, exert influence, and assert power, and some of us have a weak need for these outcomes. There are high-control people who cannot stand being controlled by others, as well as high controllers who relish managers who give them clear and continuous direction. Many variations on this control theme exist, and we frequently rely on the Fundamental Interpersonal Relationship Orientation–Behavior (FIRO-B) to identify the control type of an individual leader.

We bring this up here because it's easy to divide the world into controlling and noncontrolling types, and although it's convenient to do so for the sake of discussion (we are doing it in this chapter to a certain extent), it oversimplifies the reality. Some people, for instance, have a strong need for control but can accept coworkers who have similar needs and work well with them; they can defer to people in positions of authority and let them take charge. Others, however, cannot defer and believe they can influence every situation in which they find themselves; they often have trouble delegating and frequently reject other people's decisions and ideas.

Jason, for instance, was the head of a Canadian firm who took the FIRO-B, and his scores indicated an exceedingly high need to influence and dominate others; they also revealed he had little need to include others in decisions and was not interested in interpersonal connections with others in his office. When we went over the scores with Jason, he said, "Now I know why people hate working for me." He said it in jest, but his particular type of controlling personality caused significant problems with his direct reports. During feedback sessions, these direct reports said of Jason, "I never make a decision that he doesn't carefully review" and "He never asks for my opinion on anything."

Alexis is a group manager who was assigned a team composed primarily of recent college graduates. She has very little need to control others, and her philosophy was that you give people assignments and trust that they will do the job properly until involvement becomes necessary. The opposite of Jason, Alexis not only was not interested in influencing and dominating others, but she often wished for tight supervision from her bosses. Alexis's team complained that she provided them with almost no direction and that they were unclear about what they should do, how they should do it, and what the real deadlines were. Comments from their feedback included, "I don't know what she expects from me," "Sometimes I don't know when we've made a decision and when we haven't," and "I don't feel as if I have enough information to do my job." Alexis obviously gave up too much control.

Control sometimes has to be looked at situationally. When supervising people who are new to a work unit, project team, or without much work experience, establishing control and direction is more important than it is with a veteran team. Similarly, in times of great uncertainty and ambiguity, it might make sense for a leader to take firm control, at least until the situation stabilizes (such as during a major systems outage).

Teams represent another situation where a leader's control can be a major issue. High-control leaders tend to diminish the effectiveness of teams. They limit participation and have little tolerance for ideas other than their own. In many instances, their tight control over team meetings makes it impossible to surface spontaneous ideas or creative brainstorms and discuss them in ways that the best ones emerge. High-control leaders usually do better when they are supervising teams that have decision-making authority rather than advisory teams. In fact, they may be better able to drive the former team toward clear and compelling performance goals than low-control leaders can. These high-control people, however, diminish a team's capacity for creativity, trust, mutual support recognition, synergistic exchanges, and problem solving, all critical to most teams.

Given all this, leaders need to be aware that the unnatural rule of thumb is to give up some control but be cognizant of the various situations that can affect this rule, as well as their own particular need for control.

A Timely Argument for Less Controlling Behaviors

We suppose it can be argued that now is the time for more rather than less controlling leadership. The natural reaction to the volatility of business and the changes being wrought by e-commerce and economic uncertainty and other factors is to try to control what can be controlled. Many leaders believe that emotional edge comes from dominating people through the force of a strong personality and position and keeping them slightly off-kilter. The problem, of course, is that these are not minor or temporary issues. Attempting to clamp down on people is doomed to failure because of the futility of it in a complex environment. If you are skeptical about the need to give up some control, consider the following seven factors:

- *The frequency of matrix management.* The majority of companies today rely on some form of matrix management, creating interdependencies among units in companies. Geography and product is one interdependency, but there are many others, including global and local, product development and marketing, staff and line, and corporate and field. Given a matrix structure, where there are many gray areas with unclear authority and shared responsibility for outcomes, attempting to exert control is like trying to capture a drop of mercury.

- *The rise of project teams (including virtual teams).* Andersen's information technology group has six partner-leaders on three continents who manage teams with worldwide memberships. Project development might take place in Europe, systems development in the United States, and data processing in India. The job of these partner-leaders is to make sure people manage themselves as they promised rather than to manage each individual (an impossible task, given the geographical spread of a given team).

- *Greater reliance on partnerships and alliances.* Because of a desire to share product development and marketing costs (as well as for other reasons), companies are forming joint venture partnerships that can be managed only through influence rather than control. The give and take and shared decision making necessary for joint ventures to succeed is antithetical to control. In fact, some companies have developed reputations as lousy partners because of controlling managers who attempt to dictate terms to their partners and generally act as if they control the alliance.

- *A more mobile workforce.* Even in a shrinking economy, talented people have more opportunities than ever before. The stigma of moving from job to job has been erased, and many high-potential employees will not endure managers who overcontrol and underdevelop them. Younger workers especially confound natural leaders, who find that their motivational tactics as well as their intimidating actions are ineffective.

• *Reduced control.* Speed limits opportunities to control. When a proposal has to be completed immediately, a customer has to be responded to instantly, or cycle time for product launch shortened dramatically, the chances to check and recheck are slim to none. People need autonomy and trust to act fast, and effective leaders give it to them.

• *The new focus on personal development.* Development of people has become a priority. To develop employees effectively, leaders must take risks. An employee who is completely ready to perform a new job does not need development. Leaders need to promote people who are almost ready, empower them with strong support, and give them some freedom to fail. Micromanaging direct reports or consistently insisting they are not ready to handle a project stifles development.

• *The volatility of information.* Information moves around while people stay still. People in a company have access to enormous amounts of controlled information quickly while sitting at their computer. When leaders attempt to control information or the communication of decisions, information tends to leak out faster today than ever before, primarily because of the Internet. We know of an executive committee that was meeting to decide on a new organizational structure and after long debate agreed on a structure but haggled about how to word the internal announcement. During a break in the meeting, one of the committee members logged on to the Yahoo! chat board for his company and discovered that a discussion of the proposed structural change and people's reactions was already taking place. Controlling devices such as beefing up security, threatening leakers with punishments, and tracking down leaks may work for a while, but there are just too many holes in the information dike to hold it back for long. A better strategy is to get in front and push for more transparency of decisions and information.

Signs and Symptoms of High-Control Leaders

Certain natural acts of leadership—black-and-white decision making, for example, or unwillingness to share vulnerabilities—are relatively easy to discern. Leaders who maintain subtle control, how-ever, are not always easy to identify. As we mentioned earlier, no one admits to being a controlling person. A refusal to give up some control can manifest itself in a number of ways. Let's look at some of the most common ones:

• *Direct reports or teams who mostly do or provide what they think their boss wants them to do.* A leader may honestly believe she is not con-trolling and can point to a number of instances when she has encouraged direct reports to take risks, empowered them to act, or let them make important decisions without her input. Nonethe-less, her direct reports spend enormous amounts of time trying to figure out what she expects or wants. Executive committees often complain that their middle or upper management teams do not take enough initiative and instead look to the executive team for direction. Middle and upper managers, for their part, complain that the executive committee wants to see and sign off on every-thing before it goes forward. Thus, they are conditioned to look upward before acting, and this subtle form of control is powerful and difficult to break, especially when many other company cues reinforce the importance of the hierarchy and not making mis-takes. While managers may simply be imagining that the executive committee wants to sign off on everything before action is taken, this illusion has the same impact as the reality, and it's up to lead-ers to change the game.

• *The use of power.* This does not always involve overt displays of authority, but there can be subtle signals that the leader insists on control. Interrupting team members, having the last word in meet-ings, refusing to encourage people to speak up or disagree, and not revealing their position on issues are all controlling actions. We once worked with a leader who routinely read his mail in meet-ings with direct reports. In one-on-one meetings, he would answer any telephone call while the direct report waited. When we talked to him about these habits, he insisted that he could "process on a number of levels simultaneously" or that "customers come first." This may have been true, but the message he was sending to his team was that his time or that of any other person was more valu-able than theirs, and this power play (along with other actions) frustrated them.

- *Failure to respect boundaries.* Some leaders routinely call staff members at home during the night or on weekends, insisting that their direct reports drop what they are doing and respond immediately. Sometimes this is justified, and sometimes it just a bad habit. They also feel free to telephone direct reports with messages like, "Please interrupt your meeting and come in here. This is important." They are communicating that "your time is my time," a highly controlling message.

- *Taking on the role of seller.* Some executives sincerely believe that their position and experience give them a clearer vision than their direct reports have, and they proceed to sell their group on their ideas rather than soliciting their input. They have convinced themselves that a strong leader must be passionate about his position, and they then use their authority and position power to persuade and cajole and get others to see the correctness of their position. Eventually, these tactics discourage openness and participation, and soon this leader is the sole idea person in the group.

- *Refusing to accept bad news.* It's not that leaders explicitly say, "If you don't have anything good to say, don't say it." Indirectly, however, they communicate that they are not willing to hear bad news. Perhaps they become angry when they hear bad news and take it out on the messenger. (More than one CEO we have coached has subtly controlled a whole company with his volatility.) Perhaps they refuse to discuss a negative situation in a meaningful way or hear objections to their position as not sufficiently believing in what's possible. In this manner, they control interactions by effectively creating taboos. Leaders may do this in the belief that they are being positive and upbeat, but in fact they are being manipulative.

- *Massive e-mailing.* E-mail can be a tool of unnatural leaders to foster connectivity, but it can also be abused. Some managers bombard their direct reports with e-mail, and it becomes an indirect form of oversight. Not only are these leaders constantly sending e-mails asking for status reports or posing questions and suggestions, but they expect to receive return e-mails documenting every action or decision. Many companies are debating what to do about the deluge of irrelevant e-mails clogging their systems. Some companies have gone so far as to shut down their system for a period of time daily to reduce the oppressiveness of this over-communication.

Learning to Give Up Some Control: Initial Steps

What makes this unnatural act more difficult than some of the others is that the goal is to exert control in some areas and at some times, but not always. Some of the other unnatural acts require clear behavioral changes. Here, the objective is not to give up all control but to find the sweet spot between the control necessary to meet organizational requirements and the autonomy people need to perform. A simpler way of looking at it is turning down a leader's control thermostat a degree or two. Here are some ways to do so:

- *Intentionally remove or attack bureaucratic behavioral controls.* Our Action Learning Work Out programs help companies improve processes and reduce unnecessary work. Typically, these sessions focus on internal controls and checks that add time and tasks, but not value, to a process. One Work Out method, borrowed from GE, targets unnecessary reports, approvals, and memos. Leaders who participate in these sessions invariably become aware (often acutely so) of their reflexive insistence on time-wasting controls, and they are usually much more willing to cut back on these behaviors when they understand the costs of such behaviors.
- *Ask, "What is the worst that could happen?"* In Action Coaching sessions, we often ask this question of a high-control leader. The point is to get these leaders to confront their own anxiety and why they have such difficulty letting go. Other useful follow-up questions are, "Why do you need to be so involved in your direct reports' work?" "What keeps you from letting go of a project and allowing a direct report to take responsibility?" People become stuck in a high-control mode because they have difficulty managing their own anxiety and are unconsciously focused on what might go wrong.

When leaders begin articulating their fears and worst-case scenarios, they usually realize that the worst case is not only unlikely to happen but it sometimes is not that terrible. High-control executives we coach come to understand that they do not have to let go of control completely and can moderate their anxiety by creating clear performance expectations, taking time to coach around deliverables and how to achieve them, and allowing their direct reports to initiate communication when they need to.

• *Agree on governance mechanisms.* Anxiety about control issues can also be reduced when leaders and their direct reports agree on procedures, checkpoints, and milestones. These governance mechanisms cannot be dictated by leaders but are the result of discussions and mutual buy-in. How often a leader and direct reports should meet during a project and when and what to review between meetings are two elements of a good checkpoint road map.

• *Provide forums for self-control.* Natural leaders are often more willing to reduce their controlling impulses when they know that their direct reports are doing a good job of self-management. As a result of giving people the opportunity to assess and critique their behaviors, leaders often discover that they are perfectly capable of controlling themselves and do not need a great deal of oversight. Johnson & Johnson employee training programs regularly focus on the credo and how leaders have done in maintaining the values it espouses. As a result, Johnson & Johnson does not have to establish an elaborate and intrusive system of measurement for those values considered important. Instead, leaders can count on their employees to be vigilant in assessing and attempting to maintain these values.

• *Create informal check-ins.* Formal, routinized forms of control often demean and disenfranchise employees. Punching in and out on time clocks is perhaps the most extreme example of these formal controls, but telephone calls at a regular time demanding updates have an equally negative effect. What is unnatural is moving away from these formal control systems and using informal ones. A casual coaching session just after returning from a customer or informal discussions on the fly can provide leaders with information needed to maintain sufficient control. Direct reports who are busy and stressed usually are more appreciative of focused, brief interactions than command performances in the boss's office. The casual, spontaneous nature of the interactions is far less onerous than formal reviews.

• *Differentiate between what can and what cannot be controlled.* Effective leaders recognize that it's not possible to control how people work on projects, how they make decisions, and what their recommendations and decisions will be; they need to back off behavioral controls and concentrate instead on establishing structure around certain tasks they alone are responsible for.

Many leaders become anxious about controlling their team members because their own work approach is undisciplined and lacks focus. There are three areas where leaders should apply discipline and focus.

The first area is time. Some executives are astonishingly careless with this valuable resource. As a result, they feel as if there is always too much to do and not enough time do it, attempting to control other people's time in a vain attempt to get everything done. A much better approach is to show discipline with one's schedule, establishing priorities and sticking to them.

The second area is schedules. Some executives we have observed follow schedules that seem random. Meetings are scheduled impulsively, commitments are missed because of pressing demands, and there is much last-minute juggling of activities to fit everything in. When schedules are chaotic, most leaders respond by trying to order other aspects of their business lives, and that results in overcontrolling actions. Although no one can have a completely predictable schedule, some predictable routine in dates for one-on-one reviews, staff meetings, and planning sessions creates organizational discipline and reduces the need for interpersonal control over others.

Finally is selecting direct reports as team members. A key action is to take the selection responsibility seriously and devote the time necessary to doing it right. Many executives complain to us about the price of poor selection, and nothing creates anxiety faster than poor choices of team members. Managing or mitigating poor selection decisions can cause a leader to feel that she has lost control. We advise leaders that it is much easier to select the right person for the right job than to try to retrofit the wrong person after they have been selected. Many leaders identify issues in the selection process but go ahead anyway, hoping the person will improve on the job or their deficiencies will somehow go away.

Invariably, the result is anxiety and loss of control over results. Selecting people is as much art as science, but it helps enormously if leaders devote time and energy to the process and deploy their highest performers to do recruiting, interviewing, and hiring.

Perhaps most significant, leaders who want to learn to lessen control will hold team meetings that are open conversations concerning the team, leadership, and performance. High-performing leaders give people the opportunity to provide feedback, talk about their perceptions, and discuss management style. Constructive criticism can be encouraged and defensive reactions minimized. Leaders often do not realize the impact of their overcontrol unless they hear it firsthand.

We have helped executives as they open up their team meetings to this type of discussion. Their fears revolve around a loss of authority and respect as employees vent. By and large, our clients have found that if they approach these meetings as team-building sessions, adopt the learner's perspective, and work hard to avoid becoming defensive, they establish trust. With real trust, there is less need to control another.

Giving Up Some Control

What factors are pressuring you to give up control in your work environment?

Increased dependence on matrix management

Need for cross-organizational teams

Greater reliance on partnerships and alliances

A less captive workforce

Pressure to deliver results

Development of people

Speed of information flow

Below are some behaviors that can interfere with your ability to give up control. Rate the extent to which each is a problem for you.

Behaviors	Your Rating
Wanting to see and sign off on everything before it goes forward	1　　2　　3　　4　　5 No　　　　　　Significant Problem　　　　　Problem
Interrupting team members	1　　2　　3　　4　　5 No　　　　　　Significant Problem　　　　　Problem
Having the last word in meetings	1　　2　　3　　4　　5 No　　　　　　Significant Problem　　　　　Problem
Refusing to encourage people to speak up or disagree	1　　2　　3　　4　　5 No　　　　　　Significant Problem　　　　　Problem
Either not delegating or staying too involved	1　　2　　3　　4　　5 No　　　　　　Significant Problem　　　　　Problem
Rejecting other people's decisions and ideas because you think you have all of the answers	1　　2　　3　　4　　5 No　　　　　　Significant Problem　　　　　Problem
Carefully reviewing all decisions	1　　2　　3　　4　　5 No　　　　　　Significant Problem　　　　　Problem

Giving Up Some Control (Cont.)

Behaviors	Your Rating
Never asking for opinions on anything	1 2 3 4 5 No Significant Problem Problem
Expecting that direct reports drop what they are doing and respond immediately to your needs	1 2 3 4 5 No Significant Problem Problem
Constantly getting people to see the correctness of your position	1 2 3 4 5 No Significant Problem Problem
Scheduling meetings impulsively and expecting people to attend regardless of other priorities or schedules	1 2 3 4 5 No Significant Problem Problem

Focus on the behaviors that you assigned the highest ratings. What factors may be contributing to these ratings?

In what types of situations do your control needs kick in?

How could your need for control hurt your ability to deliver your business results?

What appropriate mechanisms and performance standards do you need to put in place to control the pace and quality of the work? What do you need to do to establish an environment of performance accountability?

Giving Up Some Control (Cont.)

What actions can you take to give up some control? List three.

1.

2.

3.

Use the paradox management tool in Chapter Ten to examine how you can find the right balance between having control and giving autonomy. Identify the negative consequences for paying too much attention to each behavior at the expense of the other. Now identify the positive benefits of both having control and giving autonomy. Think about how you can "live in the positives" and "manage the negatives" in balancing both control and autonomy. What actions can you take to achieve a desirable balance?

Steps for Developing Yourself as an Unnatural Leader

Learn how to influence others effectively in a matrix structure by building cross-organizational relationships with key people.

Engage in a meaningful dialogue with your team about your style. Encourage constructive criticism and avoid defensiveness.

Use more informal and spontaneous interactions to check in on important projects.

Set a goal to empower your staff, and give them the freedom to fail.

Pay attention to how much your staff micromanages their teams.

Make a point to respect boundaries of others by not insisting that people drop what they are doing and respond immediately.

Recruit top players who can be given independence to meet their responsibilities.

Refrain from sending too many e-mails asking for status reports.

Spend time confronting your own anxiety about why you have difficulty letting go.

Let go of control by creating clear performance expectations. Agree on checkpoints and milestones.

Don't schedule meetings impulsively unless absolutely necessary.

Pay attention to how much you trust your team, and don't be afraid to delegate the tough issues.

Chapter Thirteen

Challenge the Conventional Wisdom

The conventional wisdom is about "how we do things around here." It is the stored knowledge that organizations accumulate over time, and in the case of companies such as GE, Honeywell, Unilever, and Johnson & Johnson, it may be built up over a century. The conventional wisdom can be anything from a belief about product quality to leadership practices to codes of professional conduct. Conventional wisdom can be a positive force, providing ways to acculturate employees, organize work, create priorities, and control behaviors. In companies with strong cultures, conventional wisdom serves as an unconscious guide to behavior and saves management time negotiating with people about what is and is not appropriate.

In an age of rapid change, conventional wisdom can be misguided. Conventional wisdom is rooted and inflexible, and it is based on past experience rather than present realities. As Gary Hamel observed in *Leading the Revolution,* "The organizational pyramid is a pyramid of experience but experience is valuable only to the extent that the future is like the past."

When the unconscious rules and values of corporate culture become too ingrained and controlling, bureaucracy results. Too much bureaucracy makes it very difficult to change companies, even when change is crucial for the organization's continued success or even its survival. More than one CEO we have worked with has railed against the difficulty of changing bureaucratic ways. At GE, Jack Welch viewed bureaucracy as the enemy.

Conventional wisdom in strong cultures runs so deep through the company that it can be difficult to challenge it. To do so feels wrong. It seems disloyal to go against a sacred organizational belief such as "good planning requires thick notebooks," or "never end-run your boss." Just as problematic, people who embody the corporate culture and embody the conventional wisdom are promoted to leadership roles, and that's why they get ahead. At the top of some large institutions, a significant percentage of executives act, talk, and even look alike. Challenging the conventional wisdom therefore may require an act of courage the higher you go, because many top executives will feel challenged themselves.

We are not suggesting that good leaders should become nihilists and anarchists. You need to pick your spots when you issue a real challenge because there is a danger of being typed as a troublemaker. The risk of being thought a maverick, however, is one that unnatural leaders we have observed are willing to take. Generally, they make it an acceptable risk by challenging the conventional wisdom but also preserving the strengths of the culture; they do not want to tear down the institution as much as they want to reshape it.

Leaders who commit this particular unnatural act recognize that there are major payoffs for doing so. When executives challenge the conventional wisdom, they foment change; they bring new, energizing ideas to moribund companies; they offer organizations fresh perspectives that can lead to more effective strategies. Leaders of companies like Southwest Airlines, Dell Computer, and Wal-Mart challenged the conventional wisdom of their companies and their industries and by doing so created new markets and pioneered unique and original products and services.

With these benefits in mind, let's look at what the conventional wisdom in a given organization entails.

Two Forms of Wisdom

Conventional wisdom in companies involves how to behave (in order to survive and thrive) and how to do business. We will look at behavior first.

We are coaching a number of senior leaders who experience difficulty following written and unwritten protocols. For instance, one senior executive wants to promote talented people two levels below him into key roles, bypassing his direct reports because of the high potential of these more talented people. This is not the way promotion is done in this company, however, and he knows that if he does what he wants, he will encounter protest not only from his direct reports but from human resources. Similarly, we are working with a manager who is convinced that his boss's reorganization and product plans will inhibit revenue growth, risk market share, and may send talented people out the door. He has tried to convince his boss that the plan contains too much risk, but his boss disagrees and will not discuss the issue further. What this manager wants to do is take the risk of sharing his view with his boss's boss. This company, though, has a strong and formal hierarchy, and it is considered bad form to end-run the boss for any reason.

In these and other cases, the conventional wisdom is not spelled out in a policy manual but implied and intuited. People who have worked for a company for an extended period of time frequently follow this wisdom unconsciously. As a result, it often feels odd or counterintuitive to go against what are clearly the norms. But in the two instances just mentioned, going against the norms probably is the right thing to do and in the best interests of the organization.

The second type of conventional wisdom involves a company's business model, including deeply held beliefs about how to make money, what customers want, and how to deliver value. Many times, the conventional wisdom here is based on years of success. It's very difficult to go against practices that have been at the heart of a company's successful strategy for a long period of time, and more than a few CEO change agents have failed to convince their senior leaders of the importance of adapting a new business model. In fact, creatively destroying a successful strategy by launching new products that cannibalize current ones, abandoning an installed customer base, or retiring a successful product to make room for a new one are all risky but often necessary challenges to conventional wisdom that are difficult to pull off. Typically, many people have great emotional, psychological, and career investments in current operational approaches, products, or services, and suggesting they need to be destroyed can raise more than a few hackles.

Obstacles to Overcome

Given all the talk about the need for change and horrifying stories in the business press about companies that stubbornly adhered to the status quo, you would think that challenging the conventional wisdom would be a natural rather than an unnatural act. While going up against standard policies and practices may make intellectual sense, it often does not make practical sense. A number of obstacles stand in the way of committing this unnatural act.

The Paralyzing Weight of the Routine

We are referring to the never-ending series of meetings, performance reviews, operational discussions, and other matters that dominate a leader's time and energy. Leaders become enmeshed in putting out fires or reacting to the present rather than thinking in strategic, breakthrough ways. It's very difficult to challenge norms when there is little opportunity to think strategically or reflect on the future. In fact, leaders are most able to challenge conventional wisdom when they can find the space to think and brainstorm, free from the reactive routine of the office. The unnatural act therefore is to incorporate the mind-set of a corporate retreat into the daily aspects of running the business, to force oneself to question accepted policies and concepts and suggest alternatives.

The Need for Difficult Discussions and Unpleasant Actions

Many companies have adopted a philosophy based on the notion that everyone can be developed beyond their capabilities. Average performers are viewed as potentially above-average performers given time and development. In fact, most of them will always be average. The overly optimistic notions about development in many corporate cultures result in managerial mediocrity. Certainly, some people can change if given a chance, but not all can. Many companies we work with have identified their average or below-average performers who will not progress but choose to keep in roles viewed as noncritical because they believe they are preserving a humane corporate culture. Challenging the conventional wisdom here means having candid talks about people and making tough decisions about their future in the organization. This is a big obstacle because it may mean taking actions that are perceived as hard-hearted and defending oneself against being uncaring and unfeeling.

Emotional Investments in Tradition, the Status Quo, and a Given Position

When you act against the conventional wisdom, your action often results in a disengagement from the past. Leaders may have to kill a long-standing business or eliminate a valued part of the company's heritage (for instance, the annual and expensive Christmas party or trip to the annual sales recognition event). These actions have emotional repercussions, and some leaders retreat from challenging the conventional wisdom because they do not want to deal with messy emotions or overt resistance. When we have conducted Action Learning programs for regulated businesses such as Ameritech, BellSouth, Pacific Gas & Electric, and Sprint to prepare senior executives to enter a deregulated marketplace, they had to let go of time-honored views about customer service at any cost and embrace the bottom-line orientation of the competition. Coaching senior leaders in these companies often required challenging deeply held assumptions about the benefits of monopolistic positions and the disadvantage of abandoning captive customers. Opening up the network and scaling down the expensive customer services that regulated local telephone companies used to provide was emotionally wrenching for many leaders; they had to tell customers that depended on them for these services that they would no longer be available. There are times when leaders would prefer to avoid these changes, and so they embrace the conventional wisdom.

Demotivating Measurement Systems

People usually are not rewarded for challenging the conventional wisdom. They are rewarded for delivering results, executing commitments, and meeting objectives, and although sometimes it's necessary to go against the grain to meet these objectives, the risk often outweighs the reward. We have coached sales leaders who knew that their company's marketing propositions were flawed, but rather than build an internal coalition for change, they preferred to wring more revenue out of their sales force, knowing it was an end-game they could not win. If you do things the traditional way and they do not work, you have excuses to fall back on: "I did it the way we've always done it." Do it a new way, and you open yourself to criticism: "Why in the world did you think that would work?"

Lack of Information About What Is Happening

To take on the company's norms or lead fundamental change, leaders need solid information about global best practices or front-line feedback about customer service. In some instances, they lack these data because they do not know where to look, there are budgetary constraints, or systems are not in place to provide them with this information. We still encounter senior executives who are attempting to steer large corporations without adequate financial reports, including profit and loss by product line, customer, geography, and key services areas. Without sophisticated financial information systems, it's difficult to have a firm foundation from which to challenge conventional wisdom. Leaders may have a hunch that the current approach is wrong, but if they have no data to back up their hunches, they may be reluctant to pursue their challenge.

Facilitating Challenge: Two Simple Steps

Overcoming these obstacles is not easy, but leaders can do two things to make it easier.

First, they must work to build new perspectives on the business. Perspectives with data provide the momentum to challenge conventional thinking. When leaders change perspective and work to see their business through the eyes of a key customer or from a front-line employee vantage point, they often are more compelled to speak out. When leaders fail to talk with customers regularly or engage in meaningful dialogues with a range of employees, they usually are content to go along with the status quo. When they put themselves in a position to uncover fresh information and new ideas, they may be jarred by what they learn. It's one thing to know that the company's technology lacks functionality and wondering if it might be a good idea to investigate new investments in technology for the future. It's something else to hear a customer rage about your company's outmoded systems and praise a competitor's investment in state-of-the-art technology.

To gain a new perspective on the business, numerous options are open to leaders:

- Listening to people who are different (for example, vendors, other functions, academics, and the media)
- Putting oneself in new situations (listening to customer service center conversations, calling on accounts with a sales rep, traveling to the company's manufacturing centers in other countries)
- Inviting dissent (inviting antagonists and other critics to meetings in order to surface a range of opinions)
- Reading and listening widely (beyond the standard business books reading list and exploring ideas of theorists, futurists, and other top-tier thinkers)
- Reflecting on all these new and unusual viewpoints (taking the time to ruminate on all the fresh ideas so that one's response is reasoned, personal, and well developed)

The other way to overcome obstacles is to enroll others in the process of analyzing the conventional wisdom. There is strength in numbers, and we have found that leaders who bring in other people to examine an issue often come away with support for their challenge, making it easier for them to articulate it. Challenging conventional wisdom should not be a solitary act. Issuing the challenge can be done as a whisper rather than as a shout, brought up in a business review, a staff meeting, off-site, or on-line. Choosing the right time and place for the challenge is also part of an effective approach.

Unnatural acts do not have to be acts of reckless courage. Challenging the conventional wisdom in large corporations especially needs to be handled with some political adroitness. For this reason, we often coach leaders on political mapping and how to pick the right people to join them in their challenge. Some unnaturally minded leaders make the worst choices when deciding who to approach with their heretical ideas. They single out powerful executives who they know could change things quickly, but who also hold the conventional wisdom near and dear to their hearts. As a result, they not only waste a great deal of time and effort trying to covert the unconvertible, but they may create a powerful political enemy in the process. A better approach is to focus on people who are neutral or have no strong opinions on the subject at hand but are in positions to assist or resist. Similarly, it makes sense to figure out the networks of these position people and enlist these networks in the crusade for change.

Continuous Questioning of Basic Assumptions

We have found that challenging the conventional wisdom is not done through extensively worded briefs, broadly articulated position statements, or even extensive research. Verbose position statements of challenge and observation tend to have little impact. Instead, unnatural leaders learn to challenge the accepted way of doing things through frequent questions. By poking and prodding basic assumptions about the business, leaders keep themselves and their organizations adaptive.

Here are the questions to ask regularly that will make challenges meaningful and with an impact:

- *What business are we in?* This is an obvious question, but when it probes beyond the obvious answer and when is asked continuously, it can create enormous change in companies and business units. Because of evolving technology, every company periodically has to rethink its business model. Even the most basic product manufacturing company is in the information-providing and service business because of the Internet. A company may find its business shifting not because it is manufacturing a different product or providing a different service but because customers constantly have new options and choices. Asking this question repeatedly sets up a thought-provoking duality, with the obvious answer juxtaposed with a less obvious (though no less viable) one. Consider how the following questions force people to reevaluate basic assumptions:

Are we in the banking business or the customer satisfaction business?
Are we in the telephone business or the communication business?
Are we in the travel business or the dream fulfillment business?
Are we in the learning business or in the talent growth business?

- *Who are our customers, and why do they buy from us?* When a company thinks it knows its customers, it is in the most danger of falling prey to the conventional wisdom. For example, one executive told us without pausing, "Our customers are middle market companies, and they buy from us because we provide a low-cost alternative." He was missing a shift in his customer base that even we as outsiders could identify. His customers would soon be buying from his competitors, which were offering them a better price.

When companies regularly ask naive questions about their customers, they are startled to learn that their customers are buying or not buying from them for reasons that never even occurred to them. As executive coaches, we sometimes startle our clients by asking them to view these customers from a new perspective—for instance, "Imagine you've just completed a management buyout of your business. You've used your mortgage as collateral, and your ability to pay for your children's college education depends on the business's continuing to do well. Given this, who are your customers, why do they buy from you, and what do you do next?" When executives suspend their disbelief and enter into this scenario through dialogue, the white-hot fear of the future causes them to ask and explore the question with great seriousness. In this way, they often upend common assumptions about customers.

Most business models are founded on a core idea—for example, "universal service," "overnight delivery," or "pizza in ten minutes." The company may not change this core idea—but the customers might. What the company thinks it's selling may not be what the customer knows it's buying. Or rather, there may be a disconnect between how a customer perceives a company and how the company perceives itself. Continuously challenging the internal self-image of a company is a very productive activity for unnatural leaders.

- *Where can real business growth come from?* This question is a direct strike at strategic complacency, especially when the word *real* is emphasized. Top-line growth requires constantly reconceptualizing the business: finding new ways to serve customers, eliminating products and product lines to focus on new areas, and so on. Most high-performing leaders are obsessed with increasing their business, but they may be obsessed with incremental rather than breakthrough change—giving customers what they ask for, only better. (Most breakthrough products such as cell phones and handheld computers did not respond to customer needs; they created them.) Or they are fixated on bottom-line growth through cost controls and operational efficiencies. Organic growth of a business is a complex challenge and requires thinking about growth in untraditional ways. For instance, a convention-shattering corollary question might be, "What do customers currently not know they need but would want to buy if it were available to them?"

- *Who is our talent, and how do we attract, develop, and retain the talent that makes our business successful?* Every business in every industry is driven by talent, not "human resources" or "human capital." Focusing on talent rather than viewing people through the conventional lens of jobs and positions is a big shift most companies have not made. Leaders face the critical task of choosing and building their teams, and the conventional way of doing so is to pick those with the right levels of experience and who are "due" to be promoted, or "buddies" who are well known and have served loyally in other situations. In shifting the focus to talent, leaders instead start asking questions like, "Who can we not afford to lose?" "Who does the competition most want to recruit from here?" and "Who is going to be leading the company ten years from now?"

- *Who are the best, and what are they doing to be best?* When leaders persist in viewing their company from the perspective of their own experience, they are unable to challenge conventional wisdom because they have no real basis for comparison. It's only when they look at world-class companies such as Intel, General Electric, Emerson Electric, or other consistent high performers and observe their best practices that they say, "We need to change the way we're doing X."

Action Learning is a program and process to force executives to look outside their organizations, find the best approach, and learn how to raise their own standards. Leaders are asked to benchmark the best, uncover their own best practices, and compare them. Action Learning creates a temporary system in which participants are challenged to ask uncomfortable questions and venture controversial opinions. At BellSouth, Pacific Gas & Electric, Johnson & Johnson, Lilly, and many other companies we have seen executives challenge the conventional wisdom and help their company adapt as a result.

It's not just asking about the best companies but the best leaders that's important. Natural leaders sometimes view the world myopically; they see only what is taking place in their company, their competitors, and a narrow swatch of activity within their industries. As a result, their leadership models tend to be internal ("My boss is my model") or stereotypical. When we ask leaders whom they admire, many of them respond with obvious names—Jack Welch, Steve Case, Bill Gates—that suggest a lack of serious thinking about the subject. This is a symptom of a deeper problem: failing to develop a personal theory of the case about effective leadership. Put another way, they do not give leadership much thought, and they simply lead unconsciously and naturally. As we will see in the next section, leaders must challenge the conventional wisdom about what a leader should do and be.

Unconventional Leadership

Written and unwritten rules of natural leadership have been instilled in most people's hearts and minds. To defy the standard definition of leadership, even if only on occasion, may seem unwise. Leaders at all levels fear that if they act "unleaderlike," someone above them will sneer, "He's not leadership material." The conventional wisdom about leadership therefore is often religiously adhered to. What helps people challenge it is isolating certain precepts that comprise the wisdom and discussing why these precepts are flawed. Bringing these precepts to top-of-mind awareness and pinpointing what is wrong with them helps leaders challenge them. Let's look at some pearls of leadership wisdom, and identify the flaw in each.

- *Leaders must be willing to make whatever sacrifices are necessary for the good of the organization.* The worst leaders we work with are the ones who are obsessively devoted to their work. Lacking any semblance of life-work balance, their hyperactivity drives them and others to a frenetic pace. While this might be the proper attitude for a martyr or for someone engaged in saving lives in a war, it's inappropriate for a modern leader. As coaches, we often must say to hyperactive leaders, "Get a grip!" Although we accept the pressure of global competition and the demands for increased performance, those who complain they have no time to lead people effectively are usually in that situation because they are trying to do everything themselves. The leader who always stays late creates enormous guilt and pressure for those who work for him. Challenging the conventional wisdom here means setting and holding to personal priorities, including taking vacations, pursuing hobbies, and spending time with family so that stress is managed and the leader can truly lead.

• *Leaders are heroes who can rescue and transform organizations.* Alternatively, this could be called the myth of Jack Welch. Although Welch obviously did great things for GE, not every organization needs a Welch, and not every leader can be Jack Welch. In fact, some companies need leaders who are less passionate and more thoughtful alliance builders rather than action-oriented decision makers. Dialogue, listening, and conversation are not heroic deeds, but they are often tactics that get far better results than the heroic leader who tells people what they should do.

• *Leaders motivate people.* It takes a good deal of courage to defy this truism and not give the perfect pep talk, constantly trying to push people through words, rewards, and the threat of punishment. The reality, however, is that people motivate themselves. People used to be more accepting of the motivational leader who drew on athletic, military, and movie models to give the rousing speech designed to push people to new heights of performance. As coaches, we are constantly asked, "How do I motivate him?" Our usual answer is, "You can't." As we discussed in our book *Action Coaching,* motivation is an unmet need, and leaders must arrange the environment, including assignments, opportunities, and sanctions, for people to meet their unique needs. Most employees feel as if they have heard all the motivation messages before since we live among so much hype in the culture at large. What they do respond to is a leader who creates the right environment for the employee to motivate himself. This means engaging in continuous dialogue with direct reports, providing appropriate assignments, and coaching them over obstacles.

• *Good leaders love to win (by making others lose).* Admittedly, this is a complicated conventional notion to challenge. Much of what leadership is about is taking market share, triumphing over competitors, and gaining at someone else's expense. The capitalist system is based on the Darwinian view of winners and losers. At the same time, however, there is a growing sentiment among many people within organizations to moderate this win-at-all-costs stance. This sentiment stems from an increasing awareness that companies now partner successfully with competitors, that an industry rather than just individual companies can win, that there are conflicting constituencies and stakeholders that need to be heard, and that people deserve to be treated with dignity. Thus, while people respect leaders who want to win, they have even greater respect for leaders who do not position winning as the only worthwhile endeavor.

• *Leaders must have a compelling vision.* The conventional wisdom is that leaders are inspired and bring forth a vision of the company's future from deep within, communicating it with deep passion and creating believers out of all of their employees. Most companies we have consulted with have created specs for a CEO search that includes the phrase "visionary leader." Reacting to this visionary requirement, one executive in the pharmaceutical industry said to us, "The only people I know with visions are psychotics, and we usually suggest medication."

This is not to say that a good leader does not facilitate a picture of what the company's future could be. He does this, however, through ongoing discussions with smart people; he then achieves consensus about a direction and pursues it. Many times, he pursues it not with evangelical fervor but methodically and diligently, making a series of thoughtful decisions along the way.

• *Leadership is lonely.* When leaders subscribe to this piece of wisdom, they tend to isolate themselves. While leaders do have to make decisions alone at times and based on their intuition, they do not have to set up their secretary as a sentry, keep their office door closed, and interact with only a few trusted advisers. Unnatural leaders are unusually open with others and establish strong communication networks. They build communities of which they are part, establishing meaningful relationships with board members, direct reports, and staff. When they must make an important decision, they do not retreat into their office and then emerge with a decision they have wrestled with alone. Instead, they solicit the thoughts of others, and their decision is a natural evolution of shared knowledge and trusted relationships.

We do not want to make challenging these leadership precepts sound easier than it is or pretend that it is not without some peril. For this reason, we would like to share the story of Roger with you—a story that has only a moderately happy ending. Roger is a vice president in a well-known corporation who delights in seeing his staff members shine. He is a tremendous developer of talent, and he is well known for giving his direct reports great opportunities and visibility and promoting them when openings occur. Although his teams are innovative and productive, he is not viewed highly by everyone in management. We were called in to coach Roger because he does not fit the prototype of the heroic, charismatic leader. He is a good people developer who gets things done through others, in a company that values individual, charismatic leadership.

When we talked to Roger's boss, he complained that "Roger doesn't speak up often enough in meetings." He also questioned whether Roger was sufficiently "creative and breakthrough in his thinking." Roger's response to the latter charge was, "I nurture the creativity and breakthrough ideas of my people." Modest, laid back, and seemingly without ego, Roger has not challenged the conventional wisdom but obliterated it through his persona.

We are not saying that Roger is a model for an unnatural leader. In fact, we are working with him to be a bit more assertive and politically astute. He is still viewed with a mixture of skepticism and admiration by his bosses. At the same time, however, Roger has made a tremendous contribution to his organization precisely because he is unwilling to accept the standard definition of what a leader should be, and he has seeded the company with many talented performers.

Challenging the Conventional Wisdom

Think about the ways in which conventional wisdom about leadership affects your leadership behaviors. Rate the degree to which you believe each of the following pearls of wisdom has influenced your current leadership behaviors.

Pearls of Wisdom About Leadership	Your Rating
Leaders must be willing to make whatever sacrifices are necessary for the good of the organization.	1　　2　　3　　4　　5 Not at All　　　　　　A Lot
Leaders are heroes who can rescue and transform organizations.	1　　2　　3　　4　　5 Not at All　　　　　　A Lot
Leaders motivate people.	1　　2　　3　　4　　5 Not at All　　　　　　A Lot
Good leaders love to win (by making others lose).	1　　2　　3　　4　　5 Not at All　　　　　　A Lot
Leaders must have a compelling vision.	1　　2　　3　　4　　5 Not at All　　　　　　A Lot
Leadership is lonely.	1　　2　　3　　4　　5 Not at All　　　　　　A Lot

How is your leadership behavior challenging the conventional wisdom of what a leader should be?

Identifying and Overcoming Obstacles to Challenging Conventional Wisdom

Think about the obstacles that may be standing in the way of challenging the conventional wisdom of "how we do things around here." How much is each a problem for you?

Obstacles to Challenging Conventional Wisdom	Your Rating
The paralyzing weight of the routine	1　　2　　3　　4　　5 No　　　　　　Significant Problem　　　　　Problem
The need for difficult discussions and unpleasant actions	1　　2　　3　　4　　5 No　　　　　　Significant Problem　　　　　Problem

Challenging the Conventional Wisdom (Cont.)

Obstacles to Challenging Conventional Wisdom	Your Rating
Emotional investments in tradition and the status quo	1 2 3 4 5 No Significant Problem Problem
Demotivating measurement systems	1 2 3 4 5 No Significant Problem Problem
Lack of information about what's happening	1 2 3 4 5 No Significant Problem Problem

Focus on the obstacles that you assigned the highest ratings. What actions can you take to overcome these obstacles?

What one or two other actions could you take to gain new perspectives on your work, including the following?

Listening to people who are different

Putting yourself in new situations

Inviting dissent

Reading and listening widely

Reflecting on all these new and unusual viewpoints

Challenging Basic Assumptions

Reflect on the following assumptions about doing business, and answer the following questions:

What business are we in?

Challenging the Conventional Wisdom (Cont.)

Who are our customers, and why do they buy from us?

Where can real business growth come from?

Who is our talent, and how do we attract, develop, and retain those who make our business successful?

Who are the best, and how are they doing it?

What do my answers suggest that I may need to do to challenge the conventional wisdom about doing business given present realities?

What rules, norms, and values of our corporate culture need to be challenged and changed in order for the organization's continued success or survival?

What risks and acts of courage am I willing to take to challenge conventional wisdom and bring energizing new ideas and fresh perspectives?

Steps for Developing Yourself as an Unnatural Leader

Be aware of the assumptions you are making every time you make a key decision or take important actions.

Identify the obstacles that are standing in the way of challenging the conventional wisdom of how things are done in your organization. Set objectives, and take action to overcome these obstacles.

Make time for activities that will help you gain new perspectives on your work, including putting yourself in new situations, listening to people with different points of view, and exposing yourself to the ideas of first-class thinkers.

Enroll others in challenging worn-out assumptions and crusading for change.

Spend time reflecting and challenging basic assumptions about doing business.

Set a goal to act with courage, and challenge conventional wisdom.

Make a point of bringing new, energizing ideas and fresh perspectives into your team.

Chapter Fourteen

Giving Yourself
Unnatural Options

As you look back at the ten unnatural traits we have discussed, you may feel a bit uneasy. The cumulative effect of so many counter-intuitive behaviors and countercultural attitudes may make you feel as if you must become the opposite of the leader you have always been. Or you may believe that you are never going to be able to convince other leaders in your organization or those you coach to make 180-degree changes. In fact, we are not suggesting such dramatic changes are called for. Quite frankly, it's both unnecessary and impossible for any executive to turn into his opposite. We have learned through extensive coaching and teaching that all leaders bring numerous strengths to their jobs, especially in the areas of technical expertise, decision making, drive, and problem solving. These strengths remain strengths, both for people's organizations and their careers.

Sometimes program participants and clients misinterpret our discussion of unnatural leadership and assume they need to give up most of their work behaviors and attitudes. It's not about giving anything up as much as adding to their leadership repertoire. If they are inspirational leaders and give terrific speeches, they do not have to forsake this obvious talent. They must recognize, however, that other approaches may be called for in certain situations. They might consider the option of coaching and teaching when they would automatically respond with a talk. The best leaders learn to combine natural and unnatural traits; they know the difference between decisions with a clear right and wrong answer and ones with no right answers.

All this is not to say that it's easy to exercise these unnatural options. A certain amount of courage is called for, especially if your company today does not agree with our position, but there are compelling reasons now and in the future to be courageous.

Five Factors That Will Motivate Unnatural Acts

There is no question that some people work for bosses and organizations that espouse a rigidly natural leadership style. Although our experience tells us that this style is in decline, we still encounter highly traditional leadership cultures, even in newer companies and start-ups. As a result, you may have to employ a certain deftness in leading unnaturally (or find an organization and a boss receptive to these unnatural traits). Keep in mind that although your boss may expect you to follow a certain leadership style, you will not be effective if you acquiesce completely to his wishes. As executive coaches and in leading Action Learning programs, we have seen overwhelming evidence that "kissing up and kicking down" is highly ineffective.

Even if you work for an organization and a boss open to new leadership behaviors, committing unnatural acts still takes some resolve. What you are fighting against is your own training and the power of the conventional wisdom. In fact, we have worked with CEOs who have recognized intellectually the wisdom of unnatural leadership but have struggled a bit incorporating these traits into their own daily routines.

Whatever your situation, recognize that global business is moving in an unnatural direction and that a 100 percent natural leadership approach will be decreasingly productive with each passing quarter. Five factors are driving high performance in business today and will be even more significant drivers in the future. Not surprisingly, they are different from what drove performance in the past. The following factors will compel all sorts of leaders in all sorts of companies to exercise their option to act unnaturally:

The New Generation of Talent

Much has been written about the war for talent and the critical need for companies to find it and keep it. What has not received as much notice is that the emerging generation of talent has little patience for purely natural leaders. Although everyone wants to work for a winning company, they do not respond well to command-and-control types who tell them what to do or attempt to motivate them only through words or incentives, no matter how great the company or how much it is dominating the market. Unnatural qualities are necessary if leaders want to attract, keep, and develop this talent. Many of the talented people to emerge in information technology departments and from dot-coms have become accustomed to unnatural environments. They are used to working for people who extend trust before it is earned and connect rather than create. Faced with a boss who is a classic leader type, they are likely to rebel and quit. It's good to keep in mind that people do not leave organizations; they leave supervisors.

Constant Collaboration

Forming alliances with other companies or partnering across functions are not just occasional temporary actions. Boundarylessness is becoming routine in all types of organizations. Even the most expert of experts within an organization lacks critical knowledge because of shifts in the environment and the rapid creation of new information. For instance, the human resource staff expert must now collaborate with the external pensions expert, the finance investment expert, and the pension committee line leader in order to create policy. People in companies are learning to learn from each other every day; they are recognizing that they lessen their effectiveness by gravitating toward the same people in the same function. The interdisciplinary trend in companies can be seen in multiple, iterative performance assessment. People are evaluated not only by their functional boss but by managers in other functions, vendors, customers, and other stakeholders. The same collaborative methodology is being applied to hiring and promotion decisions as well.

Leaders who know how to connect instead of create will flourish in this collaborative paradigm. Natural leaders who want to play the rugged individualist will struggle.

Adapting to the New

Structure is a passing state of mind, and what is considered bold and innovative today is passé tomorrow. Customers are in a state of constant evolution, and companies must adapt constantly if they want to keep these customers. A relentless search for best practices is occurring in the most successful organizations, and as new best practices keep emerging, companies keep changing processes, policies, and procedures. Adapting to these changes requires unnatural traits. Leaders who are able to expose their vulnerabilities and admit they do not know are much more likely to be flexible and consider an untraditional practice. Leaders who challenge the conventional wisdom find it easier to adopt and adapt because they are willing to think about work in fresh ways.

Transparency

The energy that used to be invested in controlling information is now spent disseminating it. Information technology systems, e-mail, intranet, and Internet Web sites are being upgraded every day to ensure that more people have the right information faster and with greater clarity than ever before. Successful companies have many knowledge workers; they must possess both the facts and understanding of the ideas behind the facts if they are going to achieve high performance. The best information and communication networks are the most transparent; there are fewer blacked-out areas where people lack access to information they need to do their jobs. Information flowing back and forth and in and out requires leaders who are willing to be open and honest with everyone in their network.

Obviously, leaders who extend trust first are more willing to part with information than leaders who withhold trust. Leaders who acknowledge their shadow side are unusually open, and they are usually very willing to be as transparent about their decisions and strategies as about themselves.

Uncontrollable Speed

Things are moving so fast in just about every industry that it is impossible to understand technology, much less stay ahead of it. Relevant data pour forth like a geyser. Most executives we coach cannot begin to keep up with deluge of articles, magazines, newspapers, research reports, and other information that comes across their desk or laptop. Keeping up and figuring out how to pull ahead is critical. Speed is of the essence. Being second to market is no longer acceptable in pharmaceuticals, technology, retail, consumer electronics, and many other industries.

Natural leaders who attempt to try to control this movement are going to lose. The need is for leaders who are willing to move forward without all the data and are capable of introducing a new product even though ideally more time should be spent ramping up for the introduction. Unnatural leaders are better suited to going with the flow. Their ability to be comfortable with right-versus-right decisions allows them to operate quickly in the midst of uncertainty. Instead of being overwhelmed by new developments and trying to slow things down, they are able to keep pace.

How Much Unnatural Leadership Is Enough?

There is no hard and fast rule about these ten unnatural leadership acts. We do not want leaders to believe they have to commit to all ten to be an effective leader or that they must set a goal of performing certain ones daily. What acts they commit and when they commit them will depend on the business situations they encounter, their company's strategy, and their own personality.

If we cannot tell you when and how often you should lead unnaturally, we can provide three guidelines to keep in mind as you attempt to incorporate at least some of the traits into your leadership style.

First, focus your unnatural acts on self-awareness and performance improvement rather than transformation. Do not try to become something you are not. It is unrealistic to expect that an executive who has spent years cultivating psychological armor for the corporate tournament will suddenly start revealing all her uncertainties and acknowledging her flaws to her team. It is realistic to target certain leadership behaviors that, if changed, will result in improved performance.

The foundation for these behavioral changes is self-awareness. In our Action Learning programs, we often encourage participants to initiate dialogues with others. Receiving feedback can catalyze and inform behavioral change; 360-degree evaluations are useful for this purpose. More informally, executives should get in the habit of asking their direct reports how they can be better leaders, even to the point of requesting a list of improvements they might make. When they discover the gap between what they intend to do and the actual impact of their actions, they gain crucial information about themselves. More times than not, one of the ten unnatural leadership traits will provide them with a way to close the gap.

Second, become more empathic and accepting. This might seem like new age pabulum, but our advice goes deeper than the touchy-feely connotations of those terms. It is very difficult for people to exhibit unnatural leadership behavior when they are walking around with a chip on their shoulder or blaming others for problems. In every organization, we encounter executives who are in conflict with other executives, and they often respond to these situations by saying, "If only they would change," and build a case for why their "bad" behavior is not justified. The first step in executive Action Coaching is to help these leaders focus on changing their own behavior rather than fixating on the behavior of others. They can control the former but not the latter. Rather than complain constantly and endlessly about bosses and direct reports, the skill is to keep a laser focus on what they can change within themselves to remedy the conflict.

It is very difficult to commit unnatural leadership acts when you're suspicious of other people's motives or verbally diminishing people who disagree with you. All ten unnatural traits are much easier to incorporate into your leadership style if you give people some slack. This doesn't mean to back off on performance or accountability but to remember the essential humanness of yourself and other people.

Most leaders will acknowledge, given enough time, that their peers and direct reports are hard-working, well-intentioned individuals who want to achieve, produce, and do a good job. Similarly, we have found that most bosses are concerned about developing their team members and delivering results; they are not the control freaks we first hear about who only want to look good in the eyes of top management. The problem, of course, is that in a workplace with people who increasingly are different from each other, individuals may be construed to be egomaniacs, slackers, and other negative types simply because they are different. Rather than work to understand and accept these differences, some leaders may be quick to jump to the wrong conclusions under stress. These false assumptions are obstacles that stand in the way of extending trust before it's earned, revealing vulnerabilities, and connecting instead of creating.

Third, distinguish between form and essence. The natural leadership perspective proposes that work gets done through form—through various processes and procedures. The unnatural perspective holds that it gets done through the essence of who people are—what they want in life, what they think is important at work, why they work, and how they feel about values such as integrity. The most effective leaders today recognize and respond to the essence of a work situation rather than get caught up in the form. For instance, if a group is having difficulty meeting a deadline, they do not focus energy on more measurements or checkpoints or process improvements (though that certainly should be looked at) but examine the underlying needs, resistance, and commitment of people who are moving too slowly. Is one individual not working at full capacity because of personal difficulties? Are two other people engaging in frequent conflict? Is someone else in need of coaching to help work through a perceived obstacle? Focusing on the essence requires unnatural behaviors; you need to be open, vulnerable, and trusting if you are going to see and respond to the essence of situations.

Becoming Comfortable with the Natural and Unnatural Aspects of Leadership

We earlier quoted F. Scott Fitzgerald that the sign of a first-rate mind is the ability to hold two contradictory ideas simultaneously. Similarly, the mark of a first-rate leader is the capacity to act in seemingly contradictory ways, to accept the paradox of being a leader in the twenty-first century. The increasing complexity, ambiguity, and unpredictability of being a business executive today demand a range of behavioral options. The range of natural leadership is limited; it cannot handle the multiplicity of problems and opportunities that surface every day. With the addition of unnatural options, however, these problems and opportunities can be dealt with more effectively.

It is certainly a bit disconcerting to exhibit seemingly opposite leadership behaviors. More than one leader has balked at the requirement that she be sensitive to people's feelings and needs but at the same time be tough and disciplined. Others find it difficult to adhere to personal and organizational values but also deliver increasingly ambitious results. Still others struggle with the need to be rational and analytical but intuitive and spontaneous in other situations. And of course, some executives have trouble moving back and forth between being decisive and facilitating the process of others making decisions.

The contradictory behaviors are endless. To paraphrase an old science dictum, for every natural leadership action, there is an equal and opposite unnatural reaction. You can struggle with these opposites or accept them, and we recommend accepting them. To facilitate this acceptance, realize that your opposing leadership behaviors can coexist quite nicely. The truly great leaders we have worked with are great because they have options; they are not forced to rely on the tried-and-true leadership solutions when new issues emerge; they have the option of acting unnaturally.

As you have probably noticed by now, we are tremendously fond of the word *paradox,* and we leave you with a final one. Now and in the future, the people who contribute the most to companies will be natural leaders who can act unnaturally (or unnatural leaders who can act naturally, if you prefer). Their flexibility will enable them to handle more situations more effectively than other leaders. They will still create great ideas, but they also will be savvy enough to pursue connecting strategies when they are called for. They are willing to expose their vulnerabilities and catalyze participation from others when they say they do not know, but they also recognize instances when being assertive and acting unilaterally is the appropriate response.

In organizations throughout the world, enormously talented executives exist who have been indoctrinated in one leadership approach. It's time to learn another, complementary approach, and we hope we have given you the impetus and tools to do so.

Bibliography

Argyris, Chris. *Flawed Advice and the Management Trap: How Managers Can Know When They're Getting Good Advice and When They're Not.* New York: Oxford University Press, 1999.

Ashkenas, Ron, Ulrich, Dave, Jick, Todd, and Kerr, Steve. *The Boundaryless Organization: Breaking the Chains of Organizational Structure.* San Francisco: Jossey-Bass, 1998.

Badaracco, Joseph. *Defining Moments: Choosing Between Right and Right* Boston: Harvard Business School Press, 1997.

Badaracco, Joseph, and Ellsworth, Richard R. *Leadership and the Quest for Integrity.* Boston: Harvard Business School Press, 1993.

Bennis, Warren G., and Nanus, Burt. *Leaders: Strategies for Taking Charge.* New York: Harper Business Press, 1997.

Bennis, Warren G., Spreitzer, Gretchen M., and Cummings, Thomas (eds.). *The Future of Leadership: Today's Top Leadership Thinkers Speak to Tomorrow's Leaders.* (2nd ed.) New York: Wiley, 2001.

Blix, Jacqueline, and Heitmiller, David. *Getting a Life: Real Lives Transformed by Your Money or Your Life.* New York: Penguin, 1997.

Block, Peter. *Stewardship: Choosing Service over Self Interest.* San Francisco: Berrett-Koehler, 1996.

Bolman, Lee G., and Deal, Terrence E. *Leading with Soul: An Uncommon Journey of Spirit Revised.* (2nd ed.) New York: Wiley, 2001.

Bracey, Hyler, Rosenblum, Jack, Sanford, Aubrey, and Trueblood, Roy. *Managing from the Heart.* Westminster, Md.: DTP, 1993.

Buckingham, Marcus, and Cottman, Curt. *First, Break All the Rules: What the World's Greatest Managers Do Differently.* New York: Simon & Schuster, 1999.

Carter, Steven, and Sokol, Julia. *Lives Without Balance: When You're Giving Everything You've Got and Still Not Getting What You Hoped For.* New York: Random House, 1992.

Casman, Kevin. *Leadership from the Inside Out.* Provo, Utah: Executive Excellence, 1999.

Chappell, Tom. *Managing Upside Down: The Seven Intentions of Values-Centered Leadership.* New York: Morrow, 1999.

Charan, Ram. *What the CEO Wants You to Know: How Your Company Really Works.* New York: Crown, 2001.

Charan, Ram, and Colvin, Geoffrey. "Why CEOs Fail." *Fortune,* June 21, 1999, p. 69.

Charan, Ram, Drotter, Steve, and Noel, James. *The Leadership Pipeline: How to Build the Leadership-Powered Company.* San Francisco: Jossey-Bass, 2001.

Chinen, Allen B. *Beyond the Hero: Classic Stories of Men in Search of Soul.* Philadelphia: Xlibris Corp., 1993.

Christenson, Clay. *The Innovator's Dilemma.* Boston: Harvard Business School Press, 1997.

Ciampa, Dan, and Watkins, Michael. *Right from the Start: Taking Charge in a New Leadership Role.* Boston: Harvard Business School Press, 1999.

Cohen, Dan, and Prusak, Laurence. *In Good Company: How Social Capital Makes Organizations Work.* Boston: Harvard Business School Press, 2001.

Coleman, Daniel. *Working with Emotional Intelligence.* New York: Bantam Books, 1998.

Collins, Jim. "Level 5 Leadership: The Triumph of Humility and Fierce Resolve." *Harvard Business Review,* Jan. 2001.

Conger, Jay Alden. *Spirit at Work: Discovering the Spirituality in Leadership.* San Francisco: Jossey-Bass, 1994.

Cooper, Robert K., and Sawaf, Ayman. *Executive EQ: Emotional Intelligence in Leadership and Organizations.* New York: Putnam, 1997.

Davis, Stanley M., and Meyer, Christopher. *Future Wealth.* Boston: Harvard Business School Press, 2000.

Dixon, Nancy M. *Common Knowledge: How Companies Thrive by Sharing What They Know.* Boston: Harvard Business School Press, 2000.

Dotlich, David L., and Cairo, Peter C. *Action Coaching: How to Leverage Individual Performance for Company Success.* San Francisco: Jossey-Bass, 2001.

Dotlich, David L., and Noel, James L. *Action Learning: How the World's Top Companies Are Re-Creating Their Leaders and Themselves.* San Francisco: Jossey-Bass, 1998.

Edler, Richard. *If I Knew What I Know Now: CEOs and Other Smart Executives Share Wisdom They Wish They'd Been Told 25 Years Ago.* New York: Berkley, 1997.

Egan, Gerald. *Working the Shadow Side: A Guide to Positive Behind-the-Scenes Management.* San Francisco: Jossey-Bass, 1994.

Eliot, Robert S., and Breo, Dennis L. *Is It Worth Dying For? A Self-Assessment Program to Make Stress Work for You, Not Against You.* New York: Bantam Books, 1991.

Foster, Richard, and Kaplan, Sarah. *Creative Destruction: Why Companies That Are Built to Last Underperform the Market—And How to Successfully Transform Them.* New York: Doubleday, 2001.

Fox, Jeffrey J. *How to Become CEO: The Rules for Rising to the Top of Any Organization.* New York: Hyperion, 1998.

Fox, Matthew. *The Reinvention of Work: A New Vision of Livelihood for Our Time.* San Francisco: HarperSanFrancisco, 1995.

Friedman, Thomas. *The Lexus and the Olive Tree.* New York: Farrar, Straus & Giroux, 2000.

Garvin, David A. *Learning in Action. A Guide to Putting the Learning Organization to Work.* Boston: Harvard Business School Press, 2000.

Giber, David, Carter, Louis, and Goldsmith, Marshall. *Linkage Inc.'s Best Practices in Leadership Development Handbook: Case Studies, Instruments, Training.* San Francisco: Jossey-Bass, 2000.

Goleman, Daniel. *Emotional Intelligence.* New York: Bantam Books, 1997.

Gubman, Edward L. *The Talent Solution: Aligning Strategy and People to Achieve Extraordinary Results.* New York: McGraw-Hill, 1998.

Hamel, Gary. *Leading the Revolution.* Boston: Harvard Business School Press, 2000.

Handy, Charles. *The Hungry Spirit: Beyond Capitalism: A Quest for Purpose in the Modern World.* New York: Broadway Books, 1999.

Handy, Charles. *Waiting for the Mountain to Move: Reflections on Work and Life.* San Francisco: Jossey-Bass, 1999.

Harvey, Jerry B. *How Come Every Time I Get Stabbed in the Back My Fingerprints Are on the Knife? And Other Meditations on Management.* San Francisco: Jossey-Bass, 1999.

Heifetz, Ronald. *Leading Without Easy Answers.* Cambridge, Mass.: Belknap Press, 1994.

Hesselbein, Frances, and Cohen, Paul M. *Leader to Leader: Enduring Insights on Leadership from the Drucker Foundation's Award-Winning Journal.* San Francisco: Jossey-Bass, 1999.

James, Jennifer. *Thinking in the Future Tense: A Workout for the Mind.* New York: Touchstone Books, 1997.

Jampolsky, Gerald G., and Cirincione, Diane V. *Change Your Mind, Change Your Life: Concepts in Attitudinal Healing.* New York: Bantam Books, 1994.

Jensen, Rolf. *The Dream Society.* New York: McGraw-Hill, 1999.

Johnson, Barry. *Polarity Management: Identifying and Managing Unsolvable Problems.* Amherst, Mass.: Human Resources Development Press, 1997.

Katzenbach, Jon R. *Teams at the Top.* Boston: Harvard Business School Press, 1998.

Keeny, Bradford. *Everyday Soul: Awakening the Spirit in Daily Life.* East Rutherford, N.J.: Riverhead Books, 1997.

Koestenbaum, Peter. *The Heart of Business: Ethics, Power, and Philosophy.* Dallas: Saybrook, 1991.

Kunde, Jesper. *Corporate Religion: Building a Strong Company Through Personality and Corporate Soul.* New York: Financial Times/Prentice Hall, 2000.

Levine, Rick, Locke, Christopher, Searls, Doc, and Weinberger, David. *The Cluetrain Manifesto: The End of Business as Usual.* Cambridge, Mass.: Perseus Press, 2000.

Lundin, Stephen C., Paul, Harry, and Christensen, John. *Fish! A Remarkable Way to Boost Morale and Improve Results.* New York: Hyperion, 2000.

Lundin, William, and Lundin, Kathleen. *The Healing Manager: How to Build Quality Relationships and Productive Cultures at Work.* San Francisco: Berrett-Koehler, 1993.

Marquardt, Michael J. *Building the Learning Organization: A Systems Approach to Quantum Improvement and Global Success.* New York: McGraw-Hill, 1995.

Marquardt, Michael J., and Reyans, Reginald. *Action Learning in Action: Transforming Problems and People for World-Class Organizational Learning.* Palo Alto, Calif.: Davies-Black, 1999.

Marrs, Donald. *Executive in Passage: Career in Crisis—The Door to Uncommon Fulfillment.* Los Angeles: Barrington Sky, 1990.

Meyers, Chris. *Fast Cycle Time: How to Align Purpose, Strategy, and Structure for Speed.* New York: Free Press, 1993.

Moore, James F. *Death of Competition.* New York: HarperBusiness, 1996.

Ogilvy, James. *Living Without a Goal: Finding the Freedom to Live a Creative, Innovative, and Fulfilled Life.* New York: Doubleday, 1995.

O'Neil, John R. *The Paradox of Success: When Winning at Work Means Losing at Life—A Book of Renewal for Leaders.* New York: Tarcher, 1994.

O'Reily, Charles A., and Pfeffer, Jeffrey. *Hidden Value: How Great Companies Achieve Extraordinary Results with Ordinary People.* Boston: Harvard Business School Press, 2000.

Pearson, Carol, and Seivert, Sharon. *Magic at Work: Camelot, Creative Leadership, and Everyday Miracles.* New York: Doubleday, 1995.

Pfeffer, Jeffrey, and Sutton, Robert I. *The Knowing-Doing Gap: How Smart Companies Turn Knowledge into Action.* Boston: Harvard Business School Press, 2000.

Price Waterhouse Change Integration Team. *Better Change: Best Practices for Transforming Your Organization.* New York: McGraw-Hill, 1994.

Quinn, Robert E. *Deep Change: Discovering the Leader Within.* San Francisco: Jossey-Bass, 1996.

Rhinesmith, Stephen. "The Five Steps of Global Paradox." *Journal of Accounting and Finance,* Sept.–Oct. 2001.

Sanford, Kathleen. *Leading with Love: How Women and Men Can Transform Their Organizations Through Maternalistic Management.* Ollala, Wash.: Vashon, 1998.

Schwartz, Tony. *What Really Matters: Searching for Wisdom in America.* New York: Bantam Books, 1996.

Seuss, Dr. *Yertle the Turtle and Other Stories.* New York: Random House, 1988.

Shaw, Robert B. *Trust in the Balance: Building Successful Organizations on Results, Integrity, and Concern.* San Francisco: Jossey-Bass, 1997.

Slater, Robert. *Jack Welch and the GE Way: Management Insights and Leadership Secrets of the Legendary CEO.* New York: McGraw-Hill, 1998.

Taylor, James, Wacker, Watts, and Means, Howard. *The 500-Year Delta: What Happens After What Comes Next.* New York: HarperBusiness, 1998

Thompson, Michael C. *The Congruent Life: Following the Inward Path to Fulfilling Work and Inspired Leadership.* San Francisco: Jossey-Bass, 2000.

Ulrich, Dave. *Delivering Results: A New Mandate for Human Resource Professionals.* Boston: Harvard Business School Press, 1998.

Vella, Jane. *Learning to Listen, Learning to Teach: The Power of Dialogue in Educating Adults.* San Francisco: Jossey-Bass, 1997.

Weisinger, Hendrie. *Emotional Intelligence at Work.* San Francisco: Jossey-Bass, 2000.

Whyte, David. *The Heart Aroused: Poetry and the Preservation of the Soul in Corporate America.* New York: Doubleday, 1996.

Windham, Laurie, Samsel, Jon, and Orton, Kenneth J. *Dead Ahead: The Web Dilemma and the New Rules of Business.* New York: Allworth Press, 1999.

Index

About the Authors

DAVID L. DOTLICH has been involved with planned organizational change in academics, business, government, and consulting for twenty years. He is a former executive vice president of Honeywell and Groupe Bull and a business adviser and coach to senior executives of Johnson & Johnson, Bank of America, McDonald's, Merck, Novartis, BellSouth, and Sprint, among others. He is the coauthor of *Action Learning* (Jossey-Bass, 1998, written with James Noel) and *Action Coaching* (Jossey-Bass, 1999, written with Peter C. Cairo). He lives in Portland, Oregon.

PETER C. CAIRO is a consultant who specializes in the areas of leadership development, executive coaching, and organizational effectiveness. He is the former chair of the Department of Organizational and Counseling Psychology at Columbia University. His clients include Colgate-Palmolive, Avon Products, Andersen, Merck, Bank of America and Lilly. He is the coauthor of *Action Coaching* (Jossey-Bass, 1999, written with David L. Dotlich). He lives in New York.

BOTH AUTHORS—along with their colleague Stephen H. Rhinesmith—are founding partners of CDR International, a global consulting firm that specializes in top-tier, in-house coaching, consulting, and executive education programs to execute business strategy. CDR International delivers Executive Action Learning and Action Coaching programs that corporations use as a strategic lever to develop global business leaders, integrate acquisitions, transform organizations, and grow businesses.

CDR International's Action Learning and Action Coaching promote business and leadership performance improvement through real-time business solutions, CDR International individual assessments, and one-on-one coaching. CDR International's new Unnatural Leadership programs also provide executives with business and leadership skills needed to lead organizations in the uncertain environments and economy of the twenty-first century. To learn more about how your company can implement Unnatural Leadership programs—or to learn more about CDR International itself—visit http://www.unnaturalleadership.com. Or you may contact the company at

CDR International
120 NW Ninth Avenue, Suite 216
Portland, OR 97209
Phone: (503) 223-5678
Fax: (503) 223-5677